Ideology and Class Conflict in Jamaica

Ideology and Class Conflict in Jamaica

The Politics of Rebellion

ABIGAIL B. BAKAN

McGill-Queen's University Press
Montreal & Kingston • London • Buffalo

This work is dedicated to my parents, Mildred and David Bakan.

© McGill-Queen's University Press 1990
ISBN 0-7735-0745-0

Legal deposit second quarter 1990
Bibliothèque nationale du Québec

Printed in Canada on acid-free paper

This book has been published with the help of a grant from the Social Science Federation of Canada, using funds provided by the Social Sciences and Humanities Research Council of Canada.

Canadian Cataloguing in Publication Data

Bakan, Abigail B. (Abigail Bess), 1954–
   Ideology and class conflict in Jamaica
Includes bibliographical references.
ISBN 0-7735-0745-0
1. Jamaica – History – To 1962. 2. Jamaica – History – Slave Insurrection, 1831. 3. Slavery – Jamaica. 4. Jamaica – Social conditions. 5. Working class – Jamaica.   I. Title.
F1868.B34 1990   972.92   C90-090038-5

This book was typeset in 10/12 Baskerville
on 2506 picas by Typo Litho inc.

Contents

Acknowledgments vii

Introduction 3

1. A Labour Force in Transition:
   A Brief Historical Overview 18

2. From Slavery to Freedom:
   The "Baptist War" of 1831 50

3. Freedom without Rights:
   The Morant Bay Rebellion of 1865 68

4. Into the Modern Era:
   The Labour Rebellion of 1938 94

5. Some Implications for the
   Jamaican Political System 134

Notes 143

Index 181

Acknowledgments

I owe thanks to many individuals and institutions for their contributions to the completion of this work. Professor Rex Nettleford, Mrs. Janet Liu-Terry, and the staff of the Trade Union Education Institute at the University of the West Indies (Mona Campus) graciously welcomed me as an affiliate and offered the use of their extensive services while I was in Jamaica in 1981. Edward Dixon, Carlyle Dunkley, Audley Gayle, Lloyd Goodleigh, Damien King, and the Reverend Sam Reid patiently answered numerous questions and gave me invaluable direction. The staffs of the Library of the Institute for Social and Economic Research, the University of the West Indies, and the West India Reference Library generously provided their help and cooperation.

The Centre for Commonwealth Studies at the University of London, the Public Records Office, and the Library of the Royal Commonwealth Society provided essential material, and sincere thanks are extended to the staffs of these institutions for their patient assistance. I am also indebted to the Social Sciences and Humanities Research Council of Canada, which provided the funding for the research that made this study possible.

To Richard Hart, whose continuing interest and patient commentary on my work have been a constant source of encouragement, I owe a warm debt of gratitude. To Liisa North, who has been my teacher, adviser, editor and friend since 1973, any thanks appear to be too small. Liisa's comments, criticism and encouragement as supervisor of my doctoral dissertation, for which this work was originally drafted, were invaluable. The critical suggestions and contributions of Robert W. Cox, Judith Adler Hellman, Trevor Munroe, Jorge Nef, Patrick Taylor and Ellen Meiksins Wood helped me to develop and sharpen the arguments presented in this study. David

V.J. Bell, Trent Brady, George Eaton, Mark Goodman, Rudy Grant, Stephen Hellman, Peter Landstreet, and David McNally periodically offered advice that was of greater value than they may realize. The editorial staff at McGill-Queen's Press, notably Donald Akenson, Peter Goheen, and Lesley Andrássy, and the secretarial assistance of the Political Studies department at Queen's University, particularly that of Lannie Gallienne, have been indispensable in the preparation of this manuscript for publication. And without Paul Kellogg's advice, coaxing and unfailing confidence in my work this study might never have escaped my cluttered desk. My son, Adam, and my daughter, Rachel, have been my greatest source of inspiration.

Any errors or weaknesses are of course my responsibility alone.

Ideology and Class Conflict in Jamaica

Introduction

Jamaica is a small Caribbean island nation with a current population of about 2,100,000. The majority of this population are the descendants of African slaves, forced to leave their villages some two hundred years ago to labour on Jamaican plantations for white masters. In contemporary Jamaica, the legacy of slavery is still very much a part of popular consciousness.

Various works draw repeated analogies between the traditions established in the years of slavery and those of the modern labour movement, although widespread, sustained labour organization did not become established in Jamaica until the rebellion of 1938, one hundred years after the complete emancipation of the slaves.[1] Trade union leaders in Jamaica today often trace the origins of a tradition of resistance to the slave and peasant rebellions of the nineteenth century.[2] One lifelong labour and political organizer, Richard Hart, was so determined to disclose the legacy of slave resistance that he devoted a two-volume history to the subject.[3]

Linked to the legacy of slavery is another legacy of the Jamaican working class: the historical significance of small-scale, private agricultural cultivation and landholding. Under slavery, the planters instructed the labourers to cultivate produce for their own sustenance on provision grounds. The slaves were allowed to sell any surplus produced on these grounds at the local weekly market. Over the years the provision grounds system became an important symbol of independent slave activity. After emancipation, the former slaves attempted to support themselves primarily through private land cultivation, rather than accept subordinate, but nominally free, wage labour on the plantations.

Though a significant body of work has addressed the development of a post-emancipation peasant class upon the ashes of the slave system,[4] the effect of peasant development on later working-class organization has not been adequately considered, particularly in terms of the development of class ideology. This question is essential, given the history of the formation of the working class in Jamaica, and is central to the analysis developed in this study. In the post-emancipation period, the Jamaican peasantry was largely also engaged in agricultural wage labour to supplement its income. By the early 1900s, changing economic and social conditions led to a decline in access to peasant land relative to population trends, and to a similar decline in productivity levels, with the result that wage labour became the central, rather than a supplemental, means of support for the producing classes. The attachment to private landholding, both symbolic and real, nonetheless continued strongly to influence patterns of working-class organization and activity.

The following study attempts to provide a synthetic overview of a recurrent pattern of resistance from slavery to wage labour. What is original is the attempt to recognize and analyse the common elements in what appear to be at first glance unique and varied moments of struggle. What is not original is the discovery of these moments in the history of the Jamaican producing classes. The pivotal argument presented here is that a persistent ideology of class resistance has characterized the Jamaican labour force from the period of slavery, through the period of post-emancipation peasant development, and into the era of modern working-class activity. This is neither an unchanging nor an unbroken pattern, but it is a tenacious one. What is presented here is a Marxist interpretation of this ideological pattern traced over three formative historical flash points in the history of Jamaican politics and class struggle: the rebellions of 1831, 1865, and 1938.

This analysis spans the century of greatest transition in the development of the Jamaican labour force. It may appear that a study based on continuity would be more appropriately suited to a period encompassing less variation. The validity of the approach, however, can be demonstrated only if it stands up to the test of variation as well as to that of consistency. The period selected begins with the last and most important slave revolt, which took place in 1831 and signalled the beginning of the end of the slave era. Slavery was finally abolished with the enactment of complete emancipation in 1838. The period concludes with the first general election in Jamaican history, which took place in 1944, and signalled the beginning of the modern Jamaican political system. The foundations for this system were laid in the aftermath of the working-class revolt of 1938.

These were the mass trade union movement led by Alexander Bustamante, which brought about the incorporation of the disenfranchised black majority into the official political process, and the first permanent, stable political party, the People's National Party led by Norman Washington Manley, which marked the birth of sustained mass party politics in Jamaica. By 1944, the movement had become divided into two great political labour blocs – each represented by a trade union and a directly affiliated political party – which have continued to be the hallmarks of Jamaican politics to this day.

In considering any particular period, however, much that lies before and after is necessarily ignored. Another difficulty, perhaps a more serious one, is that many of the events falling within the broad period selected cannot be given adequate consideration. The face of the Jamaican economy underwent major changes during the years following World War II, and along with this came changes in the Jamaican work force.[5] The most notable economic change was the discovery in the early 1940s of extensive, high-quality bauxite reserves, and the consequent development of a small but strategically important mining sector within the national work force. Similarly, the labour force that preceded the development of full-scale plantation slavery under British settlement in the late seventeenth century was markedly different from those considered here. The inhabitants of the island before the first Spanish colonial settlers arrived in 1494 were indigenous Amerindians, engaged in communal agricultural production. This population, estimated at about sixty thousand, was virtually exterminated by the time of the British settlement of 1655. The small numbers of white private settlers who immediately followed British colonial settlement in 1655 were unable to withstand the attempts of large wealthy planters to monopolize the fertile lands.[6] The period under consideration, however, bears crucially upon more recent developments and can shed light on the modern Jamaican political system. Some implications of this history for the study of modern Jamaica are briefly considered in the concluding chapter of this work.

Certain assumptions have been made in this study. First, it is assumed that Jamaica's political, social, and economic history has been inextricably connected with the development of an international system. From the date at which this study begins, the international system was one in which industrial capitalism was dominant; over the period considered, industrial capitalism became increasingly pervasive on an international scale. Jamaica's history is that of an economically weak nation whose development, or lack of it, has been subordinate to the imperialist interests of capitalist expansion.[7] It is further assumed that the system of imperialism has not manifested itself primarily in terms of the presence or absence of foreign settlers, but more profoundly in the pressures of international production forces on the Jamaican class structure.

Racism has been one of the central elements in the ideology used to justify such an "internal structure of exploitation,"[8] defined here as the ideologically constructed view that the white race is physically, morally, intellectually, and culturally superior to the black race. This brings us to a second underlying assumption in this study. Racism is seen as a set of ideas that further justifies and reinforces relations of class domination or exploitation. In Jamaican society, racism and class rule are intricately linked, and one cannot be understood without the other. From the time of the institution of slavery, the ideology of racism was encouraged and legitimized by the colonial powers and those who supported colonial rule. The physical characteristics of the black African were "held to be the first and the lasting badge of his inferiority."[9] The slave origins of the modern Jamaican working class led to the development of a general correlation between class and race in the society as a whole: the fairer the skin colour, the higher the individual's social status was likely to be. This correlation was most sharply maintained and institutionalized during the years of plantation slavery. Since the eighteenth century the basic class and racial systems of a minority white ruling class managing the affairs of a society in which the majority were black slaves, black peasants, or black workers, have been more or less in place, moderated only since the 1940s by the advance of coloured (or mixed race) individuals and a number of blacks into the Jamaican middle and ruling classes.[10]

The historical condition of a permanently small proportion of white residents was perpetuated by the absentee nature of the early planter class, or plantocracy. The majority of the wealthy planters were resident in Britain. As a result, many service occupations that would normally have been preserved for the colonial rulers became open to resident Jamaicans, particularly the progeny of white male colonialists and black female slaves. Management of the plantations, legal advising, maintaining correspondence, and the like, were prestigious tasks requiring certain acquired skills offered to those of fairer complexion. The correlation between class and colour, therefore, was "neither absolute nor caste-like."[11]

The class and colour relationship weakened slightly in the years following emancipation. By 1910, of the fourteen members elected to the Legislative Council on a restricted franchise, one black and five coloured representatives won seats.[12] Racism as a predominating ideological feature of the society, however, continued to linger with a tenacity far greater than any structural correlation between race and class. Ambursley has aptly summarized this as follows: "Though a black and brown element had entered the capitalist ranks, and there were black members of the middle class, an underdeveloped agrarian capitalist Jamaica resembled its slave-based predecessor's structure sufficiently for the old racial concerns to continue to eat into the heart and spirit of its people, at all social levels, moulding their perceptions of their lives."[13] That racial divisions are primarily ideological constructs rather than fundamental structural characteristics of West Indian societies is a view that has been advanced by a number of scholars.[14] The perspective adopted here also maintains this view, and alternatively emphasizes the class basis of social division in Jamaica. Such an emphasis, however, "need not lead us to underestimate the force of racism."[15] On the contrary, the identification of the fundamental, materially rooted class interests of various sectors of Jamaican society highlights the significance of a wide range of ideological constructs — as the following study is intended to illustrate — of which racism is a critical element.

The persistence of racism as an ideology has also been a constant factor in Jamaica's subordination in the global imperial system. Racism was an element of justification for domestic class rule as well as for colonial domination of Jamaica in the British Empire. Alexander notes that racism subsided temporarily after the abolition of slavery, but recurred after 1840 in a more intense form. "Rejuvenated and more powerful, racism no longer appeared as the hand-maiden of slavery but as the ideology of empire. The new *racism of empire* had three distinguishing characteristics. It was paternalistic, 'scientific,' and nationalistic. It was to be the dominant form of racism for the next hundred years."[16]

Incorporating an understanding of race and race consciousness into an explanation of an ideology of resistance does not mean that all actions on the part of the producing classes against the racist state representatives can be immediately reduced to racial categories. In fact, in each of the rebellions considered here, there is no clear, autonomous racial theme operating independently of other sociopolitical and economic factors. Hence, white missionaries are considered by the rebels to be friends of the black slaves and enemies of the white planters; the white royal family are perceived to be friends of the black peasants and enemies of the white members of the Assembly; and a near-white labour leader is heralded as the sole voice of the black working class.

Such is the intricacy of the race and class mosaic in Jamaican society that race consciousness can only be understood in the context of the concrete, historical actions of the black majority as they have forged ideological weapons in specific moments of class conflict.

This brings us to the final assumption of this study – that Jamaican society is organized on the basis of class relations and interaction. The specific concept of class employed rests on the Marxist premise that social relations are essentially based upon the relation of human beings to the development and organization of the productive forces in society, and simultaneously upon the relationship of human beings in any given social class to those in other social classes. The two points together form a single premise, and cannot be separated from one another without distorting the meaning of the premise itself. Unfortunately, Marx never completed his life's work, and among the unfinished projects lay the definition of class.[17] Though Jamaican class development does not lend itself to readily definable categories, three terms are repeatedly used in this study to differentiate various forms of activity carried out by the direct producers – slaves, peasants, and wage workers – and therefore merit some definition or at least description. A more general elaboration of the meaning and implications of a class analysis will follow.

The category of "slave" in pre-emancipation Jamaica is fairly unambiguous. The slaves were the property of their masters; as chattels, they were forbidden to own any property. As a labouring class, they neither owned nor controlled the means of production, and the surplus they produced was extracted by means of forced labour. Nor did they own their capacity to labour, their "labour power," and therefore they were not free to sell that capacity to any employer in exchange for a wage.

The peasant producer is more difficult to define.[18] The Jamaican peasants were agricultural producers organized in family units, who maintained some form of long-term, though not necessarily permanent, access to a small plot of land. The term includes those who had legal title to such plots of land, as well as those who rented the land on which they lived and worked, and paid their rent in either cash or labour on the landlord's estate. It also includes those who squatted on previously uncultivated or abandoned properties where legal possession was unclear or contentious. Land "ownership" in the legal sense was itself a question of recurring class conflict in post-emancipation Jamaica, and is therefore of little value as a criterion for defining the peasantry as a class of producers. At some periods, and in some areas, peasant producers sold their produce on the local or export markets – mediated through "higglers" or local traders in the case of the former, and merchants or trading companies in the case of the latter. In other instances they were able to grow only enough for immediate family consumption, which may have included providing gifts of food to family members who had migrated to the urban centres of the island. The hope or intention of selling produce on the market was a common characteristic, however, whether or not it could be realized.

The wage workers in Jamaica differed from the slaves and peasants insofar as they were owners of their labour power and attempted to sell that labour power to the employing class in exchange for a wage. Because unemployment was always a problem in Jamaica, the effort to complete this exchange did not necessarily meet with success. The notion of a single wage-labouring working class – both employed and unemployed – is therefore important to the applicability of the concept.

Even such broad working definitions can be much more clearly delineated in the abstract than in the activities of the labour force. The terms are important, however, in explaining and interpreting the nature of these activities. Slave labourers, for example, not only worked in the fields, but also cultivated private plots and sold their produce on the local market. After emancipation, peasant cultivators spent part of the week or part of the year working for wages on the plantations as well as working as private producers. Peasant production and wage labour were often performed by the same individuals, or both tasks contributed to the earnings of the family as a unit. After approximately 1900, the Jamaican work force approached, at least in part, the more classical definition of a proletarian class, i.e., a class owning nothing but its ability to labour, which it sold to capital in exchange for a wage. Many, however, continued to own a piece of rural property and the legacy of landholding remained a powerful aspect of working-class organization and consciousness. The Jamaican wage labour force therefore could not be strictly described as a landless proletariat.

The general terms "slaves," "peasants" and "wage workers," as loosely described above, are used liberally as working concepts throughout this study. The more specific meaning of such terms is described in the immediate context of their usage. When a generic term is required for all three forms of labour organization, or for the large body of partly peasant, partly proletarian labourers, the term "producing classes" is employed.

This study assumes a conceptual framework where class relations are taken to be essential to understanding social interaction, though class formation itself is a far from unambiguous process. In conditions where widespread industrial capitalist development has not advanced, class formation is much more fluid than in more developed settings where the lines of demarcation may be sharper. To the extent that class analysis has come into modern usage, its definition has been based essentially on the evolution of advanced (i.e., post-nineteenth-century European) industrial capitalist societies.

The concept of class is nevertheless applicable to the social, political and economic processes of pre-industrial societies.[19] In pre-industrial capitalist societies (including pre-industrial Europe), social relations of production are not clearly defined by a sharp division between wage labour and capital. Therefore, the conceptual vocabulary of class analysis may not yet exist. Nevertheless, the process of production, or the basic means by which people interact with nature to produce a social surplus, and hence the relations of production, or the forms in which people interact with one another as they interact with nature, pose a limited set of historically specific conditions within which societies develop. Very crudely put, the labouring classes produce the social surplus but do not control it; the ruling class controls the social surplus but does not produce it. The material conditions in which societies are formed present limits to social activity and social consciousness, but human beings make their own history within these limits. The process is not predetermined but neither is it entirely arbitrary. Class as a historical category allows for the intricacies of this process in the real lives of the members of those societies to be understood.[20] The development of the Jamaican working class between 1831 and 1944 can be adequately understood only if this pattern of historical action, including the integral processes of both continuity and transformation, can be analytically incorporated.

The following study covers three broad historical periods of development in the evolution of the Jamaican labour force. Each begins and ends in the context of a colonial state and a racist state ideology, but each is distinguished by the prevalence of one particular form of production relations. These periods are: (1) the years between British colonial plantation settlement and emancipation, characterized by slave gang labour concentrated primarily on the sugar estates; (2) the era between the mid-1830s and the late nineteenth century, marked by the growth of a class of small peasant producers; and (3) the decades between the late 1800s and the mid-1940s, during which peasant production and access to land declined relative to population, and urban and agricultural wage labour expanded.

Each of these periods experienced a major rebellion among the producing classes. In 1831, an uprising of slaves, particularly in Jamaica's western parishes, was organized to demand freedom and payment for labour in wages;[21] in 1865, a peasant movement in demand of land culminated in a confrontation with the colonial authorities at Morant Bay; and in 1938, a massive rebellion involving strikes and demonstrations in demand of both land and labour rights swept virtually every corner, both rural and urban, of the island.

Each struggle expressed the frustrations and demands of the labour force dominant in the period – slaves, peasants, or wage workers. Each rebellion also marked a critical transition point in Jamaican social and political development: from slavery to emancipation, from local government to Crown Colony rule, and from non-party politics into the modern era of universal suffrage. In the following chapters, these three rebellions will be analysed. The purpose of the discussion is not to provide an extensive historical account of events, for such accounts can be obtained from other sources.[22] Rather, the aim is to identify a general and recurrent pattern of ideological resistance among the direct producers over a broad historical period of development. Despite the differences in labour force organization that characterize these three rebellions, in each instance there are clearly discernible similarities reflected in the forms of expression adopted and the dominant ideas expressed.

An approach such as this is necessarily highly selective. It neglects important areas of popular experience, concentrating instead upon moments of upheaval and social crisis. The approach is valid to the extent that the pattern of expression of the political traditions of the producing classes is shown in particularly sharp relief during periods of intense protest. In such periods of conflict class divisions are sharpened, and latent forms of discontent are more clearly brought into relief. There is, however, the risk in such an approach that the long periods of relative quiescence between these moments of upheaval, and the process of transition from latent to overt conflict, are overshadowed. Punctuated periods of struggle sharpen class divisions, and in so doing can lend analytical clarity to long-term trends. If such crises are not understood for what they are, that is, watershed marks only rather than history as a whole, then a distorted picture could emerge. It should be stressed, therefore, that these selected moments of struggle are not intended to obscure other tendencies in mass ideology in Jamaica's history, tendencies not toward resistance but toward accommodation and acquiescence. Given that the better part of mainstream first-world interpretations have seen only the latter, however, the approach presented here may act as a necessary corrective to an otherwise linear and static interpretation.

Jamaica has complex and contradictory traditions, and, as Hobsbawm has noted, "nothing marks a people more deeply than the major revolutions it has undergone."[23]

In the case of Jamaica, Hobsbawm's comment must be slightly modified. Here we are considering three struggles which qualify more accurately as rebellions or revolts than as revolutions. Revolutions involve a complete transformation of the structure of power. None of the events considered here achieved this end. The slave rebellion of 1831 was the most organized, or least spontaneous, of the three revolts, and to the extent that it aimed at the complete abolition of slavery its intentions could be considered revolutionary. But unlike the slave rebellion which culminated in revolution in Haiti in 1804,[24] the struggle in Jamaica did not aim to create a new social order led by emancipated blacks. Instead it presumed the maintenance of the power and authority of the white planters, but in conditions of free hired labour rather than slavery. The 1865 outbreak met such brutal repression at its inception that it is difficult to characterize it even as a full-scale rebellion. The revolt of 1938, even at its peak, aimed for reforms that were certainly radical in the context, but could be met within the confines of the existing colonial political system and capitalist economy.

The overt and explicit demands of a movement are not the only features which define its character. In each case discussed here, the ruling regimes were so resistant to changes that would meet the demands of the producing classes that revolutionary labour struggle was necessary to win even the most modest of reforms. In 1831 and 1865, the rebellions met with bloody massacres led by state authorities; only in 1938 were reforms granted, creating a dynamic of co-optation but also indicating the success of the movement in wrenching changes from a rigid and repressive system of rule. The fact that these struggles were for reforms within the system rather than being revolutions against the system does not weaken their significance or relevance to the development of a tradition of resistance. Indeed, in many circumstances the distinction between movements for reform and revolution is not as easily discernible in practice as it is in theory. Depending on the specific conjuncture and the subjective factors of organization and leadership, one can easily turn into the other.[25]

The approach presented here considers the effects of different and specific historical conditions, particularly on the various forms of labour-force activity, while attempting to focus on recurrent patterns of ideological resistance. At each historical conjuncture, the critical element of human will, of choice, of conscious action, was crucial to the outcome of events. With the twenty-twenty vision of hindsight, however, it is clear that a distinct series of options were recurrently selected. In order to explain this process the dynamic interaction of material necessity and human freedom, of restraint and choice, is emphasized in the developing historical context. In this endeavour the ideas of the Marxist historian George Rudé,[26] developed in his studies of the political traditions of what may be called pre-industrial labouring classes in Europe, and more centrally those of the Italian socialist Antonio Gramsci,[27] are particularly useful. Since Rudé has relied upon Gramsci's earlier work to inspire his own, a brief consideration of the views of these two theoreticians is in order.

In his *Prison Notebooks*, Gramsci sketches the basis of an analytical framework through which an ideology of resistance among the producing classes can be understood.[28] He attempts to draw a distinction between the various aspects, or components, of mass consciousness. Some aspects of consciousness reflect historically grounded, objective circumstances and interests. Certain ideas, or sets of ideas, make sense only in a given historical setting, and cease to make sense when the setting is changed. Other ideas are far less historically specific, and continue to influence generations living in very different circumstances. The former, Gramsci terms the "organic" or historically necessary aspect of ideology; the latter, he terms "willed" or "arbitrary." "To the extent that ideologies are historically necessary they have a validity which is 'psychological'; they 'organise' human masses, and create the terrain on which men move, acquire consciousness of their position, struggle, etc. To the extent that they are arbitrary they only create individual 'movements'."[29]

In considering the validity of Gramsci's approach, Rudé raises an important objection. He points out that while Gramsci stresses that ideology must be understood historically, the framework fails to show how the "willed" ideology of the producing classes interacts with the more formulated, or more dominant, ideas of the ruling classes.[30] In an attempt to address this, Rudé provides two alternative conceptual categories. He draws a distinction between what he defines as "inherent" and "derived" ideas.[31] Inherent ideas are those that make up the "sort of 'mother's milk' ideology, based on direct experience, oral tradition or folk-memory and not learned by listening to sermons or speeches or reading books."[32] Derived ideas, on the other hand, are those that are borrowed from members or groups that are not themselves part of the producing classes, and often take "the form of a more structured system of ideas."[33]

The strength of this perspective, Rudé argues, is threefold. First, it eliminates the faulty notion that working-class or peasant rebels are merely "mindless hordes," bereft of their own ideas and willing to follow any persuasive self-styled agitator. Second, it makes it clear that there is no mechanistic progression of ideas on a scale from simple to sophisticated ideologies. And third, such an approach still leaves room to explain the extensive interaction between inherent and derived ideas. For the purpose of this study, which attempts to trace the broad outlines of an ideological tradition developed over several generations, the third point is crucial. As Rudé stresses, "there is no Wall of Babylon dividing the two types of ideology, so that one cannot simply describe the second [derived ideas] as being 'superior' or at a higher level than the first. There is, in fact, a considerable overlap between them. For instance, among the 'inherent' beliefs of one generation, and forming part of its basic culture, are many beliefs that were originally derived from outside by an earlier one."[34]

Rudé's approach, however, presents some new difficulties. Unlike Gramsci's perspective, both of Rudé's categories refer to forms of consciousness that are essentially independent of the specific historical circumstances in which they develop. Rudé accounts for the fluidity and flexibility of ideas, but he fails to address the constraining element imposed by objective historical reality. In an apparent effort to redress this weakness, Rudé brings in a new element that he calls simply "circumstances and experience."[35] In the last analysis, he argues, it is experience that determines the "final mixture" resulting from the interaction of inherent and derived ideas.[36] While the ultimately determinant character of experience is undeniable, Rudé's theory fails to identify the link between experience and the planes of ideology he describes.

The most instructive approach, therefore, may be to combine the contribution of Gramsci with the best of the approach presented by Rudé. Both inherent and derived ideas could loosely be considered to fall within Gramsci's concept of "willed" ideology, as they are not historically time-bound. Further, Gramsci's notion of "organic" ideas can, for our purposes, be more narrowly defined than he had intended. We can consider certain ideas concerning available means of practical resistance that are immediately and historically specific to the organization of production to be "organic."[37] Under slavery, for example, two major forms of resistance were possible. The first was escape, usually carried out individually and in itself presenting no fundamental challenge to the system of slavery as a whole. The second was the more effective option of a collective and organized withdrawal of labour, comparable to strike action. The production process on the plantations was so highly socialized that collective action could effectively cut into the planters' profits. In 1831 in Jamaica, the idea of strike action was posed by the immediate realities of slave-gang labour. In 1865, on the other hand, the labourers were atomized, working in family units engaged in private cultivation. Though discontent was widespread and broadly expressed, only very limited mass actions were organized by either the landholding or the land-hungry peasantry. In 1938 more collectivized labour patterns in both rural and urban areas led to the re-emergence of strike action as the major bargaining tool. It was only when landholding had become ineffective as a means of maintaining either economic security or a strong bargaining position against the employers that the producing classes turned to permanent organizations for collective bargaining in the form of trade unions. In each case, the organization of production and labour force participation led to the development of certain concepts of struggle and resistance. These concepts may be described as historically "organic," and therefore variable in different conditions.

At the same time, a strong thread of continuity at the level of "willed" ideology is reflected in these rebellions. Two broad ideological themes are particularly persistent. These are: (i) the expression of producing class protest using what may be called a "religious idiom"; and (ii) an expectation of, or an appeal to, the British Crown as a benevolent and fair ruler, protective of the interests of the producing class despite its despotic tradition of government. In fact, in some respects it is precisely this despotic character that attracts peasant and working-class support. The rebels appealed to the apparently unending power of the monarchy in efforts to control the excesses of the local Jamaican rulers.

The specific form of these two ideological themes varies in the three rebellions considered. Initially, a set of ideas may have been derived from ruling class or missionary circles. In the next period this same set of ideas may have become an inherent part of the contemporary consciousness of the producing classes. The specific nature of these ideas, and their relationship to the organic ideas of the period and to each other, will be discussed in connection with each rebellion. At this point a brief definition of these two components of "willed" ideology is in order.

The term "religious idiom" identifies a religious conceptual vocabulary, both African and Christian (primarily Baptist) in origin, employed among the Jamaican producing classes to express a tradition of resistance to, and liberation from, a socially, politically, and racially oppressive society. The religious idiom is distinguished from a rigid theological school of thought as it is not based upon a coherent set of specific ideas. This distinction is one not only of degree, but also of substance. The religious idiom refers to the way in which certain ideas are expressed, not to the specific content or doctrine finding expression. Moreover, it is distinct from messianic or millenarian movements in its organizational form. Messianic movements are described by de Queiroz as being "religious in form but socio-economic and political in their aims."[38] In the Jamaican context, there is only one case of a clearly messianic movement (led by Alexander Bedward in the early 1900s).[39] Millenarianism, similar to messianism, is described by Cohn, in the context of medieval movements, as a "body of doctrine concerning the final state of the world, which was chiliastic in the most general sense of the term – meaning that it foretold of the Millenium, not necessarily limited to a thousand years and indeed not necessarily limited at all, in which the world would be inhabited by a humanity at once perfectly good and perfectly happy."[40] In Jamaica, the Ras Tafari movement could be characterized as millenarian. This movement began in the years following the coronation in 1930 of Emperor Haile Selassie in Ethiopia.[41] However, neither messianism nor millenarianism as such characterized the rebellions considered here.[42] The religious idiom may include certain features common to these movements, but it cannnot be equated with them.

The concept of the religious idiom has two essential components: (1) the use of Biblical teaching to reinforce and justify the struggle to achieve greater rights for the producing classes against the interests of the ruling authorities; and (2) the identification of political and social leadership with religious authority, either officially ordained or self-styled. In the case of the slave revolt of 1831, and in a much less direct sense in 1865, religious groups provided the organizational basis for the struggle. In all three instances, however, the understanding that the struggle was in some way religiously authorized was paramount.[43]

The recurrent interpretation of the British Crown as a benevolent despot also warrants brief elaboration. For the Jamaican labourers, be they slaves, peasants or wage workers, colonial rule was experienced in terms of a clear differentiation between the Jamaican authorities who were directly identified with the conditions of racial oppression and economic exploitation, and the more powerful but also more remote British colonial authorities. The distinction was, to some degree, a real one. The former were seen face-to-face and were challenged up to and including the level of direct violent confrontation. The latter, particularly the monarchy, took on a more abstract and even mythical character in these struggles.

A similar "medley of loyalties"[44] may be discerned in pre-industrial European political movements.[45] It is important to stress that an identification of the Crown as a protector of the interests of the producing classes is not in any sense equivalent to a loyalty to British imperialism or colonialism as an economic and political system. On the contrary, in the rebellions considered here, it was precisely the conviction that the British monarchy sympathized with the demands of the producing classes that encouraged the labourers to undertake actions that objectively undermined the stability of this very system. The themes apparent in the religious idiom and the Crown as benevolent despot reflect the dynamic and contradictory processes at work in the development of an ideology of resistance. Persistent appeals to God and Crown appear at face value to reveal only accommodation and passivity to the symbolic figureheads of the existing structure of authority. However, in the minds of the producing classes these symbols were readily and repeatedly transformed into weapons of resistance. The precise way in which these apparently contradictory sets of ideas developed will be considered in the context of each struggle.

CHAPTER ONE

A Labour Force in Transition: A Brief Historical Overview

The evolution of the labour force in Jamaica from a class of slaves working under the discipline of their masters' decree and the rule of the whip to a class of free, independent wage workers was not accomplished with the mere legal passage of the Emancipation Act in the British Parliament in 1833. The legacy of almost two centuries of slavery meant that, once free from their masters' control, the newly emancipated resisted returning to the plantations to labour for wages.[1] Moreover, the geographic and demographic conditions of early nineteenth-century Jamaica presented the former slaves with feasible alternatives. Vast areas of uncultivated land and further acres of land previously cultivated but since abandoned by bankrupt planters were occupied by the former slaves and developed into small agricultural plots. In the early years after emancipation, work for wages on the plantations was performed essentially to obtain supplementary cash income.

It was only when land availability and the profitability of small plot production were outstripped by the growth of the labour force that this "re-constituted peasantry"[2] began to function as a more fully dependent wage labour force on the agricultural estates. These conditions began to develop around the 1880s, but it was only at the turn of the century that the pattern could be fully discerned. Furthermore, as the labour force continued to expand and less land was available to the producing class, the large sugar plantations emerged from post-emancipation decline and became increasingly mechanized. Foreign corporate interests, such as the United Fruit Company of the United States and Tate and Lyle of England, became major agricultural investors in Jamaica. At the same time, Kingston and neighbouring St Andrew developed into a large urban centre, attracting many thousands of displaced rural workers.

In order to provide an understanding of the development of the labour force from its origins in slavery, the nature of slave labour itself will first be described. The historical development of the labour force from the post-emancipation years to the late nineteenth century will then be considered, followed by a discussion of the years between the late nineteenth century and the mid-1940s.

SLAVE LABOUR AND PROVISION GROUNDS PRODUCTION (EIGHTEENTH AND EARLY NINETEENTH CENTURIES)

The essential organizational unit of Jamaican society throughout the years of slavery was the plantation, or estate, specifically the sugar estate. A number of economic activities operated beyond the system of the sugar plantation, but most of these were either related to it in some way or were peripheral to the economy in terms of both numbers employed and surplus generated. Cattle breeding, for example, was dependent upon the sugar plantations as its main purchaser. Cattle were used as working stock, as were mules and to a lesser extent, horses. Stock-raising properties, or pens, were usually located near or on estate properties.

Though other agricultural products, such as coffee, ginger, logwood, and pimento were also produced, it was sugar that sustained the island's economy. In 1770, at the height of Jamaica's plantation prosperity, sugar accounted for 76 per cent of the colony's exports, and rum and molasses for an additional 13 per cent.[3]

Similarly, the greater part of secondary and tertiary production during the period of slavery was conducted either on the plantations or in small towns, which were usually located on or near the plantations. The towns functioned mainly as centres for the export of sugar, rum, and other primary products and for the import of foodstuffs, manufactured goods, and supplies.[4] The sugar estates were thus the largest purchasers of slave labour, and the vast majority of slaves brought to Jamaica laboured on the estates under the direct supervision of their masters or their masters' representatives.

It should be noted, however, that just as there were economic activities other than sugar production on the island, so were there forms of slavery beyond plantation slave labour. A small number of what were called "town Negroes," for example, were hired out for specific jobs and returned a portion of what they earned to their masters. Similarly, there were occasions when jobbing gangs of slaves would be hired out to perform specified tasks for masters other than their own.⁵ Both in the towns and on the estates there were also slaves trained in skilled handicrafts under long apprenticeships directed by white or free coloured master craftsmen. But the majority of the slaves were field workers, whose principal task was the cutting and preparing of sugar cane.

The outstanding characteristic of Jamaican slave society was therefore not its variation but its extreme rigidity and uniformity. The distinction between slave class and master class was sharply marked by the way in which production was carried on in the island. It was reinforced by the obvious differences of colour. Whites were free, blacks were enslaved. While there was some room for upward mobility for a few individuals, the line between classes was very sharply defined. It was a society in which the features of the ruling class "were whiteness, wealth, and education, in that order."⁶

The plantation was not only a manufacturing centre for sugar, rum, and molasses but also a unit of social organization. In a very real sense, the plantation operated as a village in itself. As one observer noted, "The stranger is apt to ask what village is it? – for every completed sugar works is no less, the various and many buildings bespeaking as much at first sight."⁷ The mansion house, the mill, the boiling house, the houses for curing and distillation, combined with stables, lodge, smithies, carpenters' and servants' quarters, and rows of slave dwellings to create a picture not dissimilar to a small early industrial town.

The sugar estate thus prefigured the modern industrial centre.⁸ It required massive sums of capital investment to begin profitable production, and a large and continuing labour supply to ensure the productivity of that investment. Edwards noted that "no less than thirty thousand pounds sterling" was necessary to initiate a successful sugar plantation.⁹ Of the total amount of capital necessary to establish a sugar plantation in Jamaica in 1819, one-third was devoted to the cost of land, one-sixth to equipment and factory buildings, and almost all of the remaining one-half was spent on the purchase of slaves.¹⁰

Slave labour on the plantations was highly collectivized labour. In 1831, the *Jamaica Almanac* indicated that more than half of the total slave population was employed on properties having over one hundred slaves.¹¹ Eisner estimates that the average plantation employed two hundred to three hundred slaves in unskilled and semi-skilled labour.¹² The nature of the work, both in the cane fields and in the processing factories, demanded that slave labour "must be constant and must work, or be made to work, in co-operation."¹³

On most estates, the slaves were grouped into three distinct "gangs" of labourers, ranked according to physical strength. The first gang was composed of those considered to be the best workers, primarily strong, young slaves. The second gang consisted of older slaves, pregnant women,[14] and adolescents. The third gang was made up of weaker workers – the elderly, children, and the physically handicapped.[15] On the very large estates, the slaves were often divided into four gangs, but here the distinction between the first and second gangs seemed to be based more on the need for supervision than on the physical strength of the labourers.[16] The various gangs performed different types of work – the strongest performing the most difficult tasks, the weaker the lighter tasks.

Each gang had its own driver, a favoured slave appointed by the white overseer and given the task of extracting the maximum amount of labour and productivity from the field workers. The work of the field labourers was strictly supervised and rigidly scheduled. Somewhat different work patterns prevailed depending on whether it was crop time, (which lasted about five months, roughly from July to December, though it varied among estates) or out-of-crop time. The average work day during out-of-crop time began between 4:00 A.M. and sunrise, with the sound of the head driver's cracking whip, a bell, or the blowing of a conch shell. Before the field work began, a series of small preparatory jobs had to be performed, a roll-call was taken, and any persons tardy without excuse were whipped. Then the work in the cane field continued until sunset, with two meal breaks. After the field labour for the day was done, other tasks, such as cleaning and feeding the estate mules or cattle, were completed. A final roll-call was taken when that work was finished, and the slaves usually returned to their huts between 7:00 and 8:00 P.M.

During crop time this daily cycle was greatly intensified. The work was much more strenuous and the slaves were usually given longer hours and placed on a shift schedule. The gangs were divided into at least two rotating shifts.[17] One author, on the basis of the accounts of pro-slavery witnesses only, estimated that the slaves worked an average of sixteen and one-half hours per day during the out-of-crop period, and a full eighteen hours per day during the five months of crop time, if cultivation of provision grounds was included in the calculation.[18]

The suffering endured by the slaves of Jamaica, however, extended far beyond the immediate conditions of work. The brutality which accompanied Atlantic slavery – from the destruction of African villages to the torturous conditions of the Middle Passage and the scramble for human property on the slave market – has been extensively documented by contemporary and modern authors.[19] In 1707 Sir Hans Sloane described the method of slave punishment typical of the slave era in the West Indies.

> The Punishments for Crimes of Slaves, are usually for Rebellions burning them, by nailing them down to the ground with crooked Sticks on every Limb, and then applying the Fire by degrees from the Feet and Hands, burning them gradually up to the Head, whereby their pains are extravagant.
> For Crimes of a lesser nature Gelding, or chopping off half the Foot with an Axe ... For running away they put Iron Rings of great weight on their Ankles, or Pottocks about their Necks, which are Iron Rings with two long Necks rivetted to them, or a Spur in the Mouth.
> For Negligence, they are usually whipt by the Overseers with Lance-wood Switches till they be bloody ... after they are whipt till they are Raw, some put on their Skins Pepper and Salt to make them Smart; at other times their Masters will drip melted Wax on their Skins, and use very exquisite Torments.[20]

There was, however, one important reprieve for the plantation slaves from the continuing cycle of forced labour and harsh punishment. This was the provision grounds system. All but the most privileged slaves, such as the domestics for whom food was provided by their masters, were allotted plots of estate land not suitable for sugar cultivation, usually in the mountainous areas, where they raised produce for their own diet. Only a small portion of the slaves' food, such as saltfish, which they could not produce for themselves, was provided for the majority by their masters.

The extent to which the planters relied on slave-grown rather than imported food to feed the slaves varied, but the peculiarities of Jamaica's geography ensured that this system was by and large "carried to a high pitch"[21] on the island. Only 20 per cent of the island is ideally suited for sugar estate planting. The remainder is mountainous or hilly.[22] Hence vast regions of land were never considered usable for cane production.[23]

Furthermore, heavy reliance on imports as the main source of food for the slaves would have put the Jamaican planters in a vulnerable position. Warfare among the colonial powers was frequent during the eighteenth century when Jamaican plantation production reached its peak. This meant periodic food shortages and increased prices. Severe food shortages would have led to malnourished and therefore unproductive slave labourers, in turn decreasing plantation profits. Thus the provision grounds system was preferred.

The crops cultivated by the slaves were extremely diverse and of various origins. Sweet potatoes, arrowroot, plantain, and coconuts were grown by the Arawak population before the first Spanish settlement of the island. The Spaniards introduced not only sugar cane but also the banana and numerous varieties of citrus fruit. The ackee came to Jamaica from West Africa, the mango and breadfruit from Oceana.[24] All of these crops, in addition to numerous others, were cultivated. Plantains, yams, and cocos, however, seem to have been the most notable staples. The better part of slave cultivation consisted of root crops, which were easily grown on land not suitable for sugar cane. Such crops were also less vulnerable to destruction due to hurricanes, which have ravaged Jamaica frequently over the centuries.

In addition, the slaves raised a variety of livestock, including a small number of cows, poultry, and pigs. They also produced small hand-crafted items, mostly of straw plaiting or earthenware.

The precise amount of land apportioned to each slave family varied a great deal from estate to estate, as it varied over the years of slavery. Turner estimates that the average slave holding was between three-quarters of an acre and one and one-third acres.[25] It can be concluded that over the years most slaves were granted increasing amounts of time for provision grounds cultivation. This conclusion can be drawn from the changes written into Jamaican slave laws, which tended to be simply a codification of existing custom.

In 1792, the amended slave laws recognized Sundays off and granted a further one day per fortnight, except during crop time, for the slaves to tend their provision grounds. By 1826, the act obliged the planters to allow all Sundays off – in and out of crop time – and stipulated that there should at least be twenty-six days off throughout the year (the latter condition was added in 1816). Further, the act of 1826 stated that all mills were to be shut down between Saturdays at 7:00 P.M. and Mondays at 5:00 A.M.[26] Beyond the specific days devoted to provision ground cultivation, slaves who could worked on their plots over their two-hour daily lunch break, and the very industrious tended them at night after the long day in the cane fields was over.

The slaves were also permitted to grow crops on tiny house plots, called yards or kitchen gardens, around their huts. Crops that were easily stolen, such as tree crops, or those that demanded extra attention were usually grown here, in addition to the standard root crops.

The provision grounds system was sufficiently productive, and the slaves were sufficiently industrious, to provide not only for their own well-being but also to retain a surplus. It was this surplus that provided the basis for the regular Sunday slave markets.[27] The first legal Jamaican market of any form has been traced to Spanish Town in 1662, only seven years after the English occupation of the island. This market was established upon the request of English settlers and was clearly English, rather than African, in origin.[28] Trade among slaves, however, apparently began independently of formal marketplace transactions. By the early eighteenth century, the selling of slave provision produce was acknowledged by law. By the latter part of the century the slave market had become an accepted part of the domestic slave economy.[29]

While efforts were made to repress the selling of goods stolen by the slaves from the plantations (such activity was punishable by up to thirty-one lashes of the whip), the white settlers were far too dependent upon slave produce to interfere with its marketing. Thus, by the mid-eighteenth century, the white slave-owning population had become entirely dependent upon the slaves for much of their daily diet.[30]

Long estimated that by the last quarter of the eighteenth century the slaves held about 20 per cent of the currency in circulation on the island, "the greater part of the small silver circulating among them."[31] It should be noted, however, that the remaining 80 per cent of the circulating currency was concentrated in the hands of a minority ruling class constituting less than 10 per cent of the population.

At the end of the century, weekly slave markets had been established not only in Kingston and Spanish Town, but also throughout the rural areas. It was not uncommon for slaves to retain some savings, particularly in the years before emancipation when freedom was anticipated. In other periods, however, the slaves generally earned only enough to buy the few items of food that were neither grown by themselves nor provided by their masters, and occasionally some cloth or other products for home use.[32] Prices were far from uniform across the island, and slave earnings have been estimated variously, but about one shilling per week is a fair approximation.[33]

The significance – both material and symbolic – of the provision grounds and slave marketing system cannot be overemphasized. Jamaica represented a society where the power and authority of the ruling class were based not only on colour and position, but also on landownership. For the better part of the slave era slaves were legally forbidden to own property, as they were themselves the property of their masters. The provision grounds and house plots, however, were effectively "owned" by the slaves, by custom if not by law.[34] This land gave the slave family some sense of social and economic identity as a unit. "The focus for family life was the provision grounds, which the families worked in common ... The majority of the families ... consisted of a man and a woman of marriageable age living with the woman's children ... The household – more particularly, the family households with their common property interest in their grounds and houses – enabled the slaves to establish a nucleus of family solidarities to sustain them in the vicissitudes of life."[35] The earnings from the sale of the produce went directly into the hands of the slaves. From ground to market, the production and sale of provisions represented virtually autonomous slave activity. Further, the only time when they were granted some freedom of movement was when going to or from the weekly market. An 1807 law stated the following: "be it further enacted by the authority aforesaid, that no slave, such only excepted as are going with firewood, grass, fruit, provisions, or small stock and other goods, which they may lawfully sell, to market, and returning therefrom, shall here after be suffered or permitted to go out of his or her master or owner's plantation or settlement, or to travel from one town or place to another, unless such slave shall have a ticket from his master, owner, employer, or overseer."[36]

The autonomy the slaves enjoyed in their work on the provision grounds stands in sharp contrast to the constant supervision of their estate field labour. Bryan Edwards, an eighteenth-century planter and historian resident in Jamaica, noted that the planters benefitted by allowing the slaves to cultivate their provision grounds almost without supervision. As well as providing economic advantages, it eased the constant threats of escape and rebellion. "The negro who has acquired by his own labour a property in his master's land, has much to lose, and is therefore less inclined to desert his work."[37] Moreover, the freedom from rigid scheduling, and the threat of the whip, as well as the promise of tangible benefits, made working on the provision grounds far more desirable than estate field labour.

Another contrast can be drawn between labour on the estates and labour on the provision grounds and house plots. The former was highly collectivized, involving a large number of labourers performing similar work in a single massive enterprise. The latter was atomized, family production, involving a small number of workers performing differentiated tasks in a small-scale enterprise.

Objectively the labourers were more powerful as a united class in the fields. It was sugar production on a mass scale that defined the prime interests and identity of the plantocracy, for it was sugar that brought in the profits. The socialized, collective labour of the slaves in the fields united them as a single bloc whose members greatly outnumbered their white oppressors. Any slowdown or disruption of work or any decline in labour productivity among the slaves could seriously hamper production. Such actions would curtail the surplus upon which the planters, merchants, and sections of British industrial capital were dependent. On the provision grounds, however, though the collective identity of the slaves was reflected by such things as their common ownership of cattle, the slaves' personal well-being depended upon relatively isolated, private production.[38] The surplus generated through this production contributed only indirectly to plantation profits, by increasing the well-being and the reproduction of the slave labour force.

Subjectively, the slaves' self-esteem was developed by their work on the provision grounds and diminished by estate labour. This was in part due to the traditional attitude to the land characteristic among the tribes of West Africa, where most of the slaves were originally captured. Private rights to cultivated land were recognized and respected.[39] Furthermore, the cultivation of the provision grounds encouraged the development of intellectual and social abilities, such as independence and creativity, that were antithetical to slavery as a system.[40] The dual character of slave labour was to have significant effects on the development of the labour force after emancipation. When the plantations experienced a period of economic stagnation and decline in the early decades of the 1800s, the contradictory elements of Jamaican slavery became obvious.

PRIVATE PRODUCTION AND AMALGAMATION OF THE PLANTATIONS (EARLY TO LATE NINETEENTH CENTURY)

The Emancipation Act was submitted as a bill to the British Parliament in 1833 by Lord Stanley, then Secretary for the Colonies. The key clause read as follows:

Be it enacted, that all and every, the persons who, on the first day of August, one thousand eight hundred and thirty-four, shall be holden in slavery within any such British Colony as aforesaid, shall, upon and from and after the said first day of August, one thousand eight hundred and thirty-four, become and be to all intents and purposes free, and discharged of and from all manner of slavery, and shall be absolutely and forever manumitted; and that the children thereafter born to any such persons, and the offspring of such children, shall in like manner be free from birth; and that from and after the first day of August, one thousand eight hundred and thirty-four, slavery shall be, and is hereby utterly and forever abolished and declared unlawful throughout the British colonies, plantations and possessions abroad.[41]

By the early 1800s virtually every major industrial concern in Europe strongly opposed slavery and was committed to the expansion of a system of wage labour and free trade.[42] Most of the local plantation interests in the colonies, however, were firmly opposed to all efforts to reform or eliminate the slave system. The Jamaican planters were among the most vociferous. In the decades prior to emancipation, Jamaica's economy was already suffering seriously in the face of increased international sugar competition. Between 1813 and 1833, the island's production had declined by almost one-sixth.[43]

As a partial concession to the West India lobby, the Emancipation Act provided for a system of apprenticeship, whereby the slaves were to be given a gradually increasing degree of freedom over a period of twelve years. In practice, however, the apprenticeship system proved a dismal failure. As one contemporary writer observed, "the apprenticeship system was working *most satisfactorily* – to the planters, that is, slavery had never been abolished."[44] Stipendiary magistrates were appointed to oversee the apprenticeship system and to protect the interests of the former slaves. More often than not they were incompetent and corrupt. The planters frequently bribed them with gifts of money, alcohol, and the like, in return for a blind eye to the continuing harsh treatment of the labourers.[45] There is much evidence to support the conclusion that the slaves suffered their harshest treatment during the period of apprenticeship.[46] Even the established tradition of granting the slaves one day per week to cultivate and market their provisions was withdrawn on many plantations.[47]

So obvious was the failure of the apprenticeship system that the plan was officially abandoned only four years after its introduction. On August 1838, "the freedmen of all British colonies were made fully and unconditionally free."[48] In the aftermath of the acknowledged failure of the apprenticeship system, the importance of full emancipation to the slaves was even more profound. Their sense of having achieved a moral conquest over their white rulers must have been further increased by the economic crisis that subsequently struck the plantations.

Though "the island was utterly insolvent the day the emancipation bill was passed,"[49] complete emancipation was accompanied by the further decline of the plantations. High compensation awards were granted to the slave owners (while no compensation for their years of suffering was offered the slaves), but such sums often fell short of outstanding debts.[50] Many properties had been mortgaged for far more than their actual value, and credit for working capital became increasingly difficult to secure. The result was widespread bankruptcy and the abandonment of plantations across the island. Between 1836 and 1846, the number of sugar estates declined from 670 to 513.[51] By 1850, about 400,000 acres of land had been abandoned.

The former slaves, identifying strongly with their role as cultivators of provision grounds, and rejecting their experiences as forced workers on the plantations, were reluctant to return to the plantations as wage labourers. With large tracts of land available for occupancy, private family production was carried over to the post-emancipation period. The result was the establishment of a large class of rural producers, a "re-constituted peasantry." They occupied land surrounding the plantation areas wherever it was available. This included the mountainous regions where the provision grounds had been predominantly located and the newly abandoned plantation fields. This new peasantry emerged as "a negative reflex to enslavement."[52] Though part-time plantation labour often accompanied peasant production, the work force endeavoured to remain independent of the plantation economy in general.

Landownership was the precondition of such independence, and land could be acquired through various means. Because of the general abandonment of properties, it was relatively inexpensive, between two and ten pounds per acre.[53] In anticipation of their freedom some of the former slaves had saved sufficient from the sale of provisions to purchase one or two acres. Others stayed on the provision grounds that they had come to consider their own during slavery. Initially, in an attempt to compel the emancipated labourers to work for wages, the planters levied high rents on these properties. It was common to demand rent at the rate of two days labour per week, payable in either cash or labour on the plantation.[54] The hope was that the high costs of staying on familiar land would compel the freed slaves to return to their former masters for wage work. In fact the plan backfired against the planters. A mass exodus of workers from the estates left many planters with neither tenants nor labourers.[55]

The freed slaves could acquire land by a number of other means. In some districts, over the period extending from the early to the late nineteenth century, the decline of the plantations was so dramatic that wage labour was not available even for those who sought it. In such instances, the freed slaves were compelled to turn to peasant production simply to survive.[56] Baptist missionaries in Jamaica, longtime advocates of emancipation, helped the former slaves to acquire land. Large tracts of land were purchased in the name of the Church, and then sold off in small plots. The missionaries thus established small settlements, or "free villages," from which active parishioners were recruited.[57] In addition, squatting on abandoned or unoccupied land was widespread. Local government attempts to prevent squatting were rarely successful.[58] They were foiled by local resistance and the difficulty of identifying legal title. Later in the nineteenth century, particularly after the Morant Bay rebellion, the British authorities intervened to encourage a number of land resettlement schemes, which met with only limited success.[59]

Statistics available for the period do not allow for precise estimates of either the number of peasants or the sizes of their holdings, because figures were based only on the properties that paid taxes. It is clear, however, that the acquisition of land was the rule rather than the exception among the labourers. In 1838, 2,114 persons were recorded to hold properties under forty acres; in 1841 the figure had risen to 7,919; and by 1860 the number stood at 50,000.[60]

The rural population varied a great deal in terms of the size of holdings, the level of earnings and, to a lesser extent, the types of crops grown. Those who owned properties under five acres tended to continue growing ground crops, as they had done as slaves on their provision plots, and sold their goods in the local market. Those who owned more than five acres and kept the better part of that land cultivated with ground crops would likely have had to hire outside labour. If they produced a crop such as coffee, however, wider spacing of crops would have enabled the cultivator to maintain up to fifteen acres without outside assistance.[61]

Between the mid-nineteenth century and 1900, the peasant producers became more consolidated.[62] As the large sugar plantations continued to decline both in numbers and in productivity, small cultivators took over an increasing share of the export market. This shift in the pattern of trade reflected a shift in the pattern of production. Products such as bananas, coffee, and logwood, which could be profitably produced without large capital investments, began to compete with sugar as the dominant export. In 1850, 83 per cent of peasant output consisted of subsistence products, or ground provisions, while only 11 per cent consisted of exports. By 1890 the proportion of subsistence crops had fallen to 74 per cent, and exports had risen to 23 per cent.[63] Much of this produce was sold to American merchants for the US market. By the 1880s the American-owned United Fruit Company had established itself as a major dealer in Jamaican-grown bananas.

During the initial years following emancipation, the real income of the small producers increased significantly. Between 1832 and 1850 the incomes of small agricultural producers increased from 29.6 per cent of the national income to 44.3 per cent. After this time, however, the income of the producing class ceased to increase and distribution became more unequal. The initial expansion in earnings reflected the transition from slavery to peasant production in a period of general plantation decline. Once this adjustment period had passed, earnings of the producing class remained virtually stagnant as a percentage of the national income.[64] One island clergyman observed that by 1865 "the people generally are becoming poorer."[65] The most successful cultivators were able to establish themselves as small farmers, while the majority lived at, or barely above, subsistence level. As long as land was available, however, the former slaves were resistant to the appeals of plantation owners to return to work regularly for wages.

Those sugar plantations that continued to operate therefore suffered from a chronic shortage of labour during the first decades after emancipation. For although much had changed with the enactment of emancipation, many aspects of Jamaican society remained the same. The class and racial hierarchy was not challenged. Indeed "emancipation was accompanied by no alteration of the colony's political system or economic objectives."[66] The plantation ruling class was still in control of the island's domestic economy and political processes, within the wider context of British colonial rule. If the planters were to be compelled by their British superiors to pay their workers in wages, then they would offer wages that were as low as possible, and would pay such wages irregularly and inconsistently.

The planters persistently complained of the exorbitant cost of labour. In fact few estates were prepared to pay wages which were "high or regular enough to compete with the new opportunities"[67] available since emancipation. Further, numerous estimates calculate that the wages paid to estate employees were actually *lower* per unit of output than the cost of maintaining slaves before emancipation. Sewell concluded in 1862 "that the cost of labor in sugar-cultivation was in Jamaica, under slavery, 4 37/100 cents per pound, and is now, under freedom, two cents per pound – that the slave, under compulsory work, produced annually, 2286 lbs., while the free laborer, working only six or seven hours a day, and only 170 days out of the year, produces 2500 lbs."[68]

The former slaves' reluctance to accept plantation employment was moderated by the uncertainty of conditions surrounding private production. Prices for both ground crops and exports varied greatly, and productivity itself depended largely on weather and soil conditions. Thus a pattern developed whereby freeholders supplemented their incomes with wage labour on the estates. Those who left the estates would return to work when their own plots were not in need of great attention. Even those who continued to earn their livings primarily from estate employment "worked when and for how long they pleased."[69] Hall describes the employment situation in Jamaica throughout most of the nineteenth century in terms of the following objective and subjective factors: (1) the relation of the estate to population density and alternative forms of labour depending on conditions of soil fertility for provision growing, etc.; (2) the attitude of the sugar planters to local freeholding varying from ejectment policies to encouraging settlement; and (3) the attitude of the local population to the individual planter. This factor was expressed in unpredictable ways, sometimes involving a general boycott of labour for an unpopular planter.[70]

The "re-constituted peasantry" was therefore not in fact a purely peasant class. Except for a small percentage of more established producers, the majority were a mixed peasantry and wage-labouring group. The local planters, the Legislature, and, until late in the century, the British government, identified such freed slaves as a class consisting merely of "lazy Negroes," a class that refused to accept steady employment. Asserting with confidence the racist notions of the day, Carlyle described the Jamaican worker as one who lounged about all day long, "sunk to his ears in pumpkin imbibing saccharine juices and much at ease in Creation."[71]

A number of attempts to alleviate the labour shortage on the plantations were undertaken after emancipation. One was an unsuccessful effort to import immigrant workers. The earliest immigration schemes in Jamaica were directed toward attracting white European settlers to occupy the interior hill regions, thus denying the former slaves access to the vacant land. This attempt failed because of insufficient numbers of immigrants, and incompetence and poor planning on the part of the Jamaican authorities.[72]

Other immigration programs depended upon securing indentured labourers, primarily from India. Such schemes tended to meet with "utter failure" because the faltering Jamaican planters were unable to pay the indenture fees.[73]

Another response to the labour shortage on the estates was to increase productivity. For the first time in the island's history, the plough replaced the hoe in general use in the fields. Various types of ploughs and harrows were imported from Britain and America, and some Jamaican planters devised ploughs more suited to the hard island soils.[74] Alternative means of generating power were also employed to replace human labour. Steam power, or a combination of steam and water, came increasingly into general use to drive the sugar mills. Windmills and animal-powered mills, which were much less efficient, became less common. By 1854 over two thirds of all sugar mills in Jamaica were driven by steam and water power. By 1890, of the 162 sugar factories in operation, fully one hundred were driven by steam and an additional nineteen used steam and water.[75]

Productive capacity was also increased by the use of new machinery. The vacuum pan was introduced for processing sugar, and a machine that hulled the thin skin from coffee beans came into use.[76] Such technical improvements, however, were not universally implemented. Plantation properties that were not topographically suitable for technical improvements were forced out of business under the pressure of a shortage of labour willing to work for the wages that the plantations in crisis would or could pay.

After 1846 the Jamaican sugar industry suffered a further economic setback when protective legislation from Britain was removed. The Sugar Duties Act of 1846 introduced a new set of duties, compelling the price of Jamaican sugar to compete freely against less expensively produced sugar from other sources. Increasingly, sales of Cuban cane sugar and European beet sugar were eroding British Caribbean dominance of the sugar industry. And as prices for Jamaican sugar declined, credit, which had come primarily from British merchant houses, became difficult or impossible to secure. The government of Jamaica notified the Colonial Office in 1847 that "the plain truth is that the whole body of planters and their subordinate agents here who depend on advances of money or credit from London are in a deplorable way ... one consequence of which and of other circumstances of the moment is that London houses are refusing to make for the future any further advances."[77]

After 1846, plans to introduce new machinery were largely curtailed and requests for indentured labourers were halted. Abandonment of unprofitable estates continued, while those estates that were able to continue production became larger and more centralized. The crisis in availability of both labour and credit, however, meant that the estates remaining in operation did not show a significant rise in their rate of productivity. From the mid-1850s until the mid-1870s, sugar output remained stable. Over the same period, however, the number of operating plantations declined from 426 to 266.[78] The smaller number of more efficient plantations, therefore, could only maintain the same level of productivity carried by the more numerous but less efficient properties of two decades before.

The reduction in the number of plantations was largely the result of mergers of neighbouring estates. Amalgamations of properties were usually accomplished by combining cane areas for a single processing mill. This meant that the estates remaining in production generally employed larger and more collectivized work forces, when operating at or near full capacity, than they had employed during the era of slavery.

The work force was undergoing two simultaneous processes in the post-emancipation decades. On the one hand, there was a distinct movement towards increased dispersion through the occupation of abandoned or uncultivated lands. The small producers worked independently, labouring as family units, and competing against one another in the local and, to a lesser extent, export markets. On the other hand, there was a movement towards increased collectivization of the labour force, as the estates that remained in operation became larger and required a larger number of workers engaged in socialized production.

A unique characteristic of the Jamaican labour force is that these two processes generally affected not merely the same national work force, but the very same workers. As in the period of slavery, the effect of these distinct processes was somewhat contradictory. While the producing classes played a more economically important role in national production in their capacity as workers paid in wages, they themselves placed much more importance on their role as peasant producers. From the labourers' point of view, there was no contradiction in this attitude. They believed that social and economic security were dependent upon private cultivation, and labour on the estates was taken up only because immediate economic pressures so dictated.

The significance assigned to the ownership and control of land during the slave era continued into the years following emancipation. In addition, some new conditions arose which increased this significance. First, though the essential political structure of colonial Jamaica remained unchanged in the years immediately following emancipation, one important new development occurred: those freed slaves who were able to meet the restrictive conditions of the island franchise became eligible to vote.[79] Such conditions involved holding legal title to a piece of land rated at a certain value and the payment in full of taxes on that land.[80] These conditions were not easily or often met, largely due to perpetual disputes over legal titles to land. Nevertheless, the number of eligible voters on the island did increase slightly after 1838. In that year, there were 1,796 officially registered voters; in 1854 the number stood at 2,235.[81] As there was a net decline in the white population over these years, as a result of the decline of plantation profits and the emancipation of the black population, it can be safely assumed that the majority of this increase consisted of former slaves.[82] In 1850, one writer made the following observation: "I was surprised to find how general was the desire among the negroes to become possessed of a little land, and upon what sound principles that desire was based ... A freehold of four or five acres gives them a vote, to which they attach great value."[83]

A second, and more important factor that contributed to the significance of landholding after emancipation concerned the new relationship between the labourers and the planters. If freed slaves were able to acquire even a small piece of land, they were not compelled to return to the plantations as full-time workers. As long as land was available and soil, weather and market conditions were reasonably favourable, the labourers had some means of bargaining with their former masters over the conditions of their work. The strength of this bargaining position was based on the availability of an alternative to economic dependence upon wage labour on the estate, that is, on access to land for subsistence production and market sale.[84] After almost two centuries of slavery, the period immediately following emancipation represented the first time that the direct producers were able to offer or withdraw their labour power at will. As long as they could cultivate a piece of land they were not compelled to sell their labour power back to the planters at whatever price – in the form of wages and working conditions – was offered. As one planter complained, "I have carefully watched the native and I have *never* found a case in which a really industrious man could be induced to leave his own settlement to work for others continuously, I know of some few cases where such men in their slack time will work for others, but none where they will not revert to their own cultivation so soon as their presence and labour there is requisite."[85]

The bargaining between planter and worker was not conducted according to any plan or central directive. Rather, a pattern developed as a result of individual initiative and action in response to a common condition of emancipation and access to land. In effect, the refusal of the freed slaves across the island to return *en masse* to the plantations as wage workers might be described as a prolonged labour "strike". In implementation, however, it lacked formal collective organization or planning, and therefore was without formal collective control. This exodus from plantation labour represented an extremely important form of labour action that was to become part of the tradition of working-class resistance in Jamaica but, not surprisingly, it did not immediately contribute to increased labour organization.

LAND CRISIS, MONOPOLIZATION AND URBANIZATION (LATE NINETEENTH CENTURY TO MID-1940S)

Though the exact date is difficult to identify, in the late nineteenth and early twentieth centuries, a dramatic change in the availability of Jamaican land relative to demand began to occur: the growth of the rural population seeking land began to outstrip the supply of unoccupied acreage. Scholars have placed the turning point at varying times – in the 1880s, the year 1900, or 1911.[86] The exact date, however, matters less than the implications of a sharp break in the previous post-emancipation trend toward private family settlement of easily accessible lands. The period of the late nineteenth and early twentieth century saw the decline of the era of peasant prosperity and a shift from a situation of labour shortage on the estates to one of labour surplus. Further, the land crisis provoked a trend toward internal migration from the rural areas to the urban district of Kingston and St Andrew. These general trends continued, despite other economic changes, into the mid-1940s. Since the mid-1800s Jamaica's population had been increasing steadily at a rate of approximately 1.4 per cent per year. By 1891, the population had grown to 695,000, and it continued to expand – to 858,000 by 1921, and to 1,139,000 by 1936.[87]

The rate of increase of land under cultivation was even more rapid than population growth. During the early part of this period (i.e., before the 1930s, with the exception of the years around World War I), the banana industry was gaining ascendancy over sugar as an export crop. Though this industry was suitable for peasant production because it did not require factory processing, banana cultivation involved a reduced demand for labour per acre. Between 1871 and 1911 the average number of cultivated acres per person employed in agriculture grew from 0.771 to 1.393, an increase of

Table
Trends in Size of Rural Landholdings (1882–1943)

Size of holdings	Year	No. of holdings	Per cent change	Per cent change per annum
5 to 50 acres	1882	13,674	–	–
	1930	31,038	127	2.6
	1943	30,046	–3	–0.8
1 to 5 acres	1882	38,838	–	–
	1930	153,406	295	6.1
	1943	179,788	17	1.3

Source: C. Stone, "Political Aspects of Postwar Agricultural Policies in Jamaica (1945–1970)," *Social and Economic Studies* 23 (June 1974): 151

almost 100 per cent.[88] The increased demand for new land to cultivate was therefore not only absolute, in terms of the total rural population, but also relative, in terms of the number of acres required per labourer.

Several other factors added to the decline in the accessibility of land throughout the period under consideration. Between 1882 and 1902, a significant number of small peasants (those owning one to five acres of land) were able to expand their landholdings sufficiently to enter the middle peasant category (those owning holdings between 15 and 150 acres). This trend continued, though to a much more limited degree, between 1902 and 1930. By the end of the 1930s, however, the possibility of expansion ceased to exist. From 1930 to 1943 the number of middle peasants decreased, while the number of small peasant holdings increased notably.[89] The following table illustrates these trends. Thus, while the number of small peasants was growing, the average size of the unit of land cultivated was on the decline.

Moreover, by 1943, 92 per cent of the total number of farms in operation were under twenty-five acres but occupied only 21 per cent of the total acreage under cultivation. At the same time, large holdings of two hundred acres or more occupied 66 per cent of total farm acreage, but represented only 1.4 per cent of the number of farming units on the island.[90] The diminishing average size of peasant landholdings was in part the result of the repeated subdivision of units within families over the generations. Without access to new lands, properties were divided among the farmholders' children, who would then be expected to divide their plots among their children.[91]

The increasingly intensive exploitation of the land led to a rise in soil erosion and a decline in land fertility, particularly in the small holdings. The greatest portion of the most productive land, which was flat or gently rolling, was in the large estates.[92] Productivity was further jeopardized by the extensive spread of crop disease. The Panama and Leafspot diseases were particularly damaging to the small cultivator, as they threatened banana production.

Bananas were a thriving export crop, and their cultivation offered the small producer the best opportunity for prosperity. By 1930, 39 per cent of the island's banana exports were produced by holdings of twenty acres or less.[93] However, the banana industry suffered a serious and prolonged setback. Panama disease, by far the most damaging crop disease, began to spread after World War I, and by the end of the 1930s had reached "disastrous proportions."[94] The disease not only destroys the current crop but moves rapidly through the soil, leaving it infected for many years. Small producers with limited acreage were therefore by far the most adversely affected. Procedures to control banana disease were eventually developed, but they were too costly and made available too late to help the average small producer. By the early 1950s the Lacatan banana was found to be resistant to Panama disease. Leafspot disease, which became epidemic in Jamaica shortly after the spread of Panama disease, could be controlled by chemical sprays. The necessary regular treatment required, however, cost even the large producers on flat lands approximately one-quarter of their average returns from sales and the cost of spraying on hillside lands where small plots were concentrated was even greater.[95]

Regions where peasant banana cultivation was highly concentrated were the first to be devastated by the spread of plant disease, most notably the parishes of Portland and St Mary. As early as 1930 all attempts to employ precautionary measures against Panama disease in these parishes were abandoned.[96] But by the latter part of the 1930s no part of the island was unaffected. One leading estate owner noted in 1936 that "Panama disease has hit the small settlers much more severely than the large planter ... On talking to these men one and all seem to be in a hopeless state of mind ... The small farmer is having about the worst time he has ever had in his life."[97] Any possibility of sustained recovery for peasant banana cultivation disappeared when the outbreak of World War II virtually eliminated access to overseas markets.[98]

During this same period the organization of the large plantations was changing. The sugar industry enjoyed a brief period of stability after its years of prolonged decline and stagnation. By the late nineteenth century, the United States had surpassed Britain as the largest market.[99] The industry was further encouraged by legislation, passed in 1902, offering financial incentives to planters who invested in sugar factory modernization. The gradual restoration of British imperial preferences over the early 1900s further helped to ensure that that growth could be consolidated.[100] World War I provoked a boom in cane sugar production as the British market for beet sugar was cut off, and this also helped to re-establish the growth of the industry. The price of sugar on the international market increased from eleven shillings per hundredweight in 1910 to fifty-eight in 1920.

This recovery of Jamaican capital in the sugar industry was only temporary. Renewed crisis led to further concentration of the industry in fewer hands. In 1922, following the war-induced boom, the price of sugar fell to fifteen shillings per hundredweight and by 1930 it was down to eight shillings and ninepence, the lowest levels since 1906.[101] Now, however, it was foreign corporate capital rather than local planting interests that took advantage of the crisis. By 1938 the American-owned United Fruit Company had moved in to become the largest single private landholder in Jamaica.[102] Between June and December of 1937 the West Indian Sugar Company (WISCO), a subsidiary of Tate and Lyle Investments Limited of Britain, bought out seven of the thirty-five operating sugar estates with factories.[103] By 1945 WISCO's Jamaican holdings, which included the two largest estates, or centrals, on the island, Frome and Monymusk, produced 55,768 tons of sugar, or over one-third of Jamaica's total output.[104] In the 1940s colonial government policy further encouraged foreign capital investment in Jamaica. A series of legislative incentives such as tax holidays, duty-free imports for raw materials, and subsidized factory space were offered to those industries which produced exclusively for the export market.[105]

The entrance of such large multinationals and the increased mechanization of the industry caused a decline in the economic and political influence of the Jamaican plantocracy. Unable to compete with the larger foreign firms, the local planters became unstable as a group, divided between nationalist protectionist sentiments and dependence upon foreign sources for financial and material investment. Many were bought out by the more powerful competitors who were quickly gaining monopoly control.[106]

The number of locally owned and operated plantations thus declined as amalgamations and mergers continued. This wave of amalgamations differed from that of the immediate post-emancipation period. Rather than being based on abandonment, it was based on expansion and increased capital concentration. After about 1890 lands were no longer abandoned. Nevertheless, in the crop year 1937–38, thirty-four sugar factories were in operation; by 1945 the number had fallen to twenty-six. During this period, in Westmoreland parish alone, Tate and Lyle merged five estates into the new central Frome operation. Between 1882 and 1943 the number of holdings of five hundred acres or more declined by 41 per cent.[107]

The combined effect of these two major changes in the rural organization of production – the decline of land accessibility to the small cultivator and the concentration and increased technological improvement of the large estates – profoundly altered the pattern of rural employment. Many rural labourers who would have chosen to develop private plots as their main source of livelihood were now forced to seek regular wage labour. Among those who continued to own land, limited crop production could no longer provide the major source of income. Farming units had become too small, and were insufficiently productive to offer economic security. A study conducted in 1946 indicated that many of those who continued to own small plots did not operate farm units. Of the sugar workers in the study sample, 56.7 per cent owned some land, but only 43 per cent actually worked it.[108]

Peasant production continued to supply the better part of locally consumed crops until after World War II, when imported goods became dominant.[109] However, the results of decreasing access to land, declining fertility, inadequate access to credit, poor technology, and the need to spend more time away from peasant lands in order to work for wages meant that after the 1930s small cultivators produced for subsistence rather than for the export market. The officially estimated amount of acreage necessary for family subsistence in the late 1930s was between four and ten acres depending upon location. At this time some sixty thousand peasant holdings averaged slightly over two acres; thirteen thousand averaged about seven acres; and ten thousand holdings were on average twenty acres. This meant that at least seventy-three thousand peasant properties operated at or well below subsistence production levels.[110] It was this body of cultivators that depended increasingly upon wage labour for its survival.

If during the immediate post-emancipation period the rural population could be loosely described as a peasantry which supplemented its income with wage labour, over the period following the late 1800s it could be more accurately (though still loosely) described as a rural and recently urbanized wage-labour force, a large proportion of whom supplemented their incomes with small plot production.

The West India Royal Commission Report, produced under the direction of Commissioner Moyne after the labour rebellion of 1938, specifically noted this new development in the Jamaican labour force. "Peasant proprietors with fairly substantial holdings ... have hitherto formed an important element. But, apart from the threat that arises from the adverse trend of export markets, they appear now to be a diminishing element, owing to the sub-division of holdings into excessively small units, which is a natural consequence of the growth of population, and compels an increasing proportion of small settlers to supplement their incomes with wage-work."[111]

The report further noted that "The normal peasant holding is too small to provide the means of an independent existence, and most peasants are accustomed to supplement their income by wage-work on the estates. Thus the great majority of the negro population depend at any rate in a large degree on wages for their livelihood, however much they may supplement them by work on land that they own or rent."[112]

Moreover, between 1921 and 1943 some fifty-eight thousand persons were estimated to have been forced from agriculture, and of these fully thirty-three thousand were former private cultivators. By 1943, 68.7 per cent of the population were classified as "wage earners," while only 27.5 per cent were categorized as "own account workers."[113]

As small private landholding declined as a source of economic support, increasing numbers sought regular employment on the estates. Despite the sugar industry's expanding productivity, however, the large plantations could not provide sufficient employment to offset the effects of the land crisis. Rather than a chronic labour shortage, the estates now faced a labour surplus, particularly among unskilled workers.

The nature of labour relations on the estates was further altered by the changes that occurred within this sector. Increasingly over the decades, the labourer had a large corporate monopoly rather than a single family and its representatives as an employer. The more mechanized, capital intensive organization of production created a much more alienated and impersonal relationship between the workers on one side and the estate owners and managers on the other. The Moyne Commission noted that the sugar factories had become "large and highly mechanised undertakings, approximating ... the typical machine industry of a modern industrial country."[114]

These developments affected the organization and confidence of the work force in diverse ways. On the one hand, those workers who were employed worked in even larger, more highly collectivized, and therefore potentially more powerful production teams. The work force was increasingly "proletarianized," and "acquired an increased sense of collective worker identity and class consciousness."[115] This was reflected in the adoption of the strike as a form of collective action, and the dramatic growth of unionization and formal collective bargaining after 1938.

On the other hand, the large pool of chronically unemployed and underemployed labourers represented the simultaneous atomization of a large portion of the work force. These conditions created a social and economic climate of chronic insecurity. Landownership alone no longer offered a secure alternative source of support to plantation employment. Even large sugar estates experienced decreased access to new lands for expansion. Tenancy on estate properties rather than private land ownership became increasingly common.

Tenancy, unlike landownership, offered no incentive to permanent farm development. Moreover, rather than providing the working class with bargaining power in dealings with the employer, tenancy lent the plantation owners and managers greater control over their workers. One 1944 study indicated that almost 69 per cent of all field workers had ties to the estates other than as workers, as "tenants" or "tenants-at-will."[116] By 1952, 30 per cent of all land cultivated was rented land.[117] The large landowners therefore were both employers and landlords of a large number of their workers. Organized resistance in the fields could be met by the threat of increased rental rates or eviction.

The insecurity already associated with seasonal employment on the estates was aggravated by the crisis in land accessibility. As long as small plots were available near the estates, there was an alternative means of subsistence between crop seasons. As land surrounding the estates became both less accessible and less productive, however, annual internal migration became the normal pattern for many sugar estate employees.[118] (It should be noted that factory and field workers usually provided a secure section of estate labour throughout the year, while cutters and loaders were employed on a seasonal basis.)[119] By 1944 over 39 per cent of estate labourers worked less than half the year on the estates.[120]

While more people were seeking employment on the estates, increased centralization and mechanization were reducing the demand for agricultural labourers. In 1891 there were 271,000 persons engaged in agriculture. By 1921 the figure had risen to only 286,000, despite a population increase of some 219,000 over the period. By 1943, when the population had grown by a further 379,000 over the 1921 figure, the number engaged in agriculture had fallen to 226,000.[121]

A portion of this surplus rural population emigrated from the island, in search of work in other countries, often after first moving to Kingston. Though the flow was not evenly distributed, between 1885 and 1935 an average of ten thousand emigrants left Jamaica each year.[122] Most of these emigrants went to Panama, Costa Rica or Cuba. During the Great Depression, however, these and other host countries closed their doors to immigrants. In the early 1930s Cuba instituted a number of restrictions against immigrants, and in 1933 both Panama and Costa Rica refused new entrants.[123]

Such conditions resulted in a dramatic reversal of migration patterns. Between 1915 and 1919, for example, a total of 43,909 departures from Jamaica and 24,958 returns were recorded. Between 1930 and 1934, however, the figure for departures fell to 5,899 while returns reached 28,459.[124] The closure of emigration channels during the 1930s seriously exacerbated the already severe unemployment problem, and was one of the factors leading to the working class rebellion in 1938.[125] Emigration channels remained virtually closed until after World War II.

The second major outlet for the mass of rural unemployed was the growing urban centre of Kingston and neighbouring St Andrew. Kingston had been the traditional commercial capital of the island since the English occupation, but had stagnated in the immediate post-emancipation period.[126] From the late 1800s, however, and particularly from the 1920s, Kingston entered a new period of rapid development and expansion.

A number of factors sparked the growth of Kingston.[127] As steamships came to replace sailing ships, increased investment was made in warehouses and docking facilities. Kingston provided the only deepwater port on the island that could accommodate more than one ship at a time, eliminating the need for expensive lighters to load and unload stock. Shipping companies therefore made every effort to use the Kingston docks. Furthermore, as the sugar industry became more highly mechanized, large shipments of iron, steel, and imported machinery increased the cargoes coming into the island.

As the centre of overseas trade, Kingston also became the nexus of all internal communication and transportation. The city became the major terminal for the railway system, which was built in stages, beginning in the mid-nineteenth century. It was also the centre of the road system that was developed as automobiles came into use in the 1920s. Both the railway and the automobile brought with them a wide variety of related secondary industries, from rolling stock assembly to gasoline storage facilities and service stations, which were similarly concentrated in Kingston. As Kingston expanded, its market and abundant supply of labour continued to attract new industries, which, in turn, attracted more labour from the countryside.

Displaced rural labourers converged on Kingston in search of urban employment. Four broad classifications of Jamaican parishes have been suggested by Cumper as a means of analysing the patterns of internal migration. These are: (1) the two original banana parishes of Portland and St Mary; (2) the south coast sugar parishes of Westmoreland, Clarendon, St Catherine and St Thomas; (3) the urban parishes, which include Kingston and St Andrew as well as the partly urban parish of St James, where Montego Bay is located; and (4) the remaining "residual group" of general farming and banana-growing parishes.

These patterns of population movement are traced between the years 1911 and 1943. In the early part of this period (up to the 1930s) the urban parishes were growing at a rate of one thousand persons per year. The general farming parishes saw their populations diminish at approximately the same rate. The banana and sugar parishes were gaining approximately the same number from the general farming parishes as they were losing to the urban districts. In the latter part of the period migration to the urban parishes rose even more dramatically. Between 1939 and 1943 the urban parishes increased at a rate of seven thousand per year. This influx came in approximately equal proportions from each of the other regions.[128]

This massive migration wave led the population of Kingston and St Andrew to grow much more rapidly than any other district in Jamaica. Between 1871 and 1943 the population of the island increased by 44 per cent, while Kingston grew by 120.8 per cent and St Andrew by 204.5 per cent.[129] The rural population was attracted to the wider opportunities for employment that the urban region seemed to offer. Jobs that were not dependent upon the vicissitudes of the sugar and banana industries seemed more secure than those available in the countryside. Indeed, a variety of new employment opportunities did appear with urban expansion and development.

Kingston was the seat of Jamaican government, and as the state became more directly involved in the island's economy new jobs became available.[130] These included openings for work on the railway, in schools, in hospitals, and in the civil service. Similarly, considerable expansion in secondary industries, particularly agricultural processing, increased the size of the industrial work force. Between 1939 and 1947, 134 new manufacturing businesses were established.

In 1943, 59,229 persons were reported to be gainfully employed in manufacturing.[131]

The reality of urban working-class life, however, proved very different from the anticipated vision of prosperity and security. There were far more people seeking jobs than there were jobs available. The result was the steady growth of unemployment and underemployment. In 1939 a survey conducted by the Jamaican Department of Labour indicated that 48.16 per cent of the population sampled in the Kingston area were unemployed or had "no gainful occupation." (The latter classification, however, included those such as housewives who would not normally be engaged in paid labour but who were far from idle.) A further 10.4 per cent were casually employed. Only 17.54 per cent were considered to have been employed regularly.[132]

One notable reflection of the poor employment situation was the dramatic rise in the number of domestic servants recorded over the period considered here. The proportion of domestic servants grew from about 10 per cent of the labour force in the 1880s to almost 18 per cent in 1921.[133] Domestic servants were available in such abundance and were so poorly paid that "all but the humblest of households"[134] could afford to employ them.

Even in the most coveted jobs, good working conditions and job security were far from guaranteed. White collar clerical employees, for example, usually survived on "miserable wages" while struggling "to keep up appearances" and to maintain the higher social status of their positions.[135] The Kingston docks were also considered to be among the most attractive sources of urban employment, since "the established rates of pay for the waterside workers ... were for the West Indies exceptionally high."[136] However, this work was available irregularly, and most workers were able to work only one or two days per week.[137] The limited and irregular nature of the work offset the value of the high hourly wages.

This situation of chronic unemployment and underemployment, combined with the elimination of land as a source of economic security, also produced a large group of people who would engage in intermittent or permanent "scuffling," a term that can imply "anything and everything done to make a few shillings or even pence, ranging from collecting and selling fruit to theft and prostitution."[138] As the tourist industry began to expand in the early 1900s, and especially in the decades following World War II, the market available for scufflers and petty traders also grew.[139] It should be noted that in 1943 fully 16 per cent of the Jamaican labour force, or eighty thousand people, were classified as either domestics or petty trad-

ers.[140] Another section of the urban poor was unable to make a living even by scuffling. They lived on the streets, directionless and forced into begging.[141]

Thus, one of the most serious consequences of the land crisis in the country was the employment crisis in the towns. Unemployed rural labourers in search of some means of support moved "from the rural villages to urban ghettoes."[142] In both the rural and urban districts, increasing general inequality was the inevitable corollary.

As secondary industry and manufacturing developed Kingston became the centre of power of the white elite and of the growing coloured middle class.[143] In the country, as sugar processing became more monopolized, a new division arose in the rural areas – an agricultural middle class consisting largely of small cane growers. The large sugar centrals not only grew cane, but also maintained the processing factories. The small growers sold their cane to the large estates to be processed. By 1950 approximately 30 per cent of the cane milled was provided by small growers.[144]

The general increase in class and income inequality both encouraged, and was encouraged by, an increase in racial inequality.[145] Because the black population was concentrated in the working class, and the white population constituted the majority of the ruling class, income differences reflected racial distinctions. In 1943, 58.4 per cent of all those who earned less than ten shillings per week were black, 32.1 per cent were coloured, and only 2.1 per cent were white. Among those earning one hundred shillings per week or more, however, only 0.3 per cent were black, 5.6 per cent were coloured, and 92.8 per cent were white (including Jewish and Syrian).[146]

The increasing economic activity and opportunities in the urban areas also led to growing inequalities. Once an exclusively rural-centred society, Jamaica now became divided between rural and urban areas. Moreover, 84 per cent of all Jamaican blacks lived in the rural parishes, while over 70 per cent of all whites were concentrated in Kingston and St Andrew.[147]

The urban districts also tended to attract a disproportionate number of Jamaican youth. The land crisis forced the younger generations to seek new sources of employment. For the majority of the rural population, "the young people must have [had] a very unpromising outlook before them."[148] The division between the urban and rural communities therefore also reflected to a certain degree a division between generations.

The extent of the division between the urban and rural populations, however, should not be exaggerated. A number of other factors ensured that urban and rural workers had much in common.

For example, in many ways the working-class standard of living in the urban areas was not dissimilar to that in the rural setting. Though average earnings were considerably higher in the urban areas, irregular employment, a higher cost of living, and a much heavier reliance on the cash economy for subsistence tended to offset the apparent income imbalance.[149] In fact, in 1939 the Orde-Browne Commission concluded that the position of the employed rural labourer was "decidedly more favourable" than that of the urban worker. For the worker in the countryside, rent was minimal and food cost very little or was provided from the family's home-grown crops.[150]

The general conditions of employment in the urban and rural regions also held certain similarities. In both instances a combination of collectivized wage employment and private production was the common pattern. For example, the highly socialized estate factory employment combined with private land cultivation in the rural parishes was matched by the socialized urban labour in small factories or on the docks combined with various forms of private cottage production and petty commerce in the urban districts. Rural workers periodically sought wage employment just as urban workers were occasionally compelled to seek non-wage employment to supplement casual labour.[151]

Furthermore, family ties were frequently maintained between rural and urban residents. The pattern of seasonal and casual employment, combined with the relatively short distances to travel in Jamaica, allowed frequent annual internal migration between Kingston and the rural parishes among a significant portion of the working class. Some 45 per cent of 486 working class households surveyed in Kingston between August and October of 1939 were reported to be receiving gifts of food, undoubtedly from friends and relatives in the countryside.[152]

The method of marketing foodstuffs among all levels of the peasantry also bridged rural and urban sectors. Goods were sold through a complex network of "higglers," women from the country household or area who transported the products to be sold in the town market to buyers in private households or to other higglers.[153] The food markets in the urban districts provided a meeting place where close bonds developed between working-class women and peasant higglers, particularly because the latter tried to provide for regular customers.[154]

In both the rural and urban sectors, therefore, similar patterns had developed in the structure of the labour force. In both instances two simultaneous processes were taking place. Sections of the employed working class were concentrated in socialized, collective centres of employment; at the same time, the large pool of unemployed workers, and the irregular nature of employment itself atomized the work force and compelled other sections, or the same sections when in need, to find various alternative means of support.

During the years between the late nineteenth century and the mid-1940s, more than in earlier periods considered, the factors leading to collectivization and atomization were very closely linked. On an international level, capital was becoming increasingly centralized in the hands of corporate monopolies. Nationally, the ties between local and international capital were growing stronger, and a small number of prominent Jamaican families were emerging as a distinct modern capitalist group. The ties between landownership, local industry, and foreign interests were very close indeed. For example, by 1908 the Henriques Brothers, still prominent capitalists in contemporary Jamaica, were the major group of engineering suppliers for the sugar industry. They also owned a large sugar operation, pioneered the establishment of Jamaica's match industry, and were the exclusive Jamaican dealers with Ford Motors of America.[155]

The principal economic division in the society developed into one between large concentrations of capital and a vast pool of actual and potential wage labourers. Whether or not workers were employed, and whether they were employed regularly or only on a casual or seasonal basis, the acquisition of wages for work was the predominant means of securing an income. By 1939, the very existence of the peasants as a class was dependent upon the procurement of wage labour.[156] Where employed labour was concentrated, the labour force had become more collectivized. At the same time, the weakness of Jamaican capitalism in the international economy enabled a countervailing trend to operate simultaneously. Even powerful international sources of capital such as WISCO were affected by the restrictions of world sugar quotas. Masses of workers were forced into temporary or permanent unemployment, or into alternative means of survival such as scuffling or begging.

The large pool of permanently unemployed in turn lowered the price of employed labour, including the cost of domestic service, and increased the pool of scufflers and street beggars in the urban districts. Inadequate wages and the limited number of jobs forced even those who were increasingly dependent on wage labour to rely on produce cultivated on small plots to supplement their diets. In turn, landownership contributed to lower wages because rural workers in particular were expected by their employers to grow some of their own food, and wages were adjusted accordingly. The same forces that were leading to the increasing collectivization of labour were thus also contributing to its increasing atomization. The close identification between those workers employed in highly collectivized production units and those employed, underemployed, or unemployed in atomized conditions became obvious in the course of the labour revolt of 1938.[157]

Thus private landholding, which had been the prime source of economic and social security since the time of slavery, was no longer an insurance against falling living standards among the producing classes. At best, it could operate as a modified guarantee against starvation. Access to land alone no longer implied economic security. In fact, where land tenancy on the estates had come to replace landownership, private land cultivation symbolized the casual labour system rather than economic independence.[158]

Though landholding alone no longer provided support for the majority of labourers, there is no indication that its ideological or symbolic significance had suffered a parallel decline among either rural or urban workers. The small number of cultivators who were able to increase their holdings and establish stable, medium-sized farms remained the most prosperous rural producers (excluding the large plantation owners and managers). The Moyne Commission paternalistically praised this sector of the population. "Where ... the size of the holdings remains adequate, the peasants form the solidest element in West Indian society, and it is among them that the social virtues of forethought and the care of children are most commonly to be found."[159] Moreover, while land plots had by and large become smaller and less productive, a 1944 study conducted by the Statistical Branch of the Colonial Department of Labour revealed that half of all field workers owned one acre of land.[160] The continued commitment to retain such land, undoubtedly among many with hopes of future development, is indicated by the repeated failure of government land development schemes that depended on extensive credit facilities. Small farmers were always reluctant to borrow substantially, for this would involve putting up their land titles as security. Edwards' study indicated that most small cultivators were far more comfortable relying upon "relatives, friends, and persons to whom the farmer had lent funds in the past" as unofficial sources of limited credit, rather than risking their only property to obtain larger loans.[161]

Among the newly urbanized work force, there is no doubt that a certain sector, particularly the youth, migrated in hopes of being released from the uncertainties of agricultural employment.[162] The pattern of seasonal migration, however, makes it feasible to postulate that a section of the urban work force had hopes of saving enough to return to the country to increase the productivity of their families' landholdings. The implications of these mixed interests, in both landholding and wage labour, will be considered in subsequent chapters.

During the period under review numerous political changes accompanied these economic and social transformations. In 1919 for example, organized labour action in the form of strikes was recorded for the first time. By the late 1930s such action had taken on island-wide proportions. Mass consciousness of pride in the black race was sparked by the activities of Marcus Garvey.[163] Lasting political parties were formed for the first time in the events leading up to the first general election in 1944. During the same period, trade union organization grew dramatically and became an integral part of the modern Jamaican political and social system. The historical development of the labour force – in particular the varying nature of the relationship between private landholding and socialized collective wage labour – profoundly affected the forms of organization and action adopted by the Jamaican producing classes through the years. It is this relationship that forms the background to this study.

CHAPTER TWO

From Slavery to Freedom: The "Baptist War" of 1831

WILLED IDEOLOGY — THE RELIGIOUS IDIOM

In a very real sense, religion was the primary ideological arena of class struggle in Jamaican slave society. The role of religion was central in African cultures before the arrival of the European slave traders. Its importance as a sign of African cultural resistance and autonomy was only heightened by the suffering of slavery. African resistance to colonial oppression has been frequently expressed in religious terms, whether the context is the seizure of slaves or the seizure of land from indigenous Africans.[1]

In nineteenth-century Jamaica the memory of African life was still very strong among the slaves. Though the British slave trade was officially abolished in 1807, the last years of the trade saw the largest concentration of new African arrivals, numbering 63,045 between 1801 and 1807. By 1830 the proportion of first generation Africans had diminished, but it was still relatively high and the number of slaves with parents born in Africa was higher still. A sampling of twelve plantations in 1817 recorded 1,764 Africans and 3,325 Creole (Jamaican born) slaves; in 1829 the figures were 1,021 Africans and 3,720 Creoles.[2]

Though their African cultural traditions varied depending upon the slaves' tribal, regional, or national origin, the vast majority came from West Africa and "their differences were only regional variations of a common culture."[3] Certain common religious practices and customs became an integral part of slave society. These fall broadly under the headings of "obeah" and "myalism," traditional beliefs which made up the strongest *inherent* religious element of slave ideology.

Planters and missionaries have made various interpretations of African religious practices. Patterson, on the basis of detailed examination of various accounts, describes "obeah" as a means of imposing harm on others by use of charms or poisons upon a client's payment to a professional "obeah-man," and "myalism" as a means of anti-witchcraft against the evil deeds of others. While obeah was practiced individually, however, myalism took the form of activities among groups.[4] The planters had only the vaguest understanding of the slaves' religious practices, and their interest was mixed. For example, the overt practice of African religion was outlawed, but music and dancing were considered harmless, although both were associated with many African religious ceremonies. The line between the outlawed and the acceptable activities was often unclear – to both slaves and planters.[5] The slave-owning class was opposed to, and fearful of, the practice of "black magic," which indeed frequently employed poison. African religious practices against evil sorcery were focussed against the slave masters, who were seen as the practitioners of evil. The slaves could seek comfort in the notion that the supreme being of their ancestors was with them, and myal and obeah practitioners protected those who challenged sin in the form of the white plantocracy.[6] Freedom from sorcery, sin, and the racist practices of slavery were thus fused in the minds and religious practices of the slaves.

The relationship between class struggle, racial oppression, and religion was also strengthened by the exclusion of the blacks from the state-supported Church of England. It was maintained that slaves could not be genuinely Christian. In 1727, the Lord Bishop of London published an epistle calling upon English colonists to teach their slaves the Christian faith. The practice, however, differed greatly from the preaching. Though large numbers of slaves were baptised as a formality, blacks were not allowed into the Church of England (Established Church).[7] The Church of England was "a white man's church,"[8] supportive of the local planters in the Jamaican Legislative Assembly. It was antagonistic to the acquisition of political rights by the black slaves and to their lifestyle and customs.[9]

Although Christianity was not made accessible to the slaves by the ruling class, it was to have a profound influence on slave culture through two other sources – the arrival of black Baptist slave preachers after the American Revolution, and the much later arrival of British Baptist missionaries from England. After the American Revolution several hundred United Empire Loyalists, accompanied by their slaves, emigrated to Jamaica from the United States. In the North American colonies, where ruling class resistance to religious teaching was less entrenched, it was common for slaves to become converted to Christianity. Such slaves were among those who came to Jamaica. Upon arrival, many black Baptists became unofficial missionaries, forming religious followings among groups of slaves. Curtin estimates that by the 1840s a native Afro-religious form of Christianity "had a firmer hold than European orthodoxy."[10] The process of ascendancy of Christian ideas among Jamaica's slaves was one "over which the planters were perilously ambivalent."[11] The attempt of colonial missionaries to justify the slave system by religious rhetoric was rejected by the slaves, but certain notions such as equality and brotherhood were reinterpreted "within the matrix of black religion" to inspire confidence in the struggle for freedom.[12]

This Christian ideological element was thus ultimately *derived* from white society, albeit American white society, but in its incorporation into African religious beliefs it went through a process of transformation. By the 1830s a movement of Afro-Christian sects had developed, representing a combination of orthodox Christianity and African religious ideas, but distinguishable from both. The antecedent to this tradition was a more orthodox Baptist movement among the black slaves. The most important black Baptist leader was George Lisle (or Leile), the slave of a Baptist planter formerly from the Southern United States. Lisle arrived in Kingston in 1783 and established a congregation that adhered fairly closely to official Baptist teaching.[13] Like other black Baptist preachers, he frequently faced charges of sedition for his activities among the slave population. The association of rebellious activity and Christian teaching was already beginning to be established – perhaps more so in the minds of the authorities than in those of the slaves.[14]

Other black Baptist leaders were more overtly radical in their doctrine. George Lewis, for example, was a genuine heretic who had consciously rejected orthodox Christian instruction in favour of his own more distinctly African interpretation. Other preachers such as George Gibb and Moses Baker split away from Lisle's congregation and established their own unorthodox groups, possibly the result of illiteracy rather than intended Biblical reinterpretation.

Baptist activity eventually reached almost all parishes on the island, and local leaders tended to split off and form their own followings. The groups were based on a "leader system," whereby followers were divided into permanent groups or "classes" under the direction of a single leader, who provided religious instruction. This method was probably drawn from the American experiences of the black Baptist leaders. The particular form and implications of the approach, however, were altered by the inherent traditions among Jamaican slaves.

The black Baptists saw themselves as loyal to orthodox Baptist preaching, but part of "a black church, a church of Ethiopia."[15] At the same time they were considered by the planters to display a certain loyalty to the slave system. Lisle, for example, admitted slaves to his church only if their masters permitted it.[16] The leaders became more than teachers – they were spiritual guides similar to those in myal groups. Individual rebels could be expelled, or baptism could be refused to an applicant who did not fully accept the leader's authority.

The decentralization of authority among the various leaders was reinforced by the absence of any single recognized authority or church hierarchy. Even in terms of doctrine, Christ became subordinate in influence to John the Baptist, who had been the "leader" who admitted Christ to baptism. Further, as most of the leaders were illiterate, the idea of the spirit was elevated above the written gospel. Moreover, the isolation of the estates and the forced separation of the slaves from European Christian culture left the ideological arena open to black Baptist proselytizing and interpretation. All of these factors contributed to the tendency of the converted adherents to alter and adapt Christian orthodoxy to African traditional beliefs.

Because formal political channels and means of social support were closed to the slaves, the religious circles also served as a source of secular guidance. By the early 1800s the authority of the black Baptists was stronger than that of the myal and obeah men. Christianity seemed to have "protected" white society from the drudgery of slavery, which may have made it appear superior to African religious practices. Moreover, those who were higher up in the slave labour hierarchy – the boilers, masons and drivers chosen for their apparent leadership qualities by the planters – tended to be the leaders of the Christian circles on the estates.

By the first decades of the nineteenth century Christian teaching had been expanding across the island for some forty years. The inherent African religious tradition and the derived Baptist Christian teaching had become largely intertwined. West African religious beliefs are not monistic, but rather see spirituality in ancestors and nature, as well as in a supreme being. Turner calls Christianity a "challenge" to traditional African ideas about the spirit world, social destiny, and the nature of God. The result was not only the spreading of Christian doctrine, but a proliferation of new concepts and practices combining elements of both African and Christian religious and social faith, under appropriate new titles such as "Native Baptist," "Native Methodist," or "Spirit Christian."[17] Myalism and obeah were still distinct practices, but Afro-Christian doctrine had developed its own inherent ideology, and thus provided the official Baptist Church with fertile ground for the growth of missionary influence.

The Baptist missionaries did not seriously devote themselves to mass conversion among the slaves until 1814, when Moses Baker appealed for British aid to maintain his congregation. From the outset, the official Baptists, led by William Knibb and Thomas Burchell, adopted the leader system already in operation. With the ideological ground laid by the Native Baptist tradition, the derived ideas of orthodox Christianity spread rapidly. The Montego Bay mission church, where Burchell was stationed, claimed sixteen hundred members in full communion and a further three thousand "inquirers" by the 1920s. The congregation was so widespread that to reach all its members required riding 103 miles per week.[18]

To control this large network of converts, tickets were given out to each member of the congregation. The tickets were re-issued quarterly upon the receipt of the slaves' financial contributions to the Church and could be issued only by the officially recognized missionary leader. Only ticket holders could attend services and approach the communion table. In this way the European missionaries could discipline their converts and maintain their authority over the slave leaders.

To the slave population, the tickets represented more than an organizational link to the Baptist Church. They symbolized "the Christian equivalent of the fetishes carried by Negroes in the Gambia region of West Africa, where even among non-Moslem Negroes a few words from the Koran on a scrap of paper were credited with special powers."[19] The rapid growth of the Baptist Church therefore represented not simply the adaptation of the slave population to one element of European culture – indeed the only element made accessible to them – but also the adaptation of Christianity to the African heritage and traditions of the slave population. The derived missionary influence thus met with the inherent traditions of the black labourers and, in the rebellion of 1831, was interpreted by them to meet their own interests as a class.[20]

There was also one very distinct *political* aspect to the appeal of the Baptists among the slaves of Jamaica during this period. The Baptists had been committed to the emancipation of the slaves since 1824.[21] The basic Christian doctrine that all under God are equal had profound implications in a society founded on the principle of genetic inequality. In a very real sense, the missionaries were the first members of the white population to take an active interest in the life and well-being of the slaves.

Perhaps even more significant was the reaction of the planters to the growth of missionary influence among the slaves. The missionaries were perceived to be a direct threat, which was never their intention. Simply to suggest that maltreatment of slaves was "unchristian" was to provoke the slave owners' persecution. In fact, the slaves were repeatedly advised by their ministers to simply "endure their lot until it pleased God to change it,"[22] hardly a call for active resistance.

It was because of this ideological background that the rebellion of 1831 came to be known among the slaves as the "Baptist War."[23] The rebellion erupted in the island's western parishes, "where the missions were most numerous and independent religious meetings proliferated."[24] In conditions of slavery, the mission circles operated as organizational centres for political activity. As the anti-slavery campaign in Britain reached fever pitch during the early 1830s, the slave population swelled the Baptist circles in anticipation of freedom.[25] To some extent, religious doctrine was thus transformed into political doctrine. Hope for freedom and a better life in the hereafter became hope for freedom and a better life after the abolition of slavery.[26] The most frequently quoted passages in the Bible included: "If the Son therefore shall make you free, ye shall be free indeed" (John viii. 36); "No man can serve two masters" (Matt. vi. 24); "Ye are bought with a price; be not ye the servants of men" (1 Cor. vii. 23); "There is neither Greek nor Jew; there is neither bond nor free" (Cal. iii 28); "Be not entangled with the yoke of bondage" (Gal. v.i).[27]

Though the rebellion was not directed by a single organization or under a centralized leadership, there was one leader whose work seems to have prompted the network of resistance and who led a large section of the rebels.[28] This was Sam Sharpe (or Sharp), a domestic slave and a member of the Montego Bay Baptist Church. Sharpe was a literate slave, and a passionate and intelligent convert. He became a group leader, and quickly built up an independent base of support, including his own contacts in the black Baptist and Afro-Christian movements. Going beyond the limits of official church control, Sharpe soon developed a following where he was referred to as "daddy" or "ruler." One Methodist missionary sympathetic to the cause of emancipation reported on his impressions of Sharpe when he met with him in jail after the 1831 rebellion. "Samuel Sharpe was the man whose active brain devised the project and he had sufficient authority with those around him to carry it into effect, having acquired an extraordinary degree of influence amongst his fellow-slaves. I had much conversation with him while he was in confinement; and found him certainly the most intelligent and remarkable slave I ever met with."[29]

Sharpe was an independent preacher, and he also held an independent interpretation of Biblical scripture. He became convinced that the Bible supported the freedom of the slaves. It was on the basis of this conviction that Sharpe began to organize an insurrection to attain full emancipation for Jamaican slaves. Religious gatherings were used as organizational meetings for rebellion. After the regular services, a few were supposed to stay behind and listen to plans for a slave revolt. Supporters were urged to swear "by oath not to work after Christmas as slaves, but to assert their claim to freedom, and to be faithful to each other."[30] Sharpe's owner was apparently sympathetic to the religious activity of this bright slave, and evening meetings operated as a forum for political arguments about emancipation.[31] Though other arguments were employed,[32] the religious legitimacy of a revolt to attain freedom was the most frequently heard.

The parishes of St James, Hanover, Trelawney, Westmoreland, St Elizabeth, and Manchester, an area totalling some six hundred square miles, responded to the influence of Sharpe and his co-leaders. As the revolt of Christmas 1831 approached, frequent meetings were held among the slaves to organize the resistance. In some areas such meetings were reported to occur nightly.[33] There was also a network of supporters of the rebellion under the control of Native Baptists, rather than Sharpe's official Baptist current, and there is evidence to suggest that myal men also numbered among the leadership in some districts. Contributions were collected with the stated aim of purchasing freedom on earth and the eternal safety of their souls after death.[34]

To reinforce the legitimacy of the struggle, the endorsement of the official mission pastors was needed, and "it was widely believed that the missionaries favoured freedom for the slaves."[35] The white Baptist missionaries thus provided the derived element in the religious idiomatic form of expression of the politics of resistance. Sharpe's pastor, Thomas Burchell, had left Jamaica temporarily in May of 1831. In his absence, and entirely unknown to him, Burchell became elevated to the position of a central leader of the slave rebellion. Though he did not return to Jamaica until January of 1832, Burchell was widely rumoured to be travelling among the slaves in support of the resistance. Others believed that Burchell had gone to Britain to attain the "free paper" which would order emancipation upon his return at Christmas.[36]

The missionaries, in fact, lent neither approval nor leadership to the rebellion. On the contrary, it was not until the eve of the revolt, when congregations convened for Christmas services, that the mission leaders were even *informed* of the upcoming revolt and their assumed role in it. This was true of both the Baptist missionaries and those of the other churches on the island. Mission leaders pleaded with the slaves to remain at work and to cease all plans for organized resistance. At the opening of a new Baptist Chapel in the parish of St James on 27 December, the day the rebellion was to begin, Knibb made the missionaries' position clear: "If you have any love to Jesus Christ, to religion, to your ministers, to those friends in England who have given money to help you build this chapel, be not led away by wicked men."[37]

By this point, however, the commitment to fight for freedom had become too powerful to be turned back even by the influential mission leaders. One congregation, responding to Knibb's chastisement, was "perfectly furious and would not listen to ... disuasions from engaging in such a perilous enterprise ... They accused their ministers of deserting them, and threatened to take revenge upon them."[38]

The inherent and derived aspects of slave ideology, therefore, initially combined to legitimate active political resistance against the plantocracy. At a critical moment, however, the two ideological currents came into open conflict. The slaves interpreted Christian doctrine as a legitimation and spur to revolt; the missionaries interpreted it as a barrier against such action. The derived aspect of slave ideology was, in this instance, altered to suit the interests of a class of forced labourers passionately committed to attaining their freedom.

WILLED IDEOLOGY —
THE CROWN AS BENEVOLENT
DESPOT

The religious idiom was only one central theme in the rebellion of 1831. Equally important was the belief that the slaves had already been legally granted freedom through the British Parliament, and that it was only the local Jamaican ruling class that was preventing the implementation of the "free paper." This belief was the result of the slaves' interpretation of the conflict between the Jamaican plantocracy and the British government concerning emancipation.[39] The idea that the British government advocated emancipation, that the "king had made them free" before the rebellion broke out,[40] and that the planters were doing everything in their power to keep them enslaved, was in fact *derived* from the statements and actions of the plantocracy itself.

The vast difference between the standard of living among Jamaica's white and predominantly British population and that endured by the blacks made the British heritage appear awesome. Moreover, the planters used every means available to instil fear and obedience into the minds of the slaves. The great power and authority of the omnipotent King overseas were repeatedly referred to and emphasized by the slaves' masters. Reverence for British royalty was an idea derived from the colonial ruling class.

As slavery came under increasing attack in Britain during the early nineteenth century – from humanitarian, religious and political quarters – the fear and respect for the Crown which the planters had promoted among the slaves began to turn against the planters' own interests. The emancipation discussion entered ruling class households and domestic slaves were exposed to debates concerning their futures. Conversations were overheard among the whites, and the small number of slaves who were literate – such as Sam Sharpe – were able to follow discussions in the Jamaican press. Fellow slaves were told about the issues, or information was read aloud. Slaves who accompanied their masters on journeys to Britain returned full of rumours of their pending freedom. Missionary leaders also kept their congregations informed about the emancipation movement in Britain.

Towards the end of 1830, a coalition government committed to Parliamentary reform came into power in Britain.[41] This encouraged the emancipation movement to advocate improvement in the conditions of the colonial slave population. The Jamaican rulers were incensed at what they perceived to be a threat to their "autonomy." A movement developed among the planters advocating Jamaican separation from the British Empire and a merger with the United States (where slavery was still legally practised). Parish meetings were held throughout the island between July and November of 1831. One supporter of slavery described the atmosphere in which these meetings were organized: "The colonists now considering their patrimonial property threatened with speedy and total annihilation, their future prospects irrevocably blasted, their own lives and that of their families thus thrown into imminent jeopardy, and seeing that no remonstrances would avail with the government at home, (this course having been tried,) could no longer refrain from publicly giving vent to their utmost surprise and indignation."[42] No effort was made to insulate the slaves from the full force of these discussions. Some slaves were even allowed to attend the planters' meetings if they did not speak.[43] The Jamaican press devoted pages to these developments and casual discussions everywhere revolved around the issue of emancipation.

By the summer of 1831, the slave population was becoming restless. Contrary to the view of their masters, black Jamaicans were not prepared to wait passively while the most important question in their collective future was determined by the various interests that ruled over them. As talk of Britain's interest in emancipation spread, the slave population became more confident and ready for rebellion. More slaves were reported to be running away, and overseers and bookkeepers overheard more talk of freedom among the slaves.[44]

At the same time, the information the slaves received was selective, distorted by rumour, and transferred overwhelmingly by word of mouth rather than by written documentation. In such circumstances, the idea of pending emancipation became commonly understood to mean *existing* emancipation. In the western parishes it was widely believed that the slaves were already legally free, but the local planters were preventing the royal wishes from being implemented. In some quarters, in fact, it was believed that it was the Queen who had *personally* granted the slaves their freedom.

So widespread were such rumours of emancipation, particularly among the Baptists,[45] that King William IV felt compelled to issue a proclamation to the contrary on 3 June, 1831:

whereas it has been represented to us that the slaves in some of our West-India colonies and of our possessions on the continent of South America, have been erroneously led to believe that orders have been sent out by us for their emancipation:
And whereas such a belief has produced acts of insubordination, which have excited our highest displeasure ...
We do hereby declare and make known that the slave population in our said colonies and possessions will forfeit all claim on our protection, if they shall fail to render entire submission to the laws, as well as dutiful obedience to their masters.[46]

The opposition to emancipation from the local Jamaican ruling class was well understood by the slave population. The inflammatory speeches at the planters' meetings included calls to take up arms against Britain in defence of slavery, and plans to set up an alternative governing body independent of the Crown were discussed. Rumours travelled among the slaves, in part initiated by the taunting of planters, "in terms that served to convey or strengthen the conviction that the much desired object was almost within reach."[47]

It was in this context that the slaves began to organize for the fight for their freedom in 1831. Sam Sharpe was too well informed to have actually believed that the slaves were already freed, but he apparently did tell others that he thought the "free paper" had been issued in March by King William. Bleby notes that Sharpe's strategic argument formed "the daring design of imposing upon the slaves, in that part of the island, the belief that they had actually been made free by the king."[48] Sharpe clearly understood the importance of the slaves' ideological commitment to the Crown as a benevolent despot. Logically, the slaves concluded that the King's troops would not be mobilized against the slave uprising, and some even believed that the royal forces would be fighting on the side of the slave rebels. The slaves anticipated an armed confrontation with the planters' militia, but this was the only armed opposition they expected to encounter.

The *derived* notion of the authority of the Crown was thus interpreted to further inspire the slaves' confidence in rebelling against their local masters. Despite the repeated efforts of the state and its advocates to dissuade the slaves from their commitment to rebellion the message fell on deaf ears. The desire for freedom found expression in the very language and concepts of those whose privileges depended on slavery and racial oppression. Convinced that both God and the King were on the side of emancipation, the slaves prepared to organize a mass rebellion to win their freedom.

ORGANIC IDEOLOGY — STRIKE ACTION AND THE DEMAND FOR WAGES

If the willed aspects of the ideology of resistance in the 1831 slave revolt were based on traditional loyalties to God and the King, the *organic* aspect prefigured modern industrial class conflict. The major strategic focus of rebellion, following the direction of Sam Sharpe, was the organization of a mass labour strike on the estates. The slaves were to sit down and refuse to work. Then, a rebel leader on the estate, usually a driver, was to go to the overseer and announce the refusal of the slaves to work. The overseers were to be prevented from leaving the estates until they agreed to pay wages to the slaves. The labourers were to resume work only when the overseer had acknowledged that they were free men and women by paying them wages for their work.

The *idea* of taking strike action was inextricably tied to the working conditions of the slaves. It arose from the specific historical conditions of slave labour — collective, socialized labour on large private estates. The most effective means to force concessions from the planters was to refuse to perform the labour that provided the material basis of their power. Far-sighted leaders like Sharpe and his aides could see that strike action was the best guarantee of success in the struggle to attain freedom.

Worsening conditions on the estates also encouraged the slaves to rebel. By 1831, slave labourers were no longer in ready supply. On sugar estates, where the rate of natural decrease among the slave population was the highest, the shortage of labour was particularly acute, and fewer slaves were forced to carry a heavier burden. Pressures on estate labour increased, particularly among field workers in the first gang. As a result, slaves accustomed to lighter work in the second gang were transferred to first gang duties for which they were unprepared.

The few privileges accorded to women and to coloured slaves were also gradually being withdrawn. The shortage of labour increased the burden of field labour on women. More and more women, who in earlier years were exempt from the heaviest tasks if they were pregnant or nursing young children, were now part of the first and second gangs. The tradition that slaves with white blood, or coloured slaves, were superior to blacks was cultivated by the racist ideology of the plantocracy, and coloured slaves had been given relatively privileged tasks. This had been important in enlisting some cooperation among a segment of the slave population in order to further exploit the black majority. With the shortage of field labourers, this structure of privilege was deteriorating. Even the tiny number of slaves who might have acted as loyal supporters of the system in earlier days were now victims of its harsh reality.[49]

The receptivity of the slaves to Sharpe's plan can also be understood in terms of their experience as provision grounds cultivators. A six-month-long drought followed by exceptionally heavy rains in May had made 1831 a bad year for the slave producers. Poor harvests meant poorer sales on the market, and less cash in the hands of the slaves. Cash payment at the market was the traditional symbol of the little autonomy granted to the slaves. While white overseers could beat the slaves in the fields, at the market the white masters and their representatives had to pay to receive the produce of the slaves' labour.

The organic connection between cash payment and freedom had already been made within the slave system itself. Wages paid for field labour were thus identified as an important symbol of freedom. Yet it is not clear that the fundamental aim of the rebellion was for the achievement of a stable system of wage labour and capital. On the contrary, field labour in general remained a symbol of black subordination to white plantation rule. It is more likely that "freedom" was associated with provision grounds cultivation and private marketing, given the past experiences of the slaves and the future response to emancipation. In the event, however, it was the strike as an action to obtain freedom that was particularly well planned, and the organic ideas of strike action and cash payment were widely adopted. The aftermath of a strike "may not have been so well and widely understood."[50]

These organic ideas shaped other dominant ideological elements apparent in the resistance, particularly the religious idiom. In the context of the conditions surrounding the rebellion, religious beliefs took on a distinctly secular, political role. For example, the rebellion was planned to begin during the Christmas holiday season. This was an opportune time to strike for two objective reasons. First, it was the beginning of the harvest season, when demands on slave labour were increased and when the withdrawal of labour was most effective. Second, the Christmas season was traditionally the period when plantation supervision was most relaxed. By law, three days were allowed for a slave festival in which the slaves were actively encouraged to participate by the planters. Though the militia was routinely called into active duty to discourage rebellious activity, supervision was sufficiently reduced to allow slaves to visit other estates. One visitor described the festivities he witnessed as follows: "It was Christmas-eve – a season at which the West Indian negro goes wild with excitement. Old drums, trumpets, kettles, bells, and any thing that can make a noise, are brought out; dancers dance violently, and fiddlers fiddle violently, without any regard to time or tune; and masquerading and psalm-singing are alternately kept up ... No negro will work for love or money during this carnival time."[51]

The Christmas season was also of obvious religious importance. It was respected by the Anglican planters and clergy as a time of both reverence and celebration. The orthodox Baptist missionaries saw it as an opportunity to increase the commitment to Christianity among their congregations. For the slaves, the season combined Christian doctrine with their traditional African religious festivities, in particular the ceremonial John Canoe (or Connu) dance.[52] This traditional ceremony was frowned upon by the missionaries as an immoral "pagan" exercise. It is disapprovingly described in some detail by James Phillippo, a Baptist missionary and writer resident in Jamaica.

In the towns, such processions were preceded by a tall athletic man, attired in ... grotesque habiliments, in addition to which he wore a most hideous head-dress, surmounted by a pair of ox-horns, while from the lower part of the mask large boar-tusks protruded. This hero of the party was called John Connu, after the name of a celebrated African at Axim on the coast of Guinea, with whom the practice is supposed to have originated. He bore in his hand a large wooden sword which he occasionally brandished, accompanying its evolutions by a thousand fantastic freaks. Several companions were associated with him as musicians, beating banjas and tomtoms, blowing cow-horns, shaking a hard round black seed, called Indian shot, in a calabash, and scraping the bones of animals together, which, added to the vociferations of the crowd, filled the air with the most discordant sounds.[53]

Religious holidays became accepted as a time for the legal expression of slave festivities.[54] It was also a time when the slaves expected to be away from the fields. When slaves in the area where the rebellion began were compelled to work in the fields during part of the Christmas holiday in December of 1831, this represented a direct assault on their customary practice.

Religious and political factors fused more directly as slaves were sworn into allegiance with Sharpe's forces. Those who remained behind after prayer meetings to hear of the planned revolt were asked to swear on the Bible that they would not work after Christmas.[55] In this routine exercise, the elements of willed ideology, inherent and derived, were fused with the organic idea of taking collective strike action. Further, Sharpe's role in the revolt was not merely that of preacher, but also that of political organizer and leader. He did not project himself as a prophet or a messianic hero, and though he preached as an official Baptist, he did not operate within the discipline or under the direction of the mission station. Sharp had effectively "detached the Baptist missionary organization from the white missionaries and was using it as a European trade union leader used the combined bargaining power of the workers."[56]

In the events of the revolt itself, all religious referents seemed to dissipate in the face of open and direct class conflict.[57] Preparations began around August 1831, paralleling the organization of the planters' meetings in defence of slavery. The revolt was scheduled to start on 27 December. The slaves were not, however, sufficiently organized to be assured of victory against the powerful and well-armed planter class. A full week before the rebellion was planned to begin a labour dispute on Salt Spring Estate near Montego Bay alerted the government and the white population that further disturbances could follow. On 23 December slaves anxious to win their freedom set fire to the trash house[58] on an estate in Trelawney parish, and strikes were reported on two other estates. These events provoked the government to mobilize troops and warships in the west of the island in preparation for a full scale assault.

On 27 December, the trash house on Kensington Estate in St James was set on fire, signalling the outbreak of the rebellion.[59] Soon after, estates throughout the western parishes were set ablaze by the rebellious slaves. One observer reported: "In the space of five minutes after the preconcerted signal was made, fifteen enormous fires were seen in different directions, around this once charming scene; and then it was but too plain, that the work of devastation had commenced in its most horrific form. The conche-shell was heard to blow in every quarter, accompanied by huzzas and shouts of exultation from the infatuated slaves."[60]

This rash of fires was not part of Sharpe's original strategy for the rebellion. Destruction of estate property was not central to his plan, and the original fire may have been started accidentally.[61] Given the extreme suffering endured by the slaves, however, it is not surprising that spontaneous acts of destruction would erupt. What is surprising is that the destruction of property and loss of white lives were so limited. While the burning of trash houses was widespread, the blacksmiths' shops that were on almost every estate were left intact.[62] There were certain estates in the region where no damage whatsoever was done. In some cases, rebel slaves protected occupied estates from other slaves who wanted to destroy or plunder property.[63] Remarkably, in the final tally no more than fourteen whites were reported to have been killed,[64] despite clear preparation for armed confrontation on the part of the slave rebels. A black military corps, called variously the "regiment," "company," "force," or "party," claimed some one hundred and fifty members and about fifty guns. One of its main activities was the guarding of the estates where the slaves had gone on strike.[65]

Even where the resistance was not coordinated or under clear centralized leadership, the actions of the slaves indicated that their aims were specific and directed, and largely non-violent. The slaves acted as a "discriminating crowd,"[66] carefully selecting the targets which were to be destroyed and those which were to be protected. While race and racism were definitive features of the rebellion, the rebellion cannot be reduced to a crusade of blacks against whites. It was in essence a *labour* rebellion, organized to attain freedom from slavery, and in this process the racism that supported the system was necessarily challenged directly.

The strikes were successful in isolated areas, but the organizational links from estate to estate were too weak to withstand the weight of the repression mobilized by the ruling class. In contrast to the restraint displayed by the slaves, the plantocracy, backed by British political and military power, was brutal in its repression of the revolt. Black Maroons were paid by their white superiors for each pair of ears cut from the heads of rebel slaves that they presented. "The militia were bent on vengeance and among them were individuals whose political rancour approached insanity. They raided and burnt negro villages on rebel estates, driving neighbouring slaves to take refuge in the woods for fear it was their turn next. Suspected ringleaders and known troublemakers were shot out of hand, despite the proclamation [granting amnesty for all those who returned to work]."[67]

One pro-slavery observer bemoaned the damage witnessed to estate property, but despaired at the perseverance of the rebel slaves despite brutal repression. "Notwithstanding the numerous examples that were daily made, by exhibiting the heads of the leaders of the rebels on poles, in conspicuous places throughout the district, the lessons seemed of mere effect, as few, very few returned to their properties, and not to their work."[68]

The official figure for slaves killed in the 1831 rebellion was 207, though estimates of 400 are more likely accurate. In the courts-martial that followed, at least another 376 were executed, and estimates went as high as 750 convictions.[69] Sam Sharpe was executed on 23 May 1832, after announcing proudly to Bleby that he "would rather die upon yonder gallows than live in slavery."[70]

THE AFTERMATH

Though the rebellion itself was put down in less than two weeks,[71] the long-term effect of the events of 1831 was to speed up the process of emancipation by several years. For a short period of time 20,000 slaves rose up and demanded dignity, by their actions destroying the entire structure of racist lies upon which slavery rested. Despite the restraint displayed by the slaves, the cost of the rebellion to the plantocracy was considerable. Some 1,132,000 pounds worth of property was destroyed, and an additional 161,570 pounds were spent in suppressing the uprising.[72] The political cost was still greater. The rebellion and the subsequent massacre added weight to the abolition movement raging in Britain "and led to a marked change of attitude on the part of the British government to the whole question of slavery."[73]

The lessons of the revolt were not lost on the slave population. Despite imperial support of the repression, it was the British parliament that did in fact enact legislation to free the slaves only two years later. Further, it was widely rumoured among the slaves that the white landowners no longer held legal title to their properties, but were allowed to rent the land from the Crown for the next century.[74] Royal dicta thus continued to be associated with emancipation. Moreover, the new Jamaican Governor, Lord Sligo, arrived in 1834 determined to enforce a liberal interpretation of the apprenticeship system. The local Assembly, and the planters in general, were equally determined to make apprenticeship as consistent with the slave system as possible. The identification of a benevolent Crown with the interests of the slaves was thus further reinforced in the events that followed the revolt.

The religious idiom was also reaffirmed in popular consciousness in the aftermath of the rebellion. It was primarily the Baptists and Wesleyans who were repressed, for it was these missions that predominated in the area where the rebellion was concentrated. Many of those convicted in the courts-martial following the events were self-identified Baptists. According to Craton, the way that information was introduced in these trials "suggests that a Baptist affiliation of itself was often regarded as tantamount to proof of rebel activity."[75] Though the missionaries refused to accept responsibility for the 1831 rebellion, the Jamaican plantocracy held them accountable for the slaves' actions. The leading local missionaries were arrested, and in other parts of the island missionaries were held in custody in anticipation of the spread of the revolt. Most of the missionaries were released soon after their arrest and, while martial law was in operation, few further incidents were reported. From February of 1832, however, anti-missionary sentiment became organized into a new movement, the Colonial Church Union, whose stated aim was to defend the Church of England. In reality, the Union was a reactionary planters' organization, dedicated to reversing the trend toward emancipation.

The Union appealed to leading militiamen across the island. By the summer of 1832 the Union had bases in every part of the island except Kingston, where the relatively large coloured population prevented its establishment.[76] The Colonial Church Union called for the expulsion of the dissenting missionaries from the island, and resorted to acts of terror to carry out its aims. More than seventeen chapels, primarily Baptist and Wesleyan Methodist, were destroyed and private missionary houses were threatened.

In the summer of 1832 a new governor, Lord Mulgrave, arrived and firmly declared his opposition to the Unionists.[77] In 1833 a royal proclamation declared the Colonial Church Union illegal. Events had once again confirmed the British role as the benevolent protector of the slaves' freedom. Moreover, the Crown now appeared to stand as protector of the missionary defenders of emancipation. The missionaries were again directly identified with the emancipation struggle, and their credibility as the enemies of the white planters was thus renewed in the aftermath of the rebellion.[78]

Aside from emancipation itself, the most notable development in the Jamaican political economy in the aftermath of the 1831 events was the exodus of the slaves from the plantations. The missionaries played a central role in this movement. In 1838 William Knibb began a series of land purchases. A portion of each of the properties was reserved for the erection of a chapel, and the remaining area was parcelled into holdings of one to three acres. These were sold to former slaves.[79] Knibb's aim was to establish a series of "Free Villages," populated by a "noble free peasantry."[80] By the early 1840s there were an estimated 150–200 such villages on the island, covering some one hundred thousand acres of land.[81]

The exodus of slaves from the estates, and the concomitant establishment of a peasant class rather than a wage-labour force, was met with extreme opposition from the planters. Attempts were made to refuse to sell land to Knibb, though he was able to circumvent this by employing intermediaries in the transactions.[82] Once again, the missionaries were placed in the position of giving aid to the black population against the interests of the majority of white society.

The process whereby the freed slaves became established as a peasant class can also be understood to be a critical element in the development of organic ideology. Two forms of direct action on the part of the slaves, before and after emancipation, can be identified. The first was collective strike action, planned as the central means of bargaining on behalf of the slaves during the revolt of 1831, even if only actually carried out on selected estates. The second was similar to a prolonged "strike," and was maintained after 1838 when the slaves *en masse* chose to reject estate labour as their main source of livelihood. The first was collectively organized, consciously planned and, in its immediate results, unsuccessful; the second was not organized, but based on individual initiative and, in the immediate circumstances, successful in resisting the dictates of the estate owners. The lessons of the aftermath of the rebellion thus reinforced the attachment of the producing classes to landholding as the primary source of security and autonomy, an important element of organic ideology. It is significant that the next major revolt to occur in Jamaica, the Morant Bay rebellion of 1865, which we will consider in the following chapter, focussed on the issue of access to land. Perhaps even more significant is the resilience of an ideology of resistance that incorporated both the religious idiom and the perception of a benevolent Crown as protector of the producing classes.

CHAPTER THREE

Freedom Without Rights: The Morant Bay Rebellion of 1865

BACKGROUND: JAMAICA AFTER EMANCIPATION

Jamaican society in 1865 continued to reflect the problems associated with the process of emancipation. Freedom for the slaves was granted in the interests and by the decree of the British ruling class, which was increasingly committed to a system of free trade and the more profitable organization of a free wage-labour force. Britain's economic interests, however, were international, while the Jamaican section of the ruling class was solely committed to preserving its protected position in the British Empire. The Jamaican Assembly took over the detailed direction of the island, effectively shutting out the Colonial Office. The task that had been opposed during the pre-emancipation period because it was considered impossible was now a reality – that is, "the management of a tropical, staple-producing economy under a system of free labor."[1] The white rulers, in response to the freed slaves' exodus from the plantations, attempted to improve methods of production on their estates and at the same time tried to maintain the political conditions established under slavery.

There was a critical ideological contradiction in this project. Slave society was ruled by force. The continued authority of the ruling class was based on the threat of the whip or more heinous tortures. All states are necessarily backed up by the threat and power of repression,[2] but in Jamaican slave society there was only a minimal effort to combine rule by force with rule by consent – either active or passive. To the extent that voluntary consent was expected, it involved the acceptance on the part of the slaves of the idea that their race and culture were fundamentally inferior to those of their white masters. The immediate threat of punishment was constant, whether or not the *right* of the master class to implement such punishment was accepted. In conditions of a free wage-labour force, however, economic production is largely dependent upon the voluntary participation of the producing class. In such circumstances the ruling class must develop some form of ideological "hegemony," to use Gramsci's concept, in order to rule effectively.[3]

To attain such hegemony, the Jamaican rulers would have had to provide their former slaves with a set of ideas that allowed them, as free men and women, to *choose* to support the continued rule of an exploiting class they had come to despise and fear. Curtin points out that in terms of existing bodies of thought, no set of ideas suited to these conditions was apparent. Neither the ideology appropriate to the expansive British Empire nor that suited to colonial slavery were applicable as a whole to the management of post-slavery Jamaica.[4] Certain elements of the ideology of empire, notably the notion of black inferiority to the "cultured" world of the white rulers, proved adaptable to conditions of freedom. African culture, tradition and achievements were never mentioned in the limited educational channels that were available, while white explorers, politicians and heroes were celebrated. In the absence of a coherent ideology of consent and cooperation, black history and black experience were officially denied in conditions of freedom, just as they had been in conditions of slavery.[5]

It should not be suggested, however, that the post-emancipation ruling circles in Jamaica were a united or monolithic force. The Assembly, during and after slavery, was traditionally divided into two loose caucuses referred to as political parties, but sharing none of the ideological or organizational discipline associated with the modern sense of the term. The Country Party was that of the white plantocracy. The Town Party included merchants, lawyers, and some planters, many of whom were of mixed racial background and had supported the abolition of slavery. Much of the island press identified with the Town Party. A tradition of moderate, reform-oriented politics developed among a section of the coloured middle class, but their voice remained a minority among an otherwise bitterly conservative ruling class.

The structure of government as a whole had changed little since emancipation. The governor continued to operate officially as the Crown appointee both in a military capacity as Captain-General and in a political capacity as Governor-in-Chief. The governor, along with a nominated council (appointed by the governor), performed the executive and judicial duties of the colonial government, as well as some of its legislative duties. The nominated members were selected mainly from among the leading planters and the Crown's law officers. A Legislative Assembly responsible for matters of local government was elected by a narrow franchise and represented the interests of local planters, attorneys, and other businessmen on the island. When the Council sat under the direction of the Council President, it operated as the second division of the Legislature. In the event of any matter deemed of "paramount importance," the governor could combine the votes of the Council and the Assembly in such a way as to ensure a majority in his favour. Ultimate executive authority thus rested with the governor alone.[6]

Though the franchise was expanded after emancipation it was far from approaching a system of popular democracy. In the 1864 election, out of a population of 436,807, only 1,903 were eligible to vote, and actual voters numbered no more than 1,457.[7] Though poor economic conditions had led to a steady decline in the resident white population, the planters and their attorneys continued to dominate the colony's local political positions. Every member of the Assembly was required by law to swear that he and his wife (if he had one) were "in the receipt of a clear income of nine hundred dollars a year, from real estate, or that they own real estate worth nine thousand dollars, or real and personal estate together, worth about fifteen thousand dollars."[8]

In the post-emancipation decades there was constant conflict between the local Assembly and the Colonial Office. In 1852, Governor Lord Grey stated that the major source of tension was the reluctance of the Jamaican plantocracy to adjust to the conditions of emancipation. "Although the need of well-considered legislation, to meet the wants of an entirely new state of society, was not less urgent in Jamaica than in the other former slave colonies; and though Jamaica has far greater facilities than most of these colonies for carrying into effect such measures as are required, the Statute Book of the island for the last six years presents nearly a blank, as regards laws calculated to improve the condition of the population, and to raise them in the scale of civilization."[9] Of the forty bills actually enacted into law in 1861–62, only two held any promise of improved conditions for the Jamaican producing classes and many enacted in previous years were designed to restrict the mobility and freedom of the newly emancipated slaves.[10]

The most significant change in the political system after emancipation was thus not within the formal structure or content of government, but in the fact of emancipation itself. For the former slaves, government was now a process in which they were nominally included as free citizens, albeit to a very limited extent. Unfortunately, the political officials in the most direct contact with the peasants and workers – the local magistrates or custodes in the parishes – were universally recognized to be corrupt and incompetent. One longtime resident, a member of the Island Privy Council, commented on "the acknowledged inefficiency of the courts of law; the failure of justices of the lower orders; the laxity, untrustworthiness, and improprieties of public boards; the gross and unblushing bribery and corruption practised at elections by the upper classes; [and] the licentious and gross perversions of the truth."[11]

The principal official in each parish was appointed by the governor to act as Chief Magistrate or "Custos Rotulorum." These men were almost always local planters resident in the parish and were often also members of the Assembly. The Custos in turn nominated for appointment by the governor a number of Justices of the Peace, who were largely responsible for implementing legislation regarding labour relations. The Justices of the Peace also held positions on the parish Vestry,[12] which granted them control over the local constabulary and the right to issue orders to the police – a right that otherwise rested only with the governor.[13]

One of the most notable indications of the continued legacy of slavery was the re-introduction in 1859–60 of the whip as a form of punishment for certain offences. In 1864 Governor Eyre successfully asked the Legislature to approve the use of both the whip and the treadmill as punishment for theft.[14]

These conditions were hardly conducive to the growth of stable ruling class hegemony. Ideological transformation alone would not have guaranteed hegemony for the old plantocracy. Some measure of material improvement in the lives of the producing classes was the precondition to hegemonic stabilization. Scarce island funds would have had to be expended upon various facilities and services accessible to at least a small portion of this class, sufficient to show token interest in the living standards of the majority of Jamaicans. By and large, the plantocracy was bitter over emancipation and was suffering from chronic economic decline. It could perceive nothing to be gained from such outlays of island funds. If misery and poverty were experienced among the black population, it was seen as the result of the "laziness" considered inherent in the black race.

Because it was essential to maintain a productive labour force, some island funds were spent on public health in the post-emancipation period, but the services were in some ways even poorer than they had been during slavery. During the slave era the estate owners had been responsible for providing medical services – such as they were – to the slaves. With emancipation, the cost to the planter of maintaining an estate doctor was eliminated. By the early 1860s the number of doctors practising in Jamaica had declined to about twenty-five per cent of the number employed at emancipation. Education figured even lower on the list of priorities.[15] Literacy was traditionally perceived as a dangerous and subversive skill for the slaves to acquire, and there was no incentive to alter this position in conditions of freedom.

Thus, while the ruling class could no longer rely on the constant threat or implementation of force to guarantee discipline among the work force they were not prepared to seek popular assent to their authority, on either an economic or a political level. In such conditions, a permanent "crisis of hegemony"[16] came to characterize the period between emancipation and the Morant Bay revolt in 1865.

WILLED IDEOLOGY – THE RELIGIOUS IDIOM

One important group in Jamaican society – the white missionaries – attempted, to a limited extent, to fill the vacuum of hegemony. In the post-emancipation period the missionaries continued to be "the only group of Europeans in close and friendly contact with the Negroes."[17] The churches were particularly aggressive in one arena where the plantocracy was decidedly disinterested – the field of education. Virtually every denomination, including the Church of England, took an interest in building and operating schools.[18] One indication of the relative success of this educational effort was the increase in literacy among the producing classes. While the majority of the peasants and workers remained unable to read or write, in 1862 Price estimated that about 45 per cent of 175,000 people with some elementary education could read, and that almost one-third could both read and write.[19] This meant that a significant proportion of the population was developing literacy skills.

The churches not only provided some form of education through the schools, but also, to varying degrees, actually intervened in the acculturation process of the freed slaves. The Baptist missionaries were most aggressive in this effort, relying on their historical legacy as the defenders of the black population. In the years immediately following emancipation, many former slaves became Baptists, the membership growing from about ten thousand in 1831 to thirty-four thousand in 1845.[20] With the granting of emancipation, "from one end of the island to the other, people crammed into the chapels long before services started and multitudes gathered outside."[21] Individual leading missionaries, such as William Knibb, were celebrated as heroes by the freed slaves.

This pattern of growing missionary influence among Jamaica's black population was not, however, a linear one. By the mid-1840s all of the missionary churches including the Baptists saw their numbers begin to fall. A temporary period of recovery known as the Great Revival in 1860–62 was followed by an even more profound loss in mission influence. In some congregations as much as half of the post-emancipation expansion dropped off by 1865.[22] A number of factors conspired to split apart the fusion of the inherent element of African religious tradition and the derived element of white Christian influence. The Baptist missionaries saw their role during the era of slavery clearly as defenders of the immediate interests of the slaves, and they did not hesitate to intervene on their behalf in day-to-day disputes with the planters. To intervene as unofficial "trade union shop stewards" between free men, however, was considered by the missionaries to be quite another matter.[23] The difference was not so obvious to labourers whose conditions of work seemed only nominally improved.[24]

By the mid-1840s the Baptists' Free Village System was also in decline. With the death of Knibb in 1845, and Burchell's death soon after, "the balance of opinion was increasingly tilted against the peasantry."[25] No other religious leader followed Knibb in organizing large-scale land purchases on behalf of the peasants. Thus, both on the estates and among the newly settled peasants, the major *material* incentives for loyalty to the Baptists as unofficial labour representatives were greatly reduced. Rowbotham identifies the rise and fall of the Great Revival with efforts of the believers to "launch a reform of the society by purely moral means," only to face greater despair in light of the absence of material improvements.[26]

Another cause of the increasing separation between the inherent and derived elements in the Jamaican religious tradition among the producing classes was the continued celebration and growth of Afro-Christian and African practices. Afro-Christian followings spread through the splitting away of black Baptist leaders, reflecting the aspect of Christian doctrine, originally derived, which had by this point become part of inherent ideology. Even in Kingston where European influence was the most concentrated, by 1860 Native Baptists constituted half of the entire churchgoing population. With the extremely repressive control of the slave system eliminated, African religious custom, which had been preserved as a feature of resistance, could now flourish. This was also reflected in the increase of myal and obeah practices. Both currents remained illegal, but nonetheless continued to spread in influence and expression through a tenacious culture of oral history and folklore.[27]

The increase in black religious forms of expression and organization met rising criticism from official white mission circles. The missionaries, including Baptists, were not seeking converts merely to Christianity but also, in their eyes, to a superior "civilized" society. As a result they sought to achieve moral as well as religious authority. In this sense the missionaries were seeking to play a hegemonic role in relation to the freed slaves, though their efforts met with diminishing success. Slave customs such as drumming, dancing and Christmas festivities were attacked by British leaders as immoral and provided grounds for expulsion from the Church.[28]

By the mid-nineteenth century, the relationship between European missionary practice and Afro-Christian or African tradition was strained indeed. The Great Revival, a desperate effort to bring the evangelical revival taking place in the United States, Ireland, and Britain to Jamaica, was launched by the Baptist and Moravian Churches. The movement spread, but the larger its following, the more distinctly African and the less European it became.[29] Finally, the revival was denounced and disowned by the same missionaries who had initiated it.

Despite this tension, it would be a mistake to assume that the derived missionary influence ceased to play a central role among the producing classes. In both the Afro-Christian and myal movements, selected aspects of Christian teaching and practice were evident, such as the singing of hymns and the use of Christian phraseology. Moreover, a generation of Jamaican blacks had been educated in missionary schools, where "the Bible had been their Primer."[30] The influence of the Baptist Church, because of its association with the emancipation struggle and the settlement of the peasantry, was certainly greater than that of any other single group of Europeans on the island. In a setting in which the ruling class was not even attempting to win such influence, the legacy of the mission leaders loomed even larger. Despite the decline of formal, direct contact between the mission leaders and the black population, many aspects of missionary religious teaching had, by 1865, become inherent in the ideology of the producing classes.

The chronic decline of the Jamaican economy had been exacerbated by a three-year drought. This had caused a further decline in plantation production and, more significantly, had led to a crisis in peasant agriculture.[31] These conditions provided the background to the events surrounding the Morant Bay rebellion. Discontent was rising, and official channels for the expression of discontent were virtually closed.

An atmosphere of legitimation for public grievances was established by the mass distribution of a letter written by E.B. Underhill, the Secretary of the Baptist Missionary Society in England. Underhill had visited Jamaica for several months in 1859–60 in connection with his mission responsibilities. He corresponded with the contacts he established, and when reports of profound distress among the peasantry became numerous and frequent, he wrote a lengthy letter to Edward Cardwell, then Secretary of State for the Colonies in the British government.

Underhill's letter, dated 5 January 1865, was acknowledged and forwarded to the Governor of Jamaica, Edward Eyre, who had held office since 1862. In the traditional style of Baptist missionary agitation, Underhill's letter called attention to numerous grievances which he felt demanded immediate and forceful attention. "The people, then, are starving, and the causes of this are not far to seek. No doubt the taxation of the island is too heavy for its present resources, and must necessarily render the cost of producing the staples higher than they can bear to meet competition in the markets of the world. No doubt much of the sugar-land of the island is worn out, or can only be made productive by an outlay which would destroy all hope of profitable return ... But the simple fact is, there is not sufficient employment for the people; there is neither work for them, nor the capital to employ them."[32] Underhill also called attention to the problem of those who worked for wages but whose employers would refuse to pay them, to the lack of political rights for the former slaves, and to the increase in petty larceny as a result of widespread poverty. He called for a comprehensive enquiry into island legislation enacted since emancipation.[33]

Governor Eyre chose to circulate the letter among the leading planters, parish custodes, judges, and magistrates, as well as among ministers and clergymen from all religious denominations. He requested information to help him to prepare his reply and to provide a firm refutation to the allegations. In late March, the letter was published in the Jamaican press, apparently without Eyre's knowledge or approval. The letter "became at once the topic of heated discussion in every class of the community ... Not a house, not an individual, but was made acquainted with its contents, it was common property. The field labourer equally with the planter had it before him ... Since the date of emancipation no subject had so seriously agitated the public opinion of Jamaica, or called forth more acrimonious discussion."[34] The response of Eyre, and in turn of the Colonial Office, was to dutifully forward the reports he received, the majority of which were indignant in their opposition to the Baptist charges. With the important exception of a lengthy report prepared by the Baptist missionaries in Jamaica,[35] the replies argued that there was no distress to speak of or, if there was, the prime cause was the traditional "laziness" of the Negro.[36]

In response to this exchange, a series of well-attended public meetings, which came to be known as the "Underhill meetings", were organized by various representatives of the clergy, teachers, and landholders across the island. The meetings were attended primarily by coloured middle class reformers and discontented peasants and workers. Though there was no central organization, the meetings passed a series of variously worded resolutions endorsing the contents of Underhill's letter. They provided an outlet for political expression that had been denied to the majority of the population through normal channels.

Significantly, it was a Baptist missionary officer who once again provided the catalyst for the expression of protest. And once again politics were expressed in the religious idiom. The interpretation of island conditions provided by Underhill was derived from official Baptist circles, but it touched upon the inherent elements present in the ideology of the producing classes.

Despite the later charges of Governor Eyre, however, the Underhill meetings were not principally organized or led by Baptist ministers, as the Baptists themselves were eager to confirm. Underhill stressed that out of twenty-one parishes where Baptist ministers were active, only eleven held meetings; and of thirty-six official Baptist ministers on the island, only eleven even participated in the gatherings.[37] The point to be noted is that the letter was written by a man who was not only an important official in Britain but also a Baptist missionary leader. The letter provided legitimacy and expression to the conditions among the poor black population. Moreover, it lent increased importance to Baptist missionaries as a group, though the Baptists did not actually play a leading role in the events.

The Underhill meetings provided an outlet for the expression of despair, and in the majority of cases this was sufficient to dispel any threat of further disturbances. Though this result could not have been anticipated by Underhill, whose letter was not intended for mass distribution, the meetings operated as the type of political forum that might have been provided by a ruling class attempting to resolve a prolonged crisis of hegemony. The missionaries, however, were not and could not be the ruling class of Jamaica. In the one parish where discontent went further, the reaction was far from conciliatory.

The parish of St Thomas-in-the-East, where Morant Bay is located, was one of the few regions of the island where the Baptist Missionary Society had no representative. This was not the result of a lack of effort. The local magistrates, both during the period of slavery and after, were determined to prevent the establishment of any missionary outpost, be it Baptist or any other denomination. Those who had endeavoured to gain a foothold in the parish before the 1865 events met with persecution and imprisonment. In the late 1840s Wesleyan-Methodist support was greater than in other parts of the island, but Underhill estimates that some four-fifths of the parish at the time of the rebellion were "without religious instruction" from Christian clergy.[38]

Regardless of official missionary influence, the Morant Bay rebellion clearly confirmed the religious idiomatic tradition. The identified leader of the resistance was Paul Bogle, a Native Baptist preacher, a peasant landholder[39] and a determined political agitator. Bogle was ordained by an outspoken coloured member of the Assembly, George William Gordon, who was also active in the Morant Bay district as a Baptist lay preacher.[40]

Gordon was the illegitimate son of a black slave woman and a wealthy white planter. He taught himself to read and write and became a prosperous produce merchant, sufficiently successful to arrange manumission for himself, his mother and his sisters. Gordon was able to save his white father's estate from ruin when it was threatened with bankruptcy. Having married a white woman from Kingston, by the 1860s Gordon established himself as a successful planter and large landowner in St Thomas-in-the-East and other parts of the island.[41]

Gordon's partially black heritage alone would not have kept him from common political cause with the white plantocracy, though he would have been excluded from white social circles. But his Baptist religious convictions and his political identification with the poor blacks of Jamaica made him a vocal critic of the dominant island interests, including the established Church. It was in 1861, during the peak of the Great Revival, that Gordon adopted the Baptist faith, and in 1862 he opened two mission stations near Stony Gut, the focal point of the Morant Bay rebellion. On the grounds of his adult baptism, Gordon was rejected as a Native Baptist, and removed from his elected position of July 1863 as churchwarden for the Vestry in St Thomas-in-the-East. Gordon was mistrusted for seeing his mission responsibilities as "twofold" in character, both "parochial and private."[42]

Gordon was a longstanding political enemy of Governor Eyre. For many years the Jamaican governors had formed an alliance with the Town Party to challenge the resistance of the majority of the planters to moderate reform. Governor Eyre, however, supported the Country Party, the traditional voice of the white planters. Gordon, elected to the Assembly in 1863, led the left wing of the Town Party, and became identified by Governor Eyre as his "chief personal antagonist and the leading trouble-maker on the island."⁴³ Before Gordon won a seat in the Assembly, he was the magistrate in St Thomas-in-the-East. In 1862 he had written to Eyre concerning abhorrent conditions in the local jail, and in so doing incited the hostility of the planters in the parish. Upon the request of the parish Custos and Baron von Ketelhodt, the resident leader of the planters' interests, Governor Eyre saw to Gordon's dismissal as magistrate.

Fierce opposition from the parish planters and custodes faced Gordon when he ran for election to the Jamaican Assembly. He won a seat in the election of 1863 mainly because of the support of those peasants in St Thomas-in-the-East who were eligible to meet the restricted franchise, many of whom, such as Paul Bogle, were influenced by the Native Baptist tradition.

The absence of an official missionary presence in the events leadings to the Morant Bay rebellion may have been a factor in the outbreak. Bogle, using his chapel as an organizing centre, was prepared to initiate forms of action that would have been anathema to more orthodox clergymen.⁴⁴ Bogle's primary concerns were shaped by his identification with the struggles of his race and class. His Native Baptist religious practices placed him in intimate contact with the inherent religious ideology of the producing classes, an ideology that included notions of social and economic justice. Given the hostility to formal Christian teaching harboured by the political leaders of the parish, participation in Native Baptist activities held even greater political import.

The issues at stake in the Morant Bay revolt, however, were strictly secular, as in the slave rebellion of 1831. Given the climate of discontent, the planters and Governor Eyre had been anticipating a "Negro uprising" for some months. Furthermore, as the plantation economy continued to suffer, the proportion of white residents in Jamaica steadily diminished. Governor Eyre expressed the fears of the ruling class when he stated, "European proprietors ... but above all European residents of position, education, and wealth have dwindled down to an insignificant number; their places have not been taken by colonial-born persons of corresponding status and ability ... This state of things is getting worse year by year. The European element is continually decreasing, and my firm conviction is that the day will come, though it may yet be distant, when Jamaica will become little better than a second Haiti."⁴⁵

Unrest was anticipated particularly in the northern parishes of the island, where rumours of preparation for a confrontation were rife,[46] but no signs of planning for a revolt were apparent in St Thomas-in-the-East. At the end of July 1865, a printed leaflet called upon the residents of that parish and those of St Ann's to attend a public meeting at Morant Bay Courthouse. This was one of the last localities to organize an Underhill meeting. The leaflet was unsigned, but was accredited to Gordon. "People of St Thomas-in-the-East, you have been ground down too long already. Shake off your sloth ... The Government have dared you to defend your rights ... Remember that he only is free whom the truth makes free. You are no longer slaves but free men."[47] The meeting finally took place on 12 August, but because the parish Custos had refused to allow use of the courthouse, it was held out-of-doors. Chaired by Gordon, the meeting prepared a series of resolutions concerning "the misgovernment of the island."[48] A delegation including Paul Bogle was selected to take their grievances to Governor Eyre in Spanish Town. After marching to the governor's door, the delegation was denied permission to see Eyre, and resentment rose even further.

After Eyre's refusal to see the delegation, a political division developed among the black population of the district. Bogle's efforts turned away from formal political channels, as they had proven closed to the producing classes, and he devoted himself to the organization of popular societies to challenge the discredited authorities. Bogle was hardly naïve concerning Jamaican governmental processes. For the past two years he had been involved in leading resident black peasants in self-governing committees. Bogle and his supporters had formed an independent police force and judiciary, and had elected officers to the posts of Judge, Clerk of the Peace, Inspector, Sergeant and Private. The self-governing courts issued summonses, held trials, and assigned fines to offenders.[49]

Gordon, as a politician himself and a representative of the upper class, followed a somewhat different strategy. He began a campaign to raise funds to send a delegation directly to the Queen, thereby going over the head of Governor Eyre. Significantly, both perspectives shared a common feature: political leadership of the producing classes was associated with self-styled Baptist preaching. As in 1831, in the midst of the events religion seemed to fade into the background in the face of open political class conflict.

The outbreak began on 7 October 1865, a Saturday, when a petty sessions court was in progress in Morant Bay, presided over by Custos von Ketelhodt, owner of five plantations.

The case which originally brought the demonstrators to Morant Bay Courthouse was the trial of a black peasant for charges of trespassing on the property of an absentee plantation owner. When this case was called up, some 150 persons armed with sticks entered the courthouse. The man on trial, Lewis Dick, had established himself on an abandoned plantation adjoining Stony Gut. The residents of the area, Paul Bogle and other members of his settlement, had been squatters on these lands for many years. Dick was convicted on his own plea of guilty, but Bogle came forward from the crowd and urged him to refuse to pay the fine and to appeal the conviction. Upon Bogle's intervention, an appeal of the conviction of guilty for trespass was registered.[50] The events which followed were reported in the *Colonial Standard*: "A man made a noise in the court, and was ordered to be brought before the justices. He was captured by the police outside, but immediately rescued by one Paul Bogle and several other persons, who had large bludgeons in their hands, and taken into the market-square, where some one hundred and fifty more persons joined them, also with sticks; the police were severely beaten."[51]

On the following Monday, warrants for the arrest of Paul Bogle, his brother Moses, and some twenty-five others were issued.[52] On Tuesday, six policemen and two constables arrived at Stony Gut to make the arrests. There they encountered some three to five hundred people, armed with sticks and cutlasses, prepared to assist those charged in resisting arrest. The police were held and beaten, and some were detained as prisoners. They were forced to take oaths swearing to "join their colour" and "cleave to the black."[53]

By evening, news had reached Morant Bay that on the following day an assembly would once again present the Vestry authorities with their grievances. At this point the Custos summoned the militia, and called upon Governor Eyre to provide military assistance. On Wednesday afternoon, 11 October, a crowd led by Paul Bogle assembled at the Vestry Hall, again armed with cutlasses and sticks. The Custos read out the Riot Act, and, ostensibly in response to the throwing of stones, the word was given for the militia to fire and some of the rioters fell.[54] The crowd then rushed the courthouse amidst cries of "War" and the building was set on fire. For one day, the rebels held control of the town.

On the following day, Thursday, 12 October, the rioters travelled to Bath, a town eight miles from Morant Bay, attacking several estate houses and continuing along the Plantain-garden River.[55] On that day, the first troops reached the district and the outbreak was soon crushed.

Bogle was reported to have told the police that he and his supporters were committed "to kill all the white men and all the black men that would not join them."[56] As in 1831, however, the conflict was not a purely racial war. It was a conflict between an angry black peasantry and selected agents of the white ruling class. Blacks and coloured Jamaicans perceived to be on the side of the oppressors were among those who were killed or wounded by the protestors, and there were black and coloured volunteers among those who suppressed the rioting.[57] But it is also true that, again as in 1831, when the black producers rose up, the established system of racism that supported local military and class interests was severely shaken.

The rebels were also decidedly selective, or discriminating, in their targets.[58] Among those killed during the seizure of the Morant Bay courthouse, for example, were the despised Custos Baron von Ketelhodt and the Reverend Herschell, curate of Bath, "whose oppressive acts of injustice had specially roused the passions of the people."[59] One particularly sober commentary published in Britain stated that "The Jamaica papers of dates preceding the riots show that strong party feelings existed in various districts, and that Baron Ketelhodt and the Rev. Mr. Herschell were both much disliked and distrusted by the blacks. The great questions concerning the riots in Jamaica and the measures adopted by the authorities ought not to be confused by discussions relating to the characters of individuals; and the statements here made with reference to the position in which Baron Ketelhodt and the Rev. Mr. Herschell stood towards the blacks are introduced, not as offering any judgment upon either individual, but merely because, when taken in conjunction with other facts, they throw light upon the motives which led to the murders, and give them the appearance of deeds of personal revenge."[60] When the rioters travelled to Bath, property damage to the estate houses was extensive, but only one person, the attorney or agent for Amity Hall Estate, was killed. A doctor, present at the time, was not touched. The rebels dealt harshly only with "those whites who were vicious while sparing any who were sympathetic to the cause of the blacks."[61]

In total, eighteen persons were killed and thirty-one were wounded by the rioters on 11 October. Twenty houses and shops were plundered, and five buildings, including the Morant Bay Courthouse, were burnt. These figures, however, pale in comparison with the trail of destruction left by the repression that followed. The actual numbers killed or injured by the militia in and around Morant Bay Courthouse were not recorded, but deaths by execution later came to 354 by courts-martial and an additional 85 without trial. A further six hundred men and women were whipped, and some one thousand black dwellings were destroyed.[62]

The outbreak itself was completely suppressed within three days, but a state of martial law was declared by the governor, covering the entire county of Surrey except for Kingston. Martial law stayed in force for a full month. After Thursday 12 October, no one was injured or killed at the hands of the rebels. In fact, in no instance were the soldiers even resisted.[63] Yet during this time, the full force of the revenge of the plantocracy, sometimes through the martialling of black soldiers, was given absolute licence. One white resident described the conditions as follows: "We are living in fear all the day long. Our lives were in danger during the first few days of the rioters' success, and were not less so when they were crushed. Martial law is a dreadful thing! a horrible affair! The soldiers were let loose in the country, and did their work with savage fury, shooting down good, bad, and indifferent, spreading death and desolation. The road for miles was said to have been insufferable, from the stench of the rotting bodies of men and women."[64] In the enquiry that followed, military authorities reported on the massacre, declaring how much "the soldiery enjoy it," and what "fun" they had in seeing the rebels hung.[65]

During this time, Bogle was summarily executed, and Gordon, then residing in Kingston, was arrested and taken to Morant Bay where martial law was in force. There he was tried and subsequently hanged. The Royal Commission appointed to investigate the events was compelled to conclude that "The evidence, oral and documentary, appears to us to be wholly insufficient to establish the charge upon which the prisoner took his trial."[66] Gordon was charged with having conspired to instigate the revolt at Morant Bay, though evidence suggests that he only found out about the outbreak well after it had begun.[67]

The charges against Gordon involved more than political vengeance. The religious idiom was also reconfirmed. Governor Eyre "was a thoroughgoing Anglican and hated Dissenters, Methodists and Baptists."[68] Gordon, as a self-styled Baptist preacher, was a threat to the established rulers because of "his endeavors to secure for the population the preaching of the Gospel,"[69] perceived by the planters as subversive activity. In the light of the circumstances surrounding Gordon's arrest and execution, and the later conclusions of the Royal Commission, Eyre's actions succeeded only in elevating his opponent to the level of a martyr among the Jamaican poor.

The religious idiom of political expression was also confirmed in other instances. The Baptist missionaries were repeatedly implicated during the month of martial law, despite their lack of actual direct involvement in the Morant Bay events. Governor Eyre directly named a number of Baptist ministers whom he considered responsible for the uprising, though the Royal Commission found no grounds for these charges.[70] Nonetheless, in the government's justification for its actions, the missionaries were repeatedly accused of responsibility for the outbreak. On 23 October, Eyre wrote that the rebellion broke out as a result of "the indiscreet acts, language, or writings of persons of education, as well as by political demagogues and agitators. Chief amongst these, I regret to say, are the Secretary of the Baptist Missionary Society in England, Dr Underhill, and some of the Baptist ministers in Jamaica, who have endorsed and enlarged upon his views and statements."[71] In Jamaica during the period of martial law, missionaries were harassed and arrested, their mail was censored, and there were some reports of torture.[72] Once again the Baptist missionaries were more closely associated with the interests and actions of the producing classes in the minds of the rulers than among the labourers themselves.[73]

WILLED IDEOLOGY — THE CROWN AS BENEVOLENT DESPOT

The Jamaican black population's esteem for British royalty was greatly heightened in the wake of emancipation. The single most important decree in the history of the Jamaican labouring classes, and perhaps in the history of the island as a whole, was commonly understood to have been the result of the Queen's personal intervention and assent.[74] By 1865, this notion, originally derived from ruling class legislation, had become part of the inherent ideology of the producing classes.

The apparently protective role of the interests of the freed slaves played by the British colonial government was repeatedly affirmed in the course of the debates in the Jamaican Assembly. Several laws were passed in the House in an attempt to prevent the sale of vacant lands to the small peasants, and thus force them to accept regular employment on the estates. These were almost universally overturned by the home government.[75] The identification of Governor Eyre with the interests of the plantocracy was therefore seen as an aberration in the traditional pattern. Though Eyre was a Crown appointee, he was seen as personally irresponsible, not only by the majority of the Jamaican population (including the middle class) but also, in the aftermath of the Morant Bay events, by the home government. He was perceived by discontented Jamaicans to be the dishonest and disloyal servant of a good and just master. The course of the developments at Morant Bay focussed initially on placing demands on Eyre, and when it became obvious that he would ignore these demands more militant action followed.

One of the central issues involved in the Morant Bay events was the demand for land. Prior to the publication of Underhill's letter, a meeting was held, in the parish of St Ann's, calling upon Queen

Victoria to lease unused Crown lands for private peasant cultivation.[76] The petition, entitled "The Humble Petition of the Poor people of Jamaica and parish of Saint Anns," and dated 25 April 1865, was written in a most reverent tone, but clearly stated the peasants' situation. "We the poor people of this island beg with submission to inform our Queen, that we are in great want at this moment from the bad state of our Island soon after we became free subjects ... If our most gracious Sovereign Lady will be so kind as to get a quantity of Land we will put our hands and heart to work, and cultivate coffee, corn, canes, cotton and tobacco and other produce."[77] The petition was sent to Eyre, who then forwarded it with a disparaging note to the Colonial Office. The reply, entitled "The Queen's Advice", was produced as a handbill and widely distributed across the island. Addressed to Governor Eyre, and signed on behalf of the Crown by Colonial Secretary Cardwell, the statement read:

I request that you will inform the Petitioners that their Petition has been laid before the Queen, and that I have received her Majesty's command to inform them, that the prosperity of the Labouring Classes, as well as of all other Classes, depends, in Jamaica, and in other Countries, upon their working for Wages, not uncertainly, or capriciously, but steadily and continuously, at the times when their labour is wanted, and for so long as it is wanted; and that if they would use this industry, and thereby render the Plantations productive, they would enable the Planters to pay them higher Wages for the same hours of work that are received by the best Field Labourers in this Country.[78]

The petitioners and other readers among the labouring classes were so shocked by this dismissal that they were convinced it was a forgery designed by Eyre, and that the Queen herself had never received the dispatch.[79] The passage referring to steady and continuous employment was particularly disturbing, "for the core of what the emancipated Negro understood by freedom was the right to give or withhold labour as he pleased."[80]

The publication of "The Queen's Advice," in addition to Underhill's letter, created an atmosphere of even greater public protest. The widespread belief that the reply was a forgery added to the opposition to Governor Eyre. The belief that the Queen was incapable of such a rebuff became such an entrenched part of popular consciousness that even explicit evidence to the contrary could not shake the conviction. In this instance, an inherent aspect of the class ideology of the producing classes could not be altered by an argument derived from the ruling class, despite the fact that the argument came from the office of the Crown itself.

Following the publication of "The Queen's Advice," Gordon began to collect pledges to finance a deputation to meet directly with the Queen. Gordon prided himself on his loyalty to the Crown, and challenged Eyre's authority on these grounds.[81] Bogle, on the other hand, displayed a more ambivalent attitude to the Queen. Upon his return from Kingston, when Eyre refused to see the parish delegation, Bogle vociferously denounced not only the governor and the parish Custos, but also the Queen and the white race.[82] After Bogle and his followers resisted arrest for their actions at the Morant Bay Courthouse, they drafted a further letter to Eyre. They complained that the action taken against them was illegal, but concluded with an assertion of their total loyalty to the Queen.[83] It should be noted that Gordon's approach – to appeal directly to the Queen herself – claimed a mass base of supporters in the parish of St Thomas-in-the-East.[84]

ORGANIC IDEOLOGY – LANDOWNERSHIP AND SOCIAL RESISTANCE

The report of the Royal Commission identified three essential grievances leading to the popular resistance displayed at Morant Bay. These were: (1) a desire to obtain land without rent; (2) a lack of confidence in the administration of justice; and (3) hostility to the white residents of the island, particularly those seen as political opponents of the people.[85] The second and third points followed from the first – the desire to own land.

Since 1838 the general movement of the former slaves toward land settlement had provoked numerous struggles over legal entitlement to unoccupied or abandoned acreage.[86] Grievances over land claims were numerous, but the legal system inherited from the time of slavery had been little altered to deal with conflicts arising among ostensibly free and equal citizens. The planters exercised effective control of the magisterial courts which, by the 1860s, had become "little more than a means of enforcing the rule of the planters."[87] Thus, lack of faith in the courts and in the planters who controlled them increased in proportion to the number of legal battles over land claims settled in the planters' favour. In the parish of St Thomas-in-the-East such cases were particularly frequent. Out of 256 cases brought before the parish magistrates in 1864, a black worker or peasant was defendant in 250.[88]

In 1865 the demand for land was even greater than usual. Three years of drought had struck the peasant harvests severely. The declining estate sector was also in crisis, and supplementary wage labour was not available in many districts. For those peasants who were able to produce enough surplus for export, the duties charged were extremely high. The population was forced to rely more heavily on imported food, but food items as well as textiles were very costly because of the civil war in the United States.[89]

While peasant livelihoods suffered, Jamaican government policies were designed to compel black labourers to work on the estates for extremely low wages.[90] Efforts were made to promote even greater deprivation among small property owners. One such policy was reflected in the taxation system. The policy of taxation of only a limited, propertied minority of the population was replaced by a system in which the same taxation rate was applied to all residents, regardless of income or property-holdings.[91] Other efforts to lower peasant living standards involved the destruction of produce and the repossession of lands occupied without legal title. Estate owners were reported to have allowed their cattle to trample freely over the crops of small landholders and to have refused either to compensate the losses or to repair broken fences to prevent further damage.[92]

With the onset of drought, those labourers seeking steady employment on the estates either were unable to find work, or were not paid at all for the work they performed.[93] This practice, listed among the complaints of the St Ann's petitioners, was sufficiently widespread to compel the parish Custos to attempt to justify its occurrence. Writing to the governor's secretary, he stated, "The Petitioners complain that when they do take job or contract work it is in many instances not paid for when completed. I do not believe any Employer is so ignorant of the value of regular payments as to defer it, but he has frequently to make and dispose of his crop ere he has the means of doing so, and the complaint which is not unfounded serves to show that poverty is not confined to the Laborer, it is no doubt hard on him but not the cause of his distress, often does a man take as many weeks as he ought to take days ere he finishes his job."[94]

The reaction among the peasantry to these conditions was twofold. First, there was a general increase in "praedial larceny," or "the stealing of growing crops and small stock,"[95] as a source of food. Second, significantly, the generalized demand for land increased. The significance of landownership as a source of both economic and social security did not diminish with the arrival of difficult economic conditions. On the contrary, having clear title to a few acres of land was shown to be the only effective means to resist a return to conditions very similar to those of the slave era: working long hours on the estates without compensation. Wages, so clearly identified with the struggle for freedom in 1831, were now being withheld. The only means to subsist, let alone prosper, was to be able to cultivate produce without being compelled to pay exorbitant taxes or rent. A demand for ownership and control of land, as the only lasting and effective means to resist the dictates of the planters, was the underlying theme of the struggle in 1865, it was at the heart of the petition signed by the peasants of St Ann's parish. Both the condition of peasant production and the relative decline of wages for employment were central points in Underhill's letter.

The right to own the land upon which one had lived and worked for years was under threat, and the reaction of the local population was particularly virulent. The importance of landholding in the post-emancipation period was a central element in the organic ideology of the peasantry. During slavery, the provision grounds system had provided an essential aspect of the slaves' identity, but it is notable that landownership did not figure in the overt demands of the 1831 slave rebellion. Under slavery, provision grounds cultivation was complementary to plantation export crop production and was also favoured by the slaves. With emancipation, however, provision grounds cultivation was under threat, especially because it operated as an alternative to wage labour on the plantations. Thus it became a pivotal issue in class conflict. In 1865 the objective composition of Jamaica's labour force was qualitatively different from that of 1831. Collective strike action was no longer perceived as an effective means of bargaining, particularly in the depressed conditions of 1865. Alternatively, the absolute right to own and cultivate private lands was presented as a historically specific, organic idea.

The commitment to private landholding also influenced the specific nature of the willed ideological elements referred to above. Bogle, for example, was a religious leader, conforming to the tradition established within the Jamaican producing classes. But his leadership was not confined to this domain. He was also a landholder and a militant defender of land claims among the peasants of his community. His chapel operated not only as a religious centre, but also as the political organizing centre for the peasants. Similarly, Gordon was not only a Baptist lay preacher and a politician, but also an advisor on labour questions. Gordon was clearly identified as a supporter of peasant land claims and an advocate of greater job security on the estates. Bogle stated that Gordon did not advise him to organize against white society. However, Bogle did vote for Gordon, and did collect votes for him. Bogle quoted Gordon's advice that the peasantry "were not to work except they know what wages they are to get, and they are to get good wages."[96]

The nature of the resistance surrounding the Morant Bay events reflected the attachment to private landholding among the peasants. Before the outbreak, numerous indications of discontent reached the government, including the periodic refusal to pay taxes on land.[97] The residents of Stony Gut for some time had refused to pay rent "on the ground ... that the land was free and the estate belonged to the Queen."[98] Unlike the conditions of 1831, where the central demand was for wages paid for labour on the estates, in 1865 the central issue was access to land as a means of resisting the *necessity* to work on the estates, with or without wages.

In 1865 the plantation owners were thus challenged primarily in their capacity as landlords, not in their role as employers. When the rioters entered one estate on the Plantain-garden River, a group of fifty black labourers prevented them from approaching, and even hid the white women and children who had taken refuge. The following day, the estate workers escorted the white families to the care of government troops.[99] The significance of this incident should not be exaggerated, but it can be interpreted as an indication of two characteristics of the Morant Bay revolt: (1) there was a general lack of cohesive organization and leadership among the participants in the various events; and (2) at least in this instance, there was a lack of *spontaneous* identification, possibly encouraged by depressed conditions, between the rebels who saw themselves primarily as peasants, and those who identified themselves as permanently employed estate workers.

The Morant Bay rebellion was far less organized than the brutal and extensive forces that were unleashed against it. Eyre himself stated in Kingston on 17 October that he was "of the opinion that there was no organization."[100] The revolt did, however, reflect the general atmosphere of discontent on the island. Underhill describes the situation succinctly: "That several meetings had been held in the neighbourhood, especially at Stony Gut, consequent on the refusal of Mr. Eyre and the authorities to remedy the grievances of the people, there can be no doubt. The reports of the proceedings that took place are, however, vague and contradictory, and it is altogether doubtful whether there existed any organized or combined action, beyond that which the bitter sense of common grievances, and deeply felt injuries of long duration, would produce."[101] The complete absence of resistance to the soldiers assigned to suppress the revolt is only further confirmation of the absence of extensive "organized or combined action."

The local events certainly involved some degree of preparation, as Bogle had attempted, unsuccessfully, to gain a commitment of non-intervention from the Maroons at Hayfield in anticipation of repression. Bogle was unquestionably the leader of the immediate events, but there is little evidence to suggest that he and his followers had made any specific preparations for full-scale insurrection.[102] Gordon, implicated by Governor Eyre and executed for his alleged leadership of the rebellion, was in fact neither a revolutionary nor an advocate of violent action. Before 11 October 1865 "Gordon was only one of many talkative demagogues and the official records do not contain a single mention of Bogle."[103] The events were also confined almost completely to a single parish.[104] Eyre maintained that this was only because hasty and effective suppression was organized by the government, preventing the spread of "rebellion from one end of the island to the other."[105] The threat of island-wide revolt, however, was raised only *after* the Morant Bay revolt had occurred.[106]

Thus the level of conscious organization and prepared collective action of the slave revolt of 1831 appears to be more advanced than that of the peasant revolt of 1865. The idea of mass strike action, organic in the conditions of 1831, was no longer central in the conditions of peasant production. The labour force of 1865 was largely atomized, united not by the routine process of production itself but by their common interest in attaining greater and more secure access to land. The limited organization and leadership in the Morant Bay events cannot be reduced to a pure reflection of the individualized peasant production process. It can, however, be accurately stated that mass, organized collective action was not presented as the most effective form of resistance, as it was in the conditions of large-scale socialized production that characterized the period of plantation slavery.

THE AFTERMATH

Despite the severity of the immediate repression at Morant Bay, in the aftermath of the events the Jamaican peasantry saw what they believed to be genuine reforms implemented in their interest. Once again, these changes were implemented in ways that supported the existing ideological tradition. The importance of the religious idiom in peasant and working class ideology was reconfirmed and, to an even greater extent, the association of the Crown with benevolent and protective rule was strengthened. Derived ideas and experiences thus reinforced the inherent ideological traditions.

Governor Eyre and the majority of the Assembly legislators continued to make it clear that they held the Baptist ministry responsible for the atmosphere of unrest. Shortly after martial law was revoked, the government introduced a bill aimed specifically against "all religionists who did not belong to the Church of England."[107] "A person pretending to be a minister of the Gospel was liable to a heavy fine, or in default to an imprisonment of two years. It was even provided that a person not leaving a place of worship within twenty minutes after the conclusion of Divine worship, might be fined £10, and not less than £1 and in default be committed to prison for three months with hard labour."[108] The bill was finally withdrawn after passing third reading, but it indicated the continued association of resistance among the producing classes with the Baptist Church in the eyes of the Jamaican ruling class.

The Baptist missionaries did not hesitate to take full advantage of this association. Efforts were renewed to establish a mission centre in St Thomas-in-the-East and this time met with immediate success. The minister assigned to the new mission was greeted by a "jubilant" black population, already identifying themselves as Baptists. Notably, the first services held in the parish took place at the site where Paul Bogle's chapel had formerly stood, and were attended by his widow.[109] The missionaries thus attempted to exploit the inherent tradition of the Native Baptists in order to build support for orthodox Christian doctrine, a derived set of ideas among the parish peasantry. The link between political action and religious expression was thus reinforced not only by the authorities, but also by the Baptist missionaries, and in turn by the peasant population of the Morant Bay area.[110]

The image of Britain and the Crown as the defenders of the interests of the black masses was also strengthened in the aftermath of the Morant Bay events. This is even more noteworthy given the extreme repression personally authorized by Governor Eyre, the appointed Crown representative on the island. Despite the bloody massacre of the peasants, the Morant Bay outbreak left the Jamaican ruling class with no confidence in their own ability to continue to control the population. The decline of the sugar economy, as well as the abolition of the slave system they had considered essential to its development, had for years led them to focus their animosity against the colonial authorities in Britain. In the wake of 1865, however, the black producing classes were perceived to be, for the first time, a more serious threat to the planters' interests than was the British Parliament.[111]

The prolonged crisis of ruling class hegemony came to a head following Governor Eyre's skillful manipulation of the Jamaican Legislative Assembly, when it voted by a large majority to commit "an act of political suicide."[112] On 7 November 1865, both parties were persuaded to abolish the Assembly and to petition the Colonial Office to establish Jamaica as a Crown Colony. The crisis of hegemony was not ended, for in reality there was no other class, or section of a class, that could fill the vacuum, but the signs of political defeat and demoralization within the ruling class were clear. The old constitution was revoked, and a system of Crown Colony rule was voluntarily adopted.

The institution of Crown Colony government marked a major turning point in the history of Jamaican politics. The balance between colonial Jamaica and imperial Britain was now tipped in the direction of Britain. For the white Jamaican ruling class the "prestige of Great Britain now outweighed the desire for Jamaican autonomy."[113] For a body of active political representatives consciously and willingly to surrender their authority – however limited – was indeed a "surprising and unprecedented thing."[114] It had been, however, a long desired hope of both Eyre and the Colonial Office.

It is significant that the new Crown Colony government did institute some moderate reforms affecting peasant conditions. Sir John Peter Grant, the new governor appointed to replace Eyre in August 1866, was an experienced colonial administrator committed to a system of reformed rule.[115] Under his administration, unrestrained by and unaccountable to the local Jamaican ruling class, there was a slight increase in public expenditure and an expansion of certain social services. A public medical service was formed, public utilities were expanded, and educational services were given greater government support. Moreover, the introduction of Crown Colony government led to the temporary elimination of the powers of the local magistracies, where the planters had wielded great authority, particularly on labour matters. Until 1885 parochial services were administered centrally.[116]

Most significantly, the Morant Bay events had forced the Colonial Office to acknowledge "that the peasantry was politically important."[117] In 1867 Grant established a Lands Department, enabling the government to evict those without clear title unilaterally, and to reclaim all unowned lands and rent them to resident squatters. The program was far from comprehensive land reform, but it was perceived as a moderate concession to peasant interests.

In reality, these changes represented more an alteration of approach than one of conditions. They were legal changes, and did not alter the relations between the ruling and labouring classes on any significant, structural level.[118] Even in fiscal terms the actual increase in per capita expenditure for social services was offset by the growth of the population. Nonetheless, the elimination of the Old Representative System and the institution of Crown Colony government was widely perceived to mark a victory for the interests of the black producing classes in Jamaica. The 1865 events resulted in the organization of an active movement against the objective structures of colonial government on the island. Moreover, the subsequent reforms were in large measure a necessary corrective to the conditions that had led to the rebellion initially, and to the widespread popular opposition to the repressive measures that followed. Grant's reforms were in no small measure the product of the efforts of Bogle and Gordon, and can be seen to have been "bought with their blood."[119]

The conclusions of the Royal Commission report gave further credence to the view that Britain was the fair and just protector of the labouring poor. The report, released in April of 1866, found that the punishments inflicted under martial law were excessive in the circumstances, and "That by continuance of martial law in its full force to the extreme limit of its statutory operation the people were deprived for a longer than necessary period of the great constitutional privileges by which the security of life and property is provided for."[120] Governor Eyre was recalled, returning to England in the summer of 1866. Thus Eyre's actions were effectively identified as a result of his personal failings as a colonial administrator, rather than a reflection of official imperial policy.

This interpretation was widespread not only in Jamaica but also in Britain, where the massacre following the outbreak at Morant Bay had provoked what Cardwell described as "an excitement unprecedented in our times."[121] For some three years, the British public continued to dwell on the "Jamaica case" as Governor Eyre was brought up on charges of murder for his actions.[122] It was a dispute "which had split both Liberal and Conservative parties, had separated the closest of friends, and had created a deep chasm in the world of mid-Victorian letters."[123]

In sum, Governor Eyre was perceived to be seriously remiss in his responsibilities and judgment, but Britain emerged with its credibility as an imperial power intact, having once more effectively co-opted the threat of mass opposition. British colonial policy as a whole was not developed to improve the living standards of the slave, peasant, or working-class population, but to protect the security of the Empire and colonial investments. Actual social, economic and political conditions altered little throughout the nineteenth century. Moreover, Crown Colony rule could not solve the prolonged crisis of hegemony. Despite the high esteem in which the producing classes held British royalty, the British ruling class was not, and had no wish to be in direct, regular contact with the Jamaican masses.

Constitutional concessions were gradually granted to the old plantocracy. Reforms granting greater local participation in Crown Colony government were instituted in 1883 and 1895. Since the franchise remained limited to the island's wealthiest section, however, only the island's elite were reintegrated into formal political activity.

Furthermore, Jamaica's integration into the international economy continued to shape the island's internal fiscal priorities. By 1899 the island was in the midst of another financial crisis, since a declining world market for Jamaica's exports had caused a corresponding decrease in public revenues.[124]

After 1865, however, the ideological importance of the interests of the plantocracy continued to decline since the planters had been effectively – if only temporarily – removed from political office. The hegemonic vacuum remained, filled only partially and selectively by religious influences. It was not until 1938, with the coming of changed socio-economic and political circumstances, that the basic shape of Jamaican politics began to be transformed. In that year, the working class of Jamaica took the initiative and decisively altered the political system of the country.

CHAPTER FOUR

Into the Modern Era: The Labour Rebellion of 1938

BACKGROUND: JAMAICA IN THE 1930S

Despite numerous changes in Jamaica's social and economic conditions, the political system in the 1930s continued to be closed to the majority of the island's population. In 1930, out of a total population of 1,022,152 only 78,611, or about 8 per cent, were eligible to vote. In 1935, out of a population of 1,121,823, only 68,637 or a mere 6 per cent, were eligible.[1]

Similarly, social services remained negligible. Eisner points out that in 1930 Jamaican expenditure on both education and health care represented about 1 per cent of gross domestic product for each form of service allocation.[2] Between 1936 and 1939, there were only 6.1 doctors per one hundred thousand persons, and 1.55 hospital beds for every thousand.[3] Moreover, few people could afford the costs of medical treatment. Housing conditions were also inadequate and overcrowded, with an average density rate of about five persons per one-room home. Contagious diseases were rampant. In 1933 alone, twenty-five thousand cases of malaria were reported.[4]

Educational services were slightly better than medical services. Only a very limited segment of the population received secondary school education or professional training, but some 65 per cent of the population had attended elementary school. Estimates vary considerably, but by 1943 approximately 67 per cent of the population were considered to be technically literate.[5] For a large portion of the literate or semi-literate population, however, the Bible and the Book of Common Prayer were the only texts they had ever read.[6] This was due to the historical influence of the churches in the educational process, and to the dramatic spread of churches of numerous denominations.

The mission centres no longer maintained a unique position of influence as they had in the era of slavery and in the immediate post-emancipation period. This role had been eclipsed by the widespread growth of small, independent churches and ministries. By the 1930s Jamaica had become "overchurched."[7] Chapels were present in virtually every community and region, no matter how isolated they were.

WILLED IDEOLOGY – THE RELIGIOUS IDIOM

The link between Christian religious doctrine and social reform had become an inherent aspect of the ideological traditions of the producing classes. Two new movements in particular, the overtly messianic movement led by Alexander Bedward and the political movement for black racial equality led by Marcus Garvey (both of which developed in the early 1900s), expressed this association of Christian doctrine with political reform.

Bedward was a self-educated black worker on the Mona Estate in St Andrew. He became the first successor to the founder of the Jamaica Baptist Free Church in August Town in 1891, and retained the post of minister for some thirty years. He was outspoken in his opposition to the government and the white race and appealed explicitly to the poor black population. The Bedwardite movement established camps across Jamaica, and thousands travelled miles to seek their redemption. The most powerful attraction was Bedward's promise that baptism in the Hope (or Mona) River held healing capacities for both body and spirit.[8]

The movement, though explicitly religious in form and style, "embraced social and reform objectives."[9] Bedward's approach is revealed in the following statement:

Brethren! Hell will be your position if you do not rise up and crush the white man. The time is coming! There will be a white wall and a black wall, but now the black wall is becoming bigger than the white, and we must knock the white wall down. The white wall has oppressed us for years: now we must oppress the white wall. The government passes laws that oppress black people. They take their money out of their pockets, rob them of their bread, and they do nothing for it ... The only thing that can save us is the August Town healing stream.[10]

Bedward came into open conflict with the colonial authorities because his movement was perceived to be as great a political threat to the government as it was a religious threat to traditional Christian orthodoxy.

At sixty-one, Bedward announced that he was no longer the "Shepherd," but Jesus Christ himself, and took on the title of "Lord." He further proclaimed that on 13 December 1920 he would "ascend like Elijah on a chariot of fire"[11] into heaven, and white society would subsequently be destroyed. In the event, Bedward sat in a chair specially constructed for the purpose, surrounded by some five thousand anxious spectators, many of whom had travelled great distances for the occasion, only to conclude that the proper time had not yet come.[12] In 1921 Bedward was committed to the Kingston Asylum, where he spent the last nine years of his life.

The rise of Bedward's revivalism was part of a general period of growth among Afro-Christian followers, particularly in the rural districts. The set of ideas followed by the most active adherents was referred to as "pocomania."[13] Bedwardism represented the wing of the Afro-Christian movement that carried the most overt political message, but it could not be identified as a political movement. Rather than expressing political or class interests in a religious idiom, it represented a more classical messianic movement that diverted political demands towards a conservative and escapist strategy. Mystical solutions were sought as a means of dealing with material problems. The movement reflected the widespread desperation among the producing classes. Nonetheless, when considering the preconditions of the rebellion of 1938, the question of Bedward's sanity is not the central issue. What is important "is that for nearly thirty years his church attracted the support of large numbers of the sufferers of Jamaica, and that their support was an expression of protest against prevailing conditions."[14]

In May 1921, the month that Bedward was committed to the asylum, Marcus Garvey was conducting a speaking tour throughout Jamaica. Garvey, a native Jamaican, left the island in search of employment as a young man, travelled throughout Latin America, and finally emigrated to England in 1912. Garvey was struck by the universal subjugation of black people in every country he visited, and he returned to Jamaica with the aim of founding the Universal Negro Improvement Association (UNIA) in 1914. After two years of abortive efforts, however, he emigrated to the United States, on the encouragement of Booker T. Washington, "because there was freedom of speech and press ... and the largest black population in the Western World."[15]

Garvey's movement attracted a massive following among black Americans, and soon spread among black populations across the globe. He built an international movement among black people that for the first time in history challenged the dominant racist ideology that had been an integral part of Western society since the earliest years of the slave trade. He elicited a pride in the black race and at the same time called for the rebuilding of the dispersed African nation. The focus of the UNIA's activities was to promote and organize racial pride among black peoples internationally, particularly by challenging racist images of Africa and the African heritage. To this end, Garvey founded the Black Star Line steamship company to transport cargoes of African goods to the United States, and to transport black American passengers to Africa.

Garvey's program was not only racial and political in content and appeal, but also overtly religious. In September 1921 Garvey established a new African Orthodox Church in America as an assertion of black cultural and religious autonomy. He became known as the "Black Moses," and prayers and hymns were a regular feature of UNIA chapter meetings. The following prayer was chanted routinely: "Almighty God, we beseech Thee to assist us with Thy Heavenly Grace, and to prosper the Godly aims and endeavors of this Association in bringing peace, justice, liberty and happiness to our Race ... there is but one Body and one Spirit, and one Hope of our calling, One God! One Aim! One Destiny!"[16] The UNIA's letterhead carried the Biblical quotation: "He created of one blood all nations to dwell upon the face of the earth."

In 1927 Garvey was deported to Jamaica after having been convicted for fraud in connection with promotional material for the Black Star Line. This time Garvey found a receptive audience for his ideas in his native land. Upon his arrival the Jamaican press reported that his return "was perhaps the most historic event that has taken place in the metropolis of the island," and that "no denser crowd has ever been witnessed in Kingston."[17]

The impact of the UNIA in Jamaica was dramatic and it "played a vital role in politicizing the masses, especially between 1928 and 1935."[18] Unlike Bedward's movement, it was political as well as religious in character. Though formal political channels were closed to the majority of the black population, UNIA meetings served as training grounds for black working-class activists and spokespeople.[19] In 1928, Garvey tried to found a new political party, but his efforts failed, largely due to the restricted franchise and repeated harassment from the authorities. Garvey was elected as councillor of the Kingston and St Andrew Corporation (the new name given for the merger of the two neighbouring parishes) in 1929. In 1920, he failed to win a seat in the Legislature,[20] and he left the island permanently and returned to England in 1935.

After Garvey's departure, the mass character of the movement diminished. This was only in part because Garvey played a central role in the UNIA's success. It also reflected genuine limitations in the politics of the movement. The UNIA appealed to blacks regardless of their class to take up the cause of racial advancement. Though the People's Political Party included a number of demands for labour reform – such as the eight-hour day and a minimum wage – Garvey was known to make disparaging remarks about Jamaica's working-class population in public.[21] Especially after 1935, the UNIA increasingly became the voice of the black middle class, whose concerns centred around means "to provide capital and enhance their business competitiveness."[22]

By the mid-1930s the combined effects of Bedwardism and, more importantly, Garveyism, had led to the association of the religious idiom with a radical concept of reform, more overtly political and racially identified than that established under the influence of the official missionary movement. Both Bedward and Garvey were leaders emerging from the ranks of the black labouring classes, and they expressed ideologies that were in certain respects simply more articulate versions of inherent traditional elements. Both movements were island-wide and totally independent of orthodox Christian church control, and they strongly advocated conscious pride in the black race.

At the same time, both movements expressed contradictory dynamics, displaying not only a progressive but also a conservative ideological and political message. Bedward called upon his followers to seek the source of liberation in a world beyond called heaven. Garvey sought salvation in a world of black pride, but the attainment of that goal in existing conditions of colonial Jamaica was obscured by a false trust in political allies both at home and abroad.[23] While Bedwardism was classically messianic, both movements encouraged exclusive reliance on the ostensibly God-like leadership of a single man. The UNIA was far from messianic, but by blurring class distinctions it promoted working class dependence upon individual representatives from the middle and ruling classes.

The religious idiom had thus come to express a message of black pride and the rights of the poor. It expressed the conviction that injustice and oppression were evils that could and should be overcome by some form of protest. But the means to achieve such goals were either unclear or inaccessible to the black population. The inherent ideological ground for the rebellion of 1938 was laid, but it was not until an essentially derived concept was made part of the working-class struggle that the organizational component was forged: this was the idea of trade union organization.

The concept of labour reform was derived from a variety of sources between World War I and 1938. During the 1930s a large number of reform organizations were established. They were predominantly led by the urban middle class and organized to promote its interests. Carnegie estimates that approximately eighty-three such organizations were in existence through the twenties and thirties.[24] They varied in their aims and influence, but all of these groups reflected frustration with the economic, social, and political restraints that the colonial system placed upon the aspiring coloured or black middle class.

A leading spokesman of the reform-oriented wing of Jamaica's middle class was J.A.G. Smith, a black barrister and a member of the Legislative Council from 1917 until his death in 1942. He was an articulate professional and a forthright politician, willing to publicly challenge such dominant interests as the Jamaica Imperial Association – the organization of the large planters – and the United Fruit Company. In 1921, Smith formed the Jamaica Representative Government Association, and a parallel organization was formed by H.A.L. Simpson, another representative in the Council. Neither was willing to serve under the other, and each organization was centred around its leader.[25]

These organizations called for moderate constitutional reform, seen at the time as radical, but neither was prepared to call for either full Jamaican independence or the extension of the franchise. In one regard, however, the interests of the masses of Jamaicans figured in this arena of middle class politics. Smith's popularity increased when he agreed to defend prosecuted railroad strikers in the courts. He put forward the first bills on Workmen's Compensation and Trade Union Registration, limited as they were, which became law in 1919. The idea of labour reform and the legal protection of workers' rights emerged as an important part of the derived ideology of the Jamaican working class.

Smith, though prominent, was neither the most radical nor the only supporter of labour reform. This notion was also derived from other elements beyond the limits of Jamaican society. Between 1935 and 1937 strike waves erupted in a number of the West Indian islands, including Trinidad, St Kitts and Barbados. Publicity about these events in Jamaica was widespread. In 1937 the Governor of Jamaica wrote, "While in my view there is less hardship and more employment than a year ago there is little doubt that the position has been complicated by recent disturbances in other West Indian Colonies."[26] Furthermore, two organizations in the US, the Trade Union Unity League and the Negro Labour Congress, were directly encouraging the formation of trade unions in Jamaica.[27]

The effect of international labour conditions upon Jamaican migrant workers was perhaps even more significant. The Royal Commission appointed to investigate the causes of the 1938 disturbances concluded that the effect of "the reports of West Indians who have lived and worked abroad, particularly in the United States of America, has been to create a demand for better conditions of work and life."[28] In the 1930s masses of Jamaican emigrants were forced to return to the island as local governments responded to the effects of world economic depression. Emigrant labourers returned not only from the United States, but also from Cuba and Central America. Many had gained trade union experience and returned to find conditions considerably poorer than those to which they had become accustomed.[29] For example, a large number of returned emigrants were experienced sugar workers who were unable to find agricultural jobs at home for wages comparable to those offered for the same work elsewhere.[30] As a result of such influences the Cigar Makers Union was one of the first unions organized in Jamaica. It was formed in 1907 as one of a number of unions formally affiliated to the American Federation of Labour.[31] Other Jamaican workers gained experience overseas through their enlistment in the British West India Regiment. Veterans returning after World War I played a central part in one of Jamaica's first strike waves, which erupted between 1918 and 1920, when they "were barely restrained from a mutiny."[32] These returned emigrants and veterans formed the nucleus of the nascent trade union movement in Jamaica. Thus the idea of trade union organization, derived from a variety of sources, began to influence the working class.[33]

During the period immediately following World War I a wave of strikes broke out which provoked the passage of the Trade Union Law in 1919. Little in the way of lasting labour organization remained, with the important exception of the Longshoremen's Unions. The Longshoremen's Union No. 1 was registered under the new law in 1922, and was led by A. Bain Alves. In 1926, the Longshoremen's Union No. 2 was registered, and the two unions combined with a number of other small unions to form the Jamaica Federation of Labour. These unions were sufficiently active and organized to survive in difficult conditions. Though unionization did not spread beyond the docks of Kingston, by 1938 the necessity of a permanent collective bargaining organization had become an *inherent* idea in this important segment of the working class. The Kingston dock workers were to play a central and strategic role in the labour rebellion of that year.[34]

It was not until the Jamaica Workers and Tradesmen Union (JWTU) was formed in 1936, and was registered in 1937, that a major breakthrough in Jamaican labour organization took place. It was led by two men, both of whom had had extensive experience off the island: A.G.S. Coombs and H.C. Buchanan.[35] The JWTU was neither a craft nor an industrial union but a "blanket union," drawing in workers of "no specific occupational character."[36] This organizational approach was to become the hallmark of Jamaican trade unions. Most significantly, the JWTU was able to draw agricultural workers into its ranks. Thus by December 1937 it claimed 88 per cent of the total 1,080 members of registered union bodies in Jamaica.[37]

The JWTU and both Coombs and Buchanan were to be eclipsed by the ascending personal role of another Jamaican migrant, Alexander Bustamante.[38] Bustamante was largely responsible for providing a set of ideas, albeit an eclectic and contradictory one, and a style of leadership that were to fuse the inherent religious idiom with the secular notion of permanent trade union organization, a derived and still alien idea for the majority of the Jamaican working class.

Bustamante had a varied and unclear history, for he was prone to fabricate stories to cover large periods of his background. Born Alexander Clarke, he left Jamaica at twenty-one and did not return until 1934 as a man of fifty. Bustamante claimed to have been adopted by a Spanish mariner and taken to Spain, where he was to have been given an intensive education under private tutelage and to have earned a diploma from the Royal Academy of Spain.[39] In fact, little of this story seems verifiable. Bustamante, then Clarke, had experience working in Cuba, Panama, and New York City in various occupations including tramway company employee, traffic inspector, police constable, and hospital attendant. Upon his arrival in America in 1932, he had adopted the name Alejandro Bustamanti, claiming to be a cultivated gentleman of Spanish descent.[40] As a near-white Jamaican of wealthy rural Jamaican heritage, Clarke was able to maintain such an air with some conviction. When he returned to Jamaica in 1934, now Alexander Bustamante, he claimed to have made his fortune on the New York Stock Exchange. This, however, is one of the many reports for which "Bustmante is the only source and sole authority."[41]

Upon his return to Jamaica, Bustamante set up a money-lending business, catering to the lower middle class and working poor of Kingston. Unlike Coombs and Buchanan, Bustamante was not part of the Jamaican working class, but he was to become, within a few short years, the undisputed "Labour Leader No. 1" of the Jamaican masses. He established a reputation for himself as "The Critic Bustamante"[42] by writing an extensive series of letters to the major Jamaican paper, the *Daily Gleaner*. Bustamante then went in search of public arenas in which to present himself as the representative of the working class. The JWTU, expanding its influence and membership through 1937, presented Bustamante with an accessible platform.[43] Union President Coombs, searching for a quick means to raise the JWTU's profile and solidify its financial base, invited Bustamante to become the union's treasurer. Thus began Bustamante's "first contact with labour organization."[44] After May of 1937, Bustamante became a regular speaker with Coombs on the union's platform. By October, Bustamante's appetite for recognition and power led him to offer Coombs an exchange: if Coombs would relinquish his presidency to Bustamante, then Bustamante would personally finance an island-wide campaign to expand the union's membership. Coombs agreed, and Bustamante the usurer became Bustamante the union leader.

The JWTU transformed Bustamante from a lay commentator in the press to a working-class agitator and Bustamante transformed the face of Jamaican labour from a mass of unorganized workers among whom an effective union tradition was just beginning to be established, into a labour *movement*, based not on the principles of working-class self-organization, but on Bustamante's personal leadership.

Before the end of 1937 Buchanan, incensed at the notion of having a usurer as JWTU president and seeing rising disaffection with Bustamante's leadership, had effectively organized his expulsion from the union. This, however, did not prevent him from finding other means to present himself as the undisputed leader of the Jamaican working class.

The "comet-like rise of Alexander Bustamante"[45] was the result of a culmination of events and circumstances taking place during May and June of 1938.[46] Not the least important factor was his ability to shape a working-class following on the basis of an appeal to both the most progressive and the most conservative elements of the religious idiom in working-class ideology. He did this in the process of spearheading a strictly class-based and secular struggle dedicated to fighting for working-class rights.

During the 1938 rebellion, the Jamaican working class took the offensive, rising on a scale, in terms of both sheer numbers and the intensity of the protest, unseen in Jamaican history. From the outset, the movement was distinctly identified with the politics of class conflict and workers' rights. The rebellion began only after the West Indian Sugar Company (WISCO), the Jamaican operating firm of the British multi-national Tate and Lyle, purchased several large properties and began plans to open a massive centralized factory on the Frome Estate in Westmoreland. Since unemployment was soaring and the cost of living rising, workers travelled from all over the island in hopes of finding well-paying and secure employment.[47] Conditions proved to be demonstrably different from the promises of high wages and modern cottages. Many who arrived were told there was no work available for them, while the wages paid to those who were hired were initially far lower than expected, and were later arbitrarily reduced. The workers finally reached the end of their endurance in April 1938. Post describes the course of events.

On Friday, 29 April, a misunderstanding over the paying of wages led to a riot. A strike followed, with a demand of four shillings a day for labourers and more for skilled men. More than a hundred armed police were rushed in ... On 2 May the almost inevitable result followed: a clash between strikers and police led to the latter opening fire, killing four people, two of them women, one old and another pregnant. Fourteen more were wounded (including five policemen), and eighty-five arrests made. In retaliation, company cane was fired at Frome and two other WISCO estates.[48]

By 5:00 A.M. on 3 May, Bustamante had arrived at Frome to make "first-hand observations."[49] As the Frome conflict began to quiet down, demonstrations of the unemployed were organized in the streets of Kingston. Bustamante was well-poised to take full advantage of the rising militancy.

On 19 May, the Kingston waterfront workers struck for higher wages. St William Grant, a follower of Marcus Garvey, addressed the strikers and, with Bustamante, urged them to stay out until their demands were met. On 23 May, the dock workers went on the offensive, marching through Kingston and calling upon other workers to strike in sympathy. Throughout the city, shops, factories, power stations, government railway workshops, the tramway, and public services including gasworks, were shut down. Bustamante and Grant again stepped in to fill the vacuum of organized leadership. At about noon on 23 May, some eight thousand demonstrators gathered at Parade Gardens in Kingston to hear them address the crowd. When five hundred Kingston policemen, British garrison troops and Sherwood Foresters (the British regiment stationed in Jamaica at the time) attacked the gathering, the crowd at first resisted by throwing stones, but was finally forced to disperse.[50] On the following day, Bustamante and Grant were arrested without bail, on charges of sedition and inciting to unlawfully assemble.

When Norman Washington Manley, Jamaica's most prominent criminal lawyer and coincidentially a cousin of Bustamante, offered to mediate on the workers' behalf, the striking waterfront workers responded with an outright ultimatum: "No work; we want Bustamante."[51] Even after the shipping companies had been compelled to agree to all of the strikers' wage demands, Bustamante's release remained the condition of their return to work. Bustamante was finally released, on the condition that Manley would vouch for his good behaviour.

Thus Bustamante took on the demeanour of the martyred hero of the Kingston working class. As events spread from Kingston to the rural parishes, he did not miss an opportunity to speak to crowds of angry workers and unemployed labourers. From early June, however, he no longer urged further militancy. His intervention in subsequent disputes was "almost without exception in the interests of law and order."[52] The symbolic hero of labour, once his reputation seemed established, became one of the most powerful voices for ruling class interests *within* the working-class movement itself.

After his release, Bustamante announced that he would be founding five labour unions under his own direction.[53] They were to include the maritime workers, transport labour, factory workers, municipal employees, and general labour. The plan for five separate unions was abandoned "somewhere along the way,"[54] however, and by the time of registration in January of 1939, one mass blanket union had been formed bearing the name of its leader: the Bustamante Industrial Trade Union (BITU). As early as November of 1938 the BITU could claim a membership of over six thousand, a figure more than twice that of all other unions in the island combined.

The term "membership," as it applied to the BITU, needs some explanation. Rarely in the union's history was there a year when more than half the membership paid dues. In the early years there were no local meetings, no locally elected officers or shop stewards, and no local bargaining committees. The method of "negotiation" was unofficially called "Telegraph Duke Street": a group of workers would go on strike, a telegram would be put through to Bustamante's headquarters on Duke Street and Bustamante, "The Chief," often accompanied by an assistant, would arrive to negotiate a settlement.[55] Those who identified themselves with the BITU may be more accurately described as a following than as an active and committed union membership. Thus Bustamante was more than a union leader

– he was also the leader of a movement. Historical circumstances favoured his rise, particularly the growing self-confidence and militancy of the working class and the lack of avenues for organized political expression. Bustamante's skill lay in his ability to transform the traditional religious idiomatic form of ideological expression into a permanent secular organization. The producing classes that once followed preachers or ministers now followed the "Labour Leader No. 1." Religiously authorized campaigns carrying secular demands were replaced by an explicitly class-based organization defending working-class interests.

The form and style of Bustamante's leadership, however, directly imitated the religious idiom. Bustamante called upon the militant tradition in working-class ideology by arguing that rebellion in the name of justice was not only legitimate, it was a duty. He presented himself as the only leader able to direct the noble struggle of the workers and make it understood. On the one hand, he championed the rights of the working class with a degree of determination, aggressiveness and confidence unprecedented in Jamaican history. On the other hand, he was unquestionably committed to using the working-class struggle as a means to increase his own prestige among the establishment. This meant that, although he advocated confrontation, he was extremely careful not to counterpose the *fundamental* interests of the employers and government with those of the workers. Bustamante "believed in organization; in the right to strike; in negotiation by direct confrontation of employers, including the government; in the power of public opinion; and above all in himself."[56]

Bustamante's historic achievement was the creation of an organization that effectively combined the concept of trade unionism, derived mainly from middle and upper class circles and from workers' experiences abroad, with the inherent ideological components expressed through the religious idiom. At last, the disenfranchised, impoverished working class had an organization that it could call its own: "The Union." Unlike Bedward's movement, the BITU offered a means to achieve a better life in the here and now, not in the hereafter; unlike Garvey's movement, it appealed to the working class explicitly in terms of a class identity, incorporating a racial consciousness but not identified primarily by race. But it had two weaknesses in common with both of these movements – the leader became personally identified as the workers' sole source of "salvation," and the fundamental incompatibility of the interests of workers and employers, of labour and capital, was blurred.

The BITU was, especially in its early years, something between a trade union and a mass populist movement.[57] With the rise of working-class activity and the growing prominence of Bustamante, "there was a rush to join a union regardless of worker classification or even the aims of unions. Instead of fear or indifference to union membership, it now became fashionable for workers to belong."[58] The early BITU displayed many features similar to those of the labour organizations that Hobsbawm describes as "labour sects."[59] Referring to the European context Hobsbawm notes that while "modern" working-class movements are "purely, if not militantly, secular,"[60] labour sects combined an emotional and non-theological form of religion with working-class organization. They were common among the "newest and rawest"[61] members of the proletariat recently drawn from the countryside into the cities. Hobsbawm notes:

> It is characteristic of working-class sects that they were designed for the uneducated, so that passion and morality, in which the most ignorant can compete on equal terms, were the exclusive criteria of faith and salvation ... [F]or one of the great things about the sect was that it provided a working-class community both with its own cohesion and scale of values in which the poor could outdo the rich – poverty became a symptom of grace, austerity of virtue, moral rigour contrasted with the laxity of the reprobate.[62]

The BITU differed from the early European labour sects, however, insofar as the Jamaican working class was compelled to challenge modern-day employers including major multinationals. Furthermore, the BITU developed in a period when, internationally, trade union organization was beginning to be accepted as an integral part of capitalist industrial relations.[63] The labour sects, unlike trade unions, were essentially religious and therefore other-worldly in their outlook.[64] The religious dimension of the BITU was almost entirely traceable to Bustamante's philosophy and style of leadership. In his writings and speeches Bustamante appealed to three major themes, which were emphasized selectively depending on the situation. These themes were: (1) the struggle of good against evil; (2) messianism and martyrdom; and (3) rule by divine right.[65] A few examples will illustrate how Bustamante employed these religious themes to his own advantage in the context of a militant working-class movement.

(1) Good Against Evil Though Bustamante presented himself as the supreme labour leader, he simultaneously attempted to downplay the distinctly working-class character of the trade union struggle. Hamilton understates the case when he notes that "Bustamante could not be called anti-establishment."[66] Bustamante's approach to trade unionism concentrated on the politics of compromise and col-

laboration rather than on class struggle, though he attempted to maintain the public image of an avid confrontationist. His political outlook has been aptly described as a variant of conservative populism, or "People's Toryism."[67]

As a means of instilling this perspective, particularly in conditions where class lines were very sharply drawn, Bustamante presented a view of the world in which there were those who were good and deserving of justice and those who were evil and deserving of due punishment for their sins. Individual capitalists, individual government representatives, or individual police officers were sometimes berated for their evil deeds and attitudes; but the *system* that permitted such injustices to be inflicted on the working class was regarded as fair and worthy of respect.[68]

Bustamante's liberal use of Biblical imagery also helped to support this perspective. In 1935 he wrote the following letter in reference to a continuing debate concerning the activities of the Jamaica Banana Producers' Association (JBPA):[69]

> In Spain I wrote of love and nature's beauty. In Jamaica I can only write of the miseries of injustices and of those persons who are endeavouring to deceive their countrymen and women and of those who are using their evil minds, their wicked hearts to instil in the public that other fruit companies intend to destroy the JBPA Association. This is untrue.
>
> The great Lord might have John the Devil closed up in some pen, but he certainly has let loose a lot of devils in Jamaica, sowing the evil seeds of injustice for their own personal benefit and their friends, while the masses suffer more and more, too weak to fight for themselves, praying to the Almighty God to liberate them from these of the Devil, some of whose writing make me feel they could better occupy their time by becoming theatrical clowns.[70]

Behind this extensive use of religious metaphor lay Bustamante's defence of the activities of the United Fruit Company in Jamaica. In another letter in reference to the same debate, he wrote: "Notwithstanding all that has been said about the activities of this magnificent octopus, [United Fruit] it cannot be again said that this company aside from definitely placing Jamaica on the map, has done more than any other company to develop the island's resources and to improve the condition of labouring people by instituting medical services, better houses and living conditions and at the time when this was sorely needed."[71]

Similarly, Bustamante was prepared to appeal to the most mystical and superstitious elements in the religious tradition of Jamaican labourers in an attempt to gain support. A prime example of this occurred in 1937, when Bustamante launched a public attack against then Governor Sir Edward Denham. Denham had proposed legislation to amend the Usury Act in order to limit the extent of moneylenders' abuses. Bustamante proceeded to launch a campaign under the slogan "Denham must go." A year later, in the midst of the uprising of 1938, Denham died from complications following abdominal surgery. The untimely death was widely interpreted as the fulfillment of Bustamante's "curse," a myth that Bustamante made no attempt to dispel.[72]

(2) Messianism and Martyrdom Bustamante's conception of himself as the workers' sole representative was a constant theme in his leadership. He managed to place his own directives above the initiatives of rank and file workers by appealing to the messianic tradition among the producing classes. Though he was a secular figure leading a distinctly secular movement, in many respects Bustamante presented a more clerical image than many of the politically active clergymen who had come before him. He presented himself unabashedly as the workers' "saviour." In response to the government's proposal to increase taxes, Bustamante replied:

I have one God, one soul, one life, and no matter what happens, as long as that life lasts, and as long as the failure of this Government continues, I shall continue to write pointing out its weakness – not because I love to do so, but because it is a duty to my people and my country.

The Bible says there are two places for the soul of man – Hell or Heaven. With a merciful God, I can look forward to Heaven. Can all those of the present Government say so? They who are finishing the last drop of blood of the poor of this island with extra taxes and child-like suggestions of how the money is to be spent – not invested – should only have the privilege of expecting the wrath of God.[73]

After he and Grant were arrested on 24 May 1938, Bustamante did not hesitate to exploit the opportunity to be elevated to "instant martyrdom,"[74] though he had spent only four days in jail. He repeatedly emphasized the extent of his profound personal sacrifice, made solely for the benefit of the Jamaican poor, in order to increase the workers' loyalty to his leadership.[75] Like Christ bearing the cross, Bustamante presented himself as the great sufferer on the behalf of the working class.

During the strike wave of May and June 1938, Bustamante played on this theme in order to persuade striking workers to return to their jobs. In response to the continuation of unauthorized strikes,

Bustamante told his followers "If you will only keep orderly and take a little increase today and probably a little raise in the next three or six months, you will no doubt be better off and we will be able to do greater things, but so long as these strikes continue we will never be able to do greater things for you ... You may not believe, but for nearly four weeks I have done no business of my own in the office."[76] In August 1938 Bustamante declared in the *Gleaner*:

The Unions have developed into gigantic organisations admittedly through my personal influence, but instead of being able to give labour only that per cent of time I have mentioned, I am kept occupied every day until the very early hours of the morning. What has been the result? Not one minute to attend to my own business, not even time to have my meals, but can I withdraw? No. The love I have for labour prevents me so doing, and I do not believe in a half-finished job ...

The paltry sum that labour could pay me could never compensate me for all the money I am losing now ...

The voice of labour must be heard and it shall be heard through me.[77]

This leads to the third religious theme employed by Bustamante in his agitation.

(3) Rule by Divine Right Bustamante demanded loyalty not only by making much of his personal sacrifice but also by projecting himself as the sole legitimate authority capable of leading the workers' struggle. Any challenge to Bustamante's leadership was seen as something akin to blasphemy.[78]

The title of the union itself bore Bustamante's name, reflecting the characteristic autocratic style of leadership. In 1938 the president of the small Chauffeurs Union, struggling to prevent the rising competitive influence of Bustamante's membership drive, maintained that "when you name a union after any one man, it is a sure sign that somebody is going to be dictator."[79] The solicitor for the BITU, Ross Livingstone, publicly asserted that it was upon his suggestion that the organization was so named, to prevent any confusion among illiterate workers. Bustamante stated that Livingstone urged his name to appear in the union's title "chiefly to prevent people with little petty and questionable societies extracting monies from unfortunate people by saying that I was along with them."[80]

There is no question, however, that Bustamante cherished the name of the union he led. When a wave of unauthorized strikes broke out in early 1939, the governor declared a state of emergency, and demanded that Bustamante call the labourers back to work. In reaching a negotiated settlement, Governor Richards demanded as a condition that Bustamante's name be removed from the title of the union. Bustamante was prepared to yield on a number of issues, but on this point he was intransigent. The name of the BITU remained unchanged.[81]

Bustamante's "divine rule" was further enshrined in the BITU's constitution, where he was declared "President for Life." His supporters maintained that this was the result of the membership's insistence, a protection against any sudden abandonment by an irresponsible leadership.[82] Bustamante used a similar argument to defend the appearance of his name on the union's button, maintaining that he was so widely acclaimed already that he certainly was not in need of further publicity.

My name is not upon the Unions because I want to advertise it or I want glory; for it is a known fact that my name is an international one known throughout the civilized world, but jealousy will creep in here and there in the breasts of the narrow-minded ... As it is now, tens of thousands of members have been clamouring that my name should appear on the Union button and if it does go there, it will be entirely against my desire and my will, for again it will be said that my name should not be upon the Union button.[83]

Bustamante's egocentricity reflected a wider philosophy of labour relations. He believed that there should be a sharp division between the trade union membership and its officials. He explicitly identified the rank and file as the "followers," the disciples whose duty it was to heed and obey the word of their leader. Early in his trade union career, Bustamante wrote:

A labour union is nothing more than the working people's club where they can unite for one common good, for one common cause, so that they can bring their grievances to their officers. Union members, if you want to be successful you must remember that you must follow your officers and must not expect them to follow you, and for that reason the officers should be men of intelligence, honesty and reliability. You, the workers are seeking justice from your employers, then to accomplish this you must also measure out justice and fairplay to them, however, cruel they may be.[84]

In his efforts to enforce his personal control, Bustamante was prepared to go to almost any length. He frequently insisted that the condition of this leadership was complete discipline.[85] He was even known to threaten to solicit military repression to "crush" unofficial strikes.[86] Further, Bustamante was an uncompromising individualist, a one-man show in the labour movement. He systematically eliminated any possible competitors for the leadership from the BITU, often only after fully exploiting their skills and influence in order to strengthen the union. This was how he dealt with Coombs, Grant and Buchanan, though not without resistance. In 1942 Bustamante severed his personal association and that of the BITU with Manley and the political party he founded in 1938, the People's National Party (PNP).

Other potential competitors failed to enter the ring against "the Chief." J.A.G. Smith, for example, became a relatively low-profile politician after the 1938 rebellion, acting only as Bustamante's personal barrister.[87] Garvey left Jamaica for the last time in 1935. In 1938 he conducted a tour through the West Indies, but he did not land in Jamaica.[88] Garvey's only significant immediate contribution to the Jamaican events was to write a lengthy letter to Malcolm McDonald, British Secretary of State for the Colonies, shortly after the strike wave erupted, supporting the plight of the poor and urging the appointment of a Royal Commission.[89]

Although Bustamante presented himself as the workers' sole source of salvation, he was careful not to act as an actual competitor for the special role played by the official church. On the contrary, he made it known that he was a religious man, and recognized that "all churches belong to one God."[90]

In words he would later come to regret, Manley stated that Bustamante had become "Jamaica's Labour Leader by the only test which matters and that is the support and confidence of labour."[91] By adapting the religious idiom to meet the new conditions – both objective and subjective – of Jamaica's labour force, Bustamante organized a trade union movement in his own image, and proceeded to alter the Jamaican political system.

WILLED IDEOLOGY –
THE CROWN AS BENEVOLENT
DESPOT

In the late 1930s, British colonial policy was moving in the direction of encouraging trade union organization. This reinforced the conception of the Crown as the great protector, which had long been an inherent part of the ideology of the producing classes. The idea of some means of legitimate labour reform was gaining ground, and was becoming a critical part of the derived ideology embraced by the Jamaican working class.

In Britain, the participation of the Labour Party in the government was having some bearing on Colonial Office perspectives. The Labour Party itself was not universally supportive of trade union actions, even within Britain.[92] With the coming of the second labour government in 1929, however, major directives concerning labour relations in the colonies were given to colonial governors.[93] Even before this period, the years during and after World War I witnessed a series of debates in the House concerning West Indian labour conditions.[94] By 1930, a Labour Committee made up of officials from the Colonial Office and the Ministry of Labour was formed "to prepare policies for the Colonial Office and assist in the implementation of the ILO International Labour Conventions in the colonies."[95] The secretary of state at the time was Lord Passfield (formerly Sydney Webb – the prominent Fabian Socialist),[96] who circulated a memorandum to the colonial governors on trade union matters. The statement, which became known as the "Passfield Memorandum," urged that trade unions be brought under a process of legal registration. It was argued "that without sympathetic supervision and guidance, organisations of labourers without experience of combination for any social and economic progress may fall under the domination of disaffected persons, by which their activities may be diverted to improper and mischievous ends."[97] The British government thus pressed for legalization of trade unions in the interests of offsetting or pre-empting spontaneous, "unsupervised" labour action.

The trade union legislation passed in the Jamaican Legislature in 1919 granted legal status to officially registered unions. The law did not, however, release the unions from liability for suits for damages incurred during strikes nor did it legalize peaceful picketing.[98] In practice, therefore, unions were legal only if they did not make use of the major weapon available to them in bargaining with the employers – the strike. In 1937, the British government began to argue more directly for improving the standard of living of workers in the colonies. A dispatch was issued to the colonial governors maintaining that there had been "definite improvement in the financial position of many Colonies and Colonial enterprises which had taken place after the close of the prolonged period of world economic depression, and ... that it was only right that a fair share of this benefit should be passed on to the workers in the territories concerned in the form of improved social services."[99] The British government thus became an advocate of labour reform enacted in the classical British colonial tradition of *realpolitik*, adding a further source from which the idea of trade union organization was derived. Moreover, British political support of such an apparently radical notion further strengthened the image of the Crown as the benevolent despot.

It was primarily through Bustamante's efforts that the idea of labour reform gained widespread support within the working class.

Norman Washington Manley also played an important, if less effective, role in this process. Unlike Bustamante, Manley presented a consistent and organized ideological perspective. He staunchly followed the tradition of British Fabianism, and supported the activities of the Labour Party in Britain.[100] The founding of the People's National Party under Manley's leadership in September 1938 featured Labour Party M.P. Sir Stafford Cripps as the keynote speaker.[101] At this stage in its history, however, the PNP could only gain a hearing in the working class through the support of Bustamante, and affiliation with the BITU.[102] The politics of the PNP appealed to the reform-oriented wing of the Jamaican middle class, but found few points of contact with the inherent ideological tradition within working-class circles. Manley's primary distinction was his acceptability to the employers and government.[103] At the same time, the PNP's commitment to national independence and social democratic reform placed it politically well to the left of Bustamante. In the early years, despite reservations on both sides, the affiliation of trade union and political party was opportune for both leaders: the union leader gained a political arm, and the politician acquired a base in the workers' movement.

Despite the BITU's initial formal allegiance to the PNP, Bustamante maintained his own distinct interpretation of the British political tradition and approached it in his own way. The derived notion of labour reform through peaceful and official channels was challenged by the militant, spontaneous uprising of May and June of 1938. Bustamante's credibility depended largely on his role as a mass agitator prepared to publicly berate the symbols, if not the system, of colonial authority. At the same time he was a firm supporter of the Crown and, until many years later, a staunch opponent of colonial independence.[104]

Bustamante thus adapted the historical, inherent notion of Britain as the benevolent ruler to a climate of social protest and mass action against colonial authority. He accomplished this by making outspoken, deliberate charges against individual representatives of the colonial system, in the name of complete loyalty to the Crown and British colonial rule. In a letter expressing this dual-edged approach to the government, Bustamante defended a hunger march organized in Kingston as follows:

It is no good telling the people that Government is not concerned with them, for Government tells them what to do and what not to do, where and what to buy and how much to pay for it. Government poses as a paternal Government, and as one looks to one's natural parents, so the people naturally look to Government when they are unable to help themselves ...

Hungry men and women and children have a right to call attention to their condition and to ask of people fulfillment of promises made to them as long as they do so without using violence or being disorderly ...

What Jamaica needs is practical and sympathetic men interested in the country and its people, and not charlatans and self-seekers making long speeches about nothing; men who by their handling of the country's affairs will make such things as hunger marches unnecessary.[105]

In similar vein, Bustamante called not for constitutional reform, but for more aggressive individuals in a Legislature that was structured to hold only minimal independent authority. "What we need in the island is not more men but men with courage, with the spirit of fighting for justice for all and more so for the less fortunate; independent men who will sacrifice their own interests for their unfortunate sisters and brothers; well thinking men who will speak straight from their shoulders according to the dictates of their conscience and not submit and say 'yes' when their conscience says 'no.'"[106]

Bustamante's reverence for the Crown approached worship, and exemplified the inherent conception of British royalty. Upon the death of King George v, Bustamante wrote: "I think not of him alone as a King, but a man beloved by his subjects – by his people; beloved and respected by the entire universe – not through his once mighty, earthly power, but for his just ways, not alone to the strong, but to the weak, to all ... He lived not for himself and his Royal people; he was unselfish, he lived for all. His entire and exemplary life was like that of an angel watching over his people and praying for the good of mankind."[107] In addressing a mass demonstration on 4 May 1938, Bustamante denounced the local Jamaican government for thinking itself too powerful, claiming it considered itself on a par with the Crown as "a black royal family."[108] At one stroke he both attacked the local government and increased the prestige of the real, white royal family.

Bustamante also took full advantage of the status of British parliament and the British press in his efforts to project his own authority. In February 1938, he wrote a prophetic letter to Major Attlee, Leader of the Labour Party Opposition in the British House of Commons. "The people are suffering from hunger and if they dare to make peaceful manifestation the Police clubs are broken upon their heads and limbs. There have been strikes here and there: trouble is brewing, there is a volcanic feeling but people are loyal to their King and are bearing, but no one can tell when their patience should come to be ended, what will happen."[109] In April, a *Daily Gleaner* front page carried a special report from London stating that the British House had heard of abhorrent conditions of poverty and hunger in Jamaica.[110] The *Jamaica Standard*, which had been launched in late February 1938 and was struggling to compete against the long-established *Daily Gleaner*, attacked Bustamante for irresponsible behaviour. Hart describes how Bustamante, "a man with no more scruples in his money-lending business than the worst of Kingston's usurers,"[111] exploited the events that followed to secure his position as leader of the Jamaican working class. Writing on 1 June 1938, Hart notes:

Bustamante countered by holding a monster meeting to attack the Standard for their attitude, and another, and another, and each time the crowds grew larger. What exactly it was that inspired him to write I don't know, but it made him, although he did not exaggerate the facts.

From that point on, his motive force has been insatiable vanity. The battle with the Standard continued until he was firmly established as the head Labour Leader in Kingston.

Here was a man, almost fair of complexion, financially independent (a fact which he did not cease to remind them) who was echoing the grievances of the masses. They rallied to him in their thousands, and the publicity drove him on ... Crowds at the parade meetings numbered 5000 to 6000 and Bustamante's agitation was dynamite.[112]

While Bustamante's personal status was raised by his association with British society, the prestige of the British establishment was increased through Bustamante's growing influence. Bustamante thus secured for himself a place at the head of a movement that was *socially* radical, but the nature of his leadership, combined with selected elements in working-class ideology, ensured that it was *politically* conservative.

It is important to stress the dialectical relationship between Bustamante and the Jamaican workers' movement. The 1938 uprising of some one hundred thousand workers and unemployed labourers[113] did not passively adhere to the whims and fancies of Alexander Bustamante. In fact, the movement was in many instances beyond the control of any single authority. Though this was not Bustamante's goal, there is little doubt that it was the final nail in the coffin of the old Crown Colony system. As a direct result of the events of 1938, "fundamental changes [were made] in the living conditions and legal rights of the Jamaican masses."[114]

ORGANIC IDEOLOGY — STRIKE
ACTION, LANDOWNERSHIP
AND COLLECTIVE BARGAINING

The rebellion of 1938 was more widespread – numerically and geographically – than either the slave revolt of 1831 or the peasants' struggle of 1865. It was also more effective in forcing major reforms from the colonial system. Unlike the previous outbreaks, the 1938 revolt did not give rise to vicious ruling-class revenge. There was no massacre before concessions were granted, although attempts were made to repress the rebellion by force.

Bustamante and Grant were imprisoned. The local police were reinforced by six platoons of Sherwood Foresters, almost five thousand armed Special Constables, and two Royal Navy cruisers waiting offshore.[115] These reinforcements indicate the ineffectiveness of the police force.[116] In some cases, estate overseers and bookkeepers were sworn in as Special Constables and given authority to shoot at rebellious crowds.[117]

When repression failed, the government attempted to employ the other traditional British colonial approach of yielding moderate concessions in an effort to co-opt and undermine the resistance. These measures included the appointment of a Conciliation Board, "which did valuable work in settling strikes."[118] Private employers were pressured to increase wages, and at length an announcement was made of a major five hundred pound land settlement scheme.

The ineffectiveness of repression combined with the effectiveness of concessions in quelling the unrest meant that the total casualty list of the 1938 revolt was remarkably small. The final tally recorded only eight persons killed, thirty-two wounded by gunshot, and 139 otherwise injured.[119] Even more notably "not a single white person, planter, employer, or bureaucrat or member of the forces of law and order died at the hands of the workers."[120] As in 1831 and 1865, the masses were extremely discriminating in the selection of targets. The rebellion was unquestionably violent, but property was destroyed rather than people. In Kingston striking workers barricaded the streets and broke street lights to prevent police from operating effectively at night. In the rural areas, cane fields were set ablaze, roads were blocked to prevent police access, and telephone wires were cut to impede communication among the authorities.[121] The clear aim of all these acts was to compel the employers to recognize the demands of the striking workers. Since burnt sugar cane can be salvaged if cut within twenty-four hours, in certain cases estate fires may have been set as a pressure tactic to force management to make a quick settlement.

The strikers' selectivity is illustrated by the motor omnibus drivers' strike in Kingston, as observed by Richard Hart on 23 May. Striking workers were patrolling the streets to ensure that no trams were operating during the strike when they encountered a street vendor who had been looted by youths. The strikers took up a collection to repay the vendor for the loss.[122]

Although the 1938 uprising was both more widespread and more effective than those of 1831 and 1865, it was also less organized. Bustamante, Grant and Manley arrived relatively late in the day, placing themselves before crowds of people. No individual or single group had issued the call for strike action on such a scale. There was no prepared plan of action, no stated aim that directed the course of the rebellion. The 1938 revolt was spontaneous, but this did not prevent it from spreading rapidly from one end of the island to the other.

One of the primary reasons for the spontaneous identification of various sectors of the working class with one another was the re-emergence of a largely collectivized labour force in both the rural and the urban parishes. Similar to conditions of plantation slavery in this one regard, the particular work of each individual worker in a cane field or factory depended upon the related activities of all the other workers. As a largely proletarian work force, the Jamaican working class experienced broadly similar concerns and was able to resort to broadly similar forms of action. Marx identified this feature as a central characteristic of a wage-labour force.

[I]ndustry concentrates in one place a crowd of people unknown to one another. Competition divides their interests. But the maintenance of wages, this common interest which they have against their boss, unites them in a common thought of resistance – *combination* ...

Economic conditions had first transformed the mass of the people of the country into workers. The combination of capital has created for this mass a common situation, common interests ... The interests it defends become class interests. But the struggle of class against class is a political struggle.[123]

By the 1930s the increasingly limited access to land relative to population had forced most members of the producing classes to depend primarily on wages, and therefore on alienated wage labour, for their livelihoods. It was in such conditions that the *idea* of taking strike action became once more organically posed. Strike action as a tactic was certainly not new to the Jamaican work force. It had been central to the slave rebellion of 1831, and illegal strikes had been recorded among free workers on some sugar estates as early as 1863.[124] What was unique in the circumstances of 1938 was the *widespread* adoption of the strike tactic. Strikes developed in some instances as a result of immediate grievances against a particular employer. More significantly, strikes often developed in sympathy with other sections of the work force, sometimes as a result of a conscious effort to spread resistance through the use of the "rolling strike." This tactic involved striking workers travelling *en masse* in demonstration from work place to work place, or estate to estate, calling labourers off the job to join the marching strikers.[125]

The events of May and June 1938 were characterized by various methods of resistance, including looting, riots, hunger marches, stone throwing and property damage as well as strike action. But it was the strike wave that was central to the extent and strength of the struggle, and compelled the employers and the government to treat the demands of the Jamaican producing classes with a seriousness unprecedented in the island's history. The workers' increasing dependence upon wage labour was only a corollary of the increasing dependence of the ruling class upon a socialized work force. The objective ability of the working class to withdraw their labour power and thereby curtail production stood as the most profound threat that could be posed to the interests of both the local and the colonial sections of the ruling class.

The extent of the "strike contagion"[126] that swept the island marked the spread of an awareness of the power of the mass strike as an emergent part of the organic ideology of the working class. From 22 May on, city street cleaners struck in sympathy with waterfront workers, and they were followed by domestics, Public Works Department workers, tobacco plant labourers, shoe factory employees, machinists, restaurant workers, clerks in clothing operations, hospital workers, construction labourers, cane cutters, and banana workers.[127]

The strike wave united workers from both rural and urban sectors, and the employed and unemployed sections of the labour force in common action. Over two thousand unemployed labourers in Kingston, though unable to strike themselves, acknowledged the strike weapon as among their strongest tactics. They compelled some 250 public works employees in Kingston's Trench Pen slum region, where hiring practices were in question, to stop further work.[128] At Frome Estate, where the rebellion initially erupted, employed workers demanding better pay and improved housing conditions fought side by side with unemployed workers who had gathered in a shanty town around the estate factory in the hope of finding work.[129]

Though the rebellion of 1938 indicated a new level of solidarity among the working class, it also marked a separation of interests within this segment of society. The "pure" peasantry, those who were securely established and able to maintain a livelihood without selling their labour power for a wage, was not centrally involved in the uprising.[130] This bears out Orde-Brown's observation that where secure peasant cultivation was established, relatively "little extreme hardship"[131] was experienced.

Conversely, as one Hanover landowner observed at a meeting held in early June of 1938, "The majority of the discontented labourers were those who had no lands of their own."[132] These included the large numbers of new migrants who had swelled both the employed and unemployed sections of the labour force in Kingston, as well as the masses of workers in the rural parishes who had become dependent upon wage labour to supplement or replace their earnings from private cultivation. Squatters, tenants, and those with a passionate desire to acquire productive lands were all actively involved in the rebellion. In fact, the most militant pocket of protest in 1938 came from those districts where the land crisis had become particularly acute due to the spread of banana disease. In May and June 1938, it was the banana estate workers who were the most active of the rural population. In the parishes where these workers were the most numerous – St Ann, St Mary and Portland – "the most deliberate damage was done, and there was the most resistance to the Crown Forces."[133]

Landownership, the historic symbol of social independence and economic security among the producing classes, had steadily declined in both available acreage and levels of productivity. Land hunger now added further fuel to the demands of the discontented labourers. The importance of landholding was indicated in a number of ways during the 1938 events. With the increase of rural tenancy, rent strikes involving "hundreds of tenants"[134] took place. This movement was encouraged by the widespread belief that after emancipation the planters had been allowed to maintain their holdings only by lease from the Crown for a period of one hundred years. It was believed that these lands were to revert to the slaves or their descendants in August of 1938, and therefore the withholding of rent appeared legitimated.[135]

This form of protest was particularly concentrated in upper Clarendon where an organization of squatters and tenants was formed under the leadership of Robert E. Rumble. By March 1938 Rumble had become president of an organization claiming more than eight hundred members, the Poor Man's Improvement Land Settlement and Labour Association (PMILSLA). The mixed character of the producing classes as a peasant/wage-labour force is reflected in the inclusion of the word "labour" in its title, and in its demand for a minimum wage law.[136] In the aftermath of the struggle of May and June 1938, Rumble became a member of the new PNP, and the PMILSLA no longer functioned actively.[137]

More significant, however, was the importance of the access to land in the course of the labour rebellion itself. Three demands arose repeatedly throughout the strike wave. They were for increased wages, secure employment, and greater access to land. The first demand was the most widely and clearly articulated by the strikers. The workers at Frome expected a daily minimum wage of one dollar per day, or four shillings and two pence,[138] but before the outbreak on 2 May, general labourers were offered only two shillings per day. Even the highly skilled workers, including mechanics, masons, and blacksmiths, earned only three shillings and six pence per day, an amount less than that expected for general unskilled labour.[139] Wage increases were also among the most important demands of many sections of the Kingston working class, including the striking dock workers. Secure employment was also demanded repeatedly by demonstrations of unemployed workers. Among other actions, the Legislative Council was besieged, and the demonstrators demanded jobs "that would last long."[140]

The importance of land in the events of 1938 is indicated less in the clearly articulated demands of the workers than in the rise and decline of the most militant pocket of resistance, the banana estate workers in the parishes of Portland, St Mary and St Ann. The confrontation between banana estate workers and unemployed on one side and the police, Sherwood Foresters, and Special Constables on the other led one newspaper to report that St Mary was "like an armed camp."[141] On 3 June, that parish was the scene of the most serious violence witnessed during the rebellion. After a crowd of striking workers armed with sticks congregated in the town of Islington, telephone wires were cut and some looting occurred. When the police arrived, one man refused to give up his stick. In the confrontation that followed he was bayoneted, and his back was broken by the policemen's rifle butts. When the crowd responded by throwing stones at the police, four of the demonstrators were shot dead.[142] This incident was responsible for half the total number of deaths recorded during the 1938 events.[143]

Bustamante and Manley attempted to cool the temper of the strikers, but their appeals were futile. Even when higher wages were offered as a concession, "if anything militancy grew."[144] An editorial appearing on 4 June in the *Jamaica Standard* reported: "It is revealed that those who rioted at Islington yesterday did so in defiance of the advance of wages granted by a meeting of planters with the Conciliation Board. The men argue that it is not a question of the day's wages being insufficient, but that the amount of work available is insufficient."[145]

A settlement was considered only after Acting Governor C.C. Woolley, who replaced Denham after his untimely death, announced on 5 June that a major land scheme was to be implemented, involving a budget of five hundred thousand pounds to be spent on new settlements. It was heralded as a massive "New Deal" designed to benefit the Jamaican producing classes. Within a few days, the rebellion died down, having wrenched from the government what was perceived to be one of the most significant concessions since emancipation.

Though it was annnounced by Woolley, Denham had laid the groundwork for the proposal during his term as governor. In a memorandum to the Secretary of State for the Colonies dated 20 September 1937, Denham wrote:

There is inflammable material and it is not easy to say what question in Jamaica may not lead to a political agitation which brings in the large numbers of unemployables and casual labour most of whom are youths in the town of Kingston who are ripe for mischief and disorder. Fortunately, every Jamaican has an attachment to his parish and an insatiable desire to own land in it. Consequently, Land Settlement combined with Agricultural development, as I have already pointed out in numerous despatches, affords the best solution for the future welfare of the Colony.[146]

By 1938 the colonial government, and even significant sections of the large planters,[147] had ostensibly come to the same belief that the Jamaican producing classes had held since the time of slavery: that private land cultivation was the most secure single source of income available. In the conditions of the 1930s, however, landownership no longer constituted an effective means of bargaining against the dictates of the employers. In fact, the effectiveness of land as a means of bargaining had declined in inverse relationship to the rising effectiveness of an alternative, collective bargaining tool, the strike.

In an increasingly collectivized wage-labour force, albeit one that in large measure still struggled to supplement its wages through the cultivation of small plots of land, the strike tactic presented itself as part of the organic ideology of the working class. The continuing identification with private cultivation, however, was also an essential part of this ideology, acting to some extent as a deterrent to the development of a more coherent "trade union consciousness."[148] Historically, rather than turning to collective organization at the work place as a means of bargaining in defence of their interests, the Jamaican producing classes had sought to limit their dependence upon wage labour by developing private landholdings.

The earliest recorded strikes in Jamaica's post-emancipation history broke out in the sugar industry[149] in 1863. Yet this industry had virtually no history of permanent trade union organization prior to the growth of the JWTU. Trade unionism was not presented as an inherent idea in the historical experiences and traditions of the majority of Jamaican workers. Early attempts to form lasting organizations to protect workers' rights did appear in the urban district of Kingston and St Andrew, where the links to the land were relatively weak. Notably, the first abortive attempts to form trade unions developed among urban skilled artisans. Other early efforts involved skilled craftsmen in the printing and tobacco industries,[150] who had a strong sense of their importance and power as *workers*, and thus developed the idea that trade unions were a means to protect that power.

The dock workers of Kingston had the longest successful history of trade union organization. Effective organization began with the development of Kingston as the commercial centre of the island and the subsequent increase of urbanization around the early 1920s. As Kingston expanded into Jamaica's major port, the strategic importance of the dock workers' contribution to the island's economy increased. Concentrated in large numbers and employed in a common industry, the dock workers began to use their strength to attempt to improve their wages and working conditions.[151] Following the outbreak at Frome, it was the strike among the dock workers that initiated the offensive in May and June 1938; and, equally important, it was the dock workers who catapulted Bustamante to the status of Jamaica's "Labour Leader No. 1."

Their established tradition of organization and collective bargaining gave the dock workers both the objective leverage and the subjective confidence to demand Bustamante's release from jail as the ultimate condition for their return to work. In one of the few instances in Jamaican history, "the workers of Jamaica, by refusing to work unless their chosen leader was released, imposed their will upon the Colonial administration."[152] For this segment of the Jamaican working class, the idea of strike action as an *organic* idea was combined with the *inherent* notion of collective trade union organization. In 1938, it was the dock workers who became the first members of the newly launched Bustamante unions.[153]

The other major component of Bustamante's original support came from among the rural working class, in particular those employed on the sugar estates. Significantly, these were workers with little or no trade union experience. They were also the largest section of agricultural workers that had come close to becoming "dependent solely upon the sale of their labour power."[154] Only since the expansion of the activities of the JWTU in 1937 had agricultural workers been introduced to permanent collective bargaining organization, and by 1938 these activities were still limited.[155] Bustamante's BITU thus combined the elements in the working class that were the most and the least experienced in trade union organization. The six thousand members of the BITU recorded in November 1938 were classified as two thousand waterfront workers and four thousand agricultural workers, most of whom were employed on the sugar estates.[156] For the former, Bustamante offered an aggressive agitational style and a level of courage in the face of the employers and the government never before seen. For the latter, Bustamante provided something that had historically only been made possible by an alternative source of economic security to the plantations: an emotional element of confidence in challenging the plantation owners. In this sense, Bustamante's unconventional style of leadership served an important function. "The sugar worker could now make vocal his protest to his overseer in a way in which he never could before. 'Busta' was there to defend him by shutting down the estate if necessary."[157]

Bustamante thus adapted the trade union to operate as an alternative to the productive ownership of land as a means of bargaining. Further, in the new conditions of the Jamaican economy, the weakness of the collective tradition of resistance in the rural areas operated as a "negative" aspect of organic ideology, enabling Bustamante to elevate his personal role almost to that of a deity. Though the BITU was a mass collective organization, it was extremely weak at the level of rank and file control, and far from democratic.[158]

These factors provided the organic ideological basis that allowed Bustamante to exploit both the religious idiom and the identification of the Crown as a benevolent despot to achieve prestige and power in Jamaican politics. He interpreted the religious idiom in such a way as to increase his own power and authority among workers unfamiliar with the underlying strength of collective organization, and he used the historic conception of the Crown in order to portray himself as the gallant knight, singlehandedly challenging individual opponents in his quest to defend a noble and just kingdom.

It should also be noted, however, that the other major section of Bustamante's base, the dock workers, repeatedly held unauthorized strikes, without the direction or the support of "The Chief." As early as July 1938, Bustamante threatened to resign unless the workers agreed to strike on the waterfront only on the union's direction.[159]

This tenacity among some segments of the Jamaican work force caused constant tension in the BITU, and in time enabled Bustamante's monopoly of the leadership in the labour movement to be broken.

THE AFTERMATH

In the aftermath of the labour rebellion of 1938, the Jamaican producing classes benefitted from some significant reforms. Most immediately, wage increases were widely granted. At Frome, for example, daily rates of pay for general labour rose from between one shilling and nine pence and two shillings to a starting rate of two shillings per day (still far below the original demand for "one dollar per day"). In addition, hours of work were reduced by forty-five minutes per day over a six-day week.[160]

Other legislative reforms were also instituted. Within one year of the uprising, a bill granting universal suffrage was passed, the Trade Union Law of 1919 was amended to allow for legalized peaceful picketing, and a guaranteed minimum wage was enacted into law. By 1941 legislation had been passed providing for mediation, conciliation, and arbitration of labour disputes as well as for the definition of safety regulations for factory work, and the protection of the employment rights of trained nurses.[161] In 1943 the Secretary of State for the Colonies presented the outline of a new constitution that provided for internal self-government.[162] In 1944 the first general election took place in Jamaica.

The most significant reform, the "New Deal" in land settlement, proved to be at best only a partial success. By 1939 some seven thousand people had been provided with land, but it was not the poorest rural labourers who benefitted from the program. Rather, it was the middle peasants and more secure agricultural labourers, who had the available cash necessary to make the required downpayment, who could take advantage of the policy.[163]

The plan presented by Governor Woolley was intended to relieve the pressure for jobs. But the planters, still dominant in the Legislative Council in 1938, were opposed to a scheme that would seriously diminish the ready supply of cheap labour. The Council ensured that each land purchase would go directly through its offices, rather than through the newly established Land Settlement Department.[164] In this way the local ruling class was able to quell the mood of resistance without altering the fundamental balance of power between classes.

The consequences of this series of reforms were nonetheless dramatic. Many of the most basic democratic freedoms, anticipated but not delivered since the time of emancipation, were finally granted to black Jamaica: the right to vote, the right to strike, and the right to participate in political parties.

Most of these reforms followed from the recommendations presented in the reports of two Royal Commissions assigned to investigate the events: the *Report on Labour Conditions in the West Indies* prepared by Major Orde-Browne, and the *West India Royal Commission Report* prepared under the direction of Commissioner Moyne. The latter report was considered to be so sweeping in its criticisms of the colonial administration that it was withheld from publication until World War II had ended, for fear that it could be used as enemy propaganda.[165] So influential were these reports that one contemporary Jamaican unionist maintains that "the framework for the modern industrial relations system of the country was traceable to the Moyne Commission and by extension the Orde-Browne Report."[166] Thus the implementation of these reforms once again placed the British Crown in the role of caretaker and protector of the Jamaican poor. Once more a derived idea coincided with the inherent ideological tradition of the Jamaican poor.

In fact, Britain's efforts were less benevolent than appearances indicated. Both the Moyne and Orde-Browne reports aimed, above all, to promote reforms that would offset further outbreaks such as those that occurred in May and June 1938. Emphasis was placed on promoting greater accommodation of workers' and employers' interests, rather than on increasing the strength and participation of Jamaican workers as a class or the autonomy of Jamaica as a nation.[167] The stress was on trade union organization as a means of increasing supervision over workers' recently discovered and powerful bargaining tool, the mass strike.

The wave of workers' resistance in the Caribbean was taken with utmost seriousness by the colonial government, and with just cause. Rosa Luxemburg succinctly explains the potential political threat embodied in the mass strike.

Instead of the fixed and hollow scheme of a sober political "action" executed with prudent plan decided by the highest committees, we see a vibrant part of life in flesh and blood which cannot be cut out of the large frame of the revolution. The mass strike is bound by a thousand veins to all parts of the revolution ... In a word, the mass strike ... is not a crafty means discovered by subtle reasoning to make the proletarian struggle more effective, but it is the *mode of movement of the proletarian mass, the phenomenal form of the proletarian struggle in the revolution.*[168]

Trade unions were advocated by the Colonial Office in an effort to offset the potential political threat embodied in unplanned and unauthorized strike actions. The intent was to eliminate outbreaks of working-class resistance that could threaten the social, economic, and political stability of colonial capitalism. To this end, elaborate legislation strictly regulating industrial relations was advocated. Moreover, an emphasis was placed on the development of a layer of labour officials who could adeptly control workers' militancy and yet maintain rank and file support.

Orde-Browne's conception of trade unions was suited to this general legalistic perspective. He maintained that they should operate within the governmental system to enforce labour legislation. Orde-Browne opposed what he described as "a general tendency to regard a trade union as a weapon for precipitating strikes at the most inconvenient moment with a view to the extortion of higher wages ... The lawless and criminal element in the population took advantage of such developments to initiate mob action quite beyond the control of the reputable labour leaders."[169] In both the Orde-Browne and the Moyne reports, strong emphasis was placed on the recruitment and training of "responsible" trade union officials, including the provision of courses at the Ministry of Labour in London, as a means of promoting greater control over the labour movement.[170]

The first labour adviser to the Jamaican government, F.A. Norman, whose duties included the formation of a Labour Department, took office in June 1939. The purpose of such a position, according to Orde-Browne, was to administer labour legislation, mediate employer/employee grievances, and keep the government informed, with "a view to eliminating actual strife."[171] It was through such an approach that the employers and government were "able to deflate the militancy of the masses"[172] in the wake of the 1938 revolt.

This effort was given further impetus by the outbreak of World War II soon after the events of 1938 had died down. In wartime conditions even greater emphasis was placed on control and supervision within the labour movement.[173] The pressure from the British government for the formation of a layer of professional trade union officials to regulate working-class action was part of the institutional and philosophical framework already operative in many of the advanced western countries.[174] Hyman notes this trend when he comments on the development of industrial relations in Britain. "Governments ... have sought to capture the unions by kindness – particularly in time of war or economic difficulty. By co-opting union leaders on to numerous (though typically ineffectual) consultative committees, and by offering knighthoods and similar rewards for good conduct, the attempt is made to ensure a 'responsible' trade union movement."[175] Moreover, some of the major corporations that represented management in the collective bargaining process, such as Tate and Lyle and United Fruit, had become accustomed to dealing with trade unions in other countries, and were experienced in the arts of repression and co-optation. Bustamante reported in August 1938 that "Messrs. Tate and Lyle are really in favour of Labour Union. In a talk with Mr. Kirkwood this evening I was informed that the Company in England is accustomed to deal with labour organisations. Mr. Kirkwood himself prefers to deal with labour by this medium rather than when they are just a scattered mass."[176]

The institutionalized aims and structures demanded by the government for Jamaican trade unions were therefore almost entirely drawn from international corporate and government interests. Even the style of leadership was dictated. The Moyne report called for "men of character, experience, capacity and integrity"[177] to act as Labour Commissioners, and suggested that such leaders were only to be found in the United Kingdom itself.

This derived institutional and philosophical approach added more weight to the already top-heavy structure advocated by Bustamante in the BITU. Bustamante himself was far too intemperate to fit the requirements of the colonial government's ideal labour leader. This was indicated in his perpetual criticisms of the Labour Department for the first fifteen years of its operation, and by his early withdrawal of the BITU from the Trade Union Advisory Council (which soon became known simply as the Trade Union Council, or TUC). The TUC was an apparently self-appointed body formed early in 1939, and included Norman Manley among its leading enthusiasts. It was formed with the aim of organizing "the orderly and progressive development of the trade union movement, to prevent frivolous strikes, to unify policy, to eliminate strike amongst the workers' organisations and between labour and capital and to pool all the labour resources of the country for the common good."[178]

Though Bustamante may not have agreed with the TUC's notion of what constituted a "frivolous strike," in one crucial respect he agreed wholeheartedly with the perspective on industrial relations that dominated official Jamaican circles after 1938. This was the commitment to strike action as only the last and most regrettable resort available to the working class. In an open letter to trade unionists in the pages of the *Gleaner*, Bustamante wrote: "Strikes must be the last thing on your minds, they must only come about – if they have to come – after we have exhausted every arbitrary method with the capitalists and Government and both turn their backs on us;

then and only then it is time for us to make up our minds not alone to starve for one common cause, but if needs be to die for it with a smile upon our quivering lips."[179]

The derived idea that trade union officials should act as a body of regulating agents to moderate working-class militancy thus reinforced the autocratic framework maintained by Bustamante, which was also derived though far closer to the hearts and minds of working-class Jamaicans. As a whole, however, this approach contrasted sharply with the organic ideological foundation of the Jamaican working class. The weak traditions of collective bargaining and trade union organization meant that there were few Jamaican workers who qualified for recruitment as professional negotiators and mediators. There was also little incentive for Bustamante to train representatives who would weaken his exclusive claim to authority. Thus trade union leadership by professionals, most of whom were coloured, more socially acceptable than Bustamante, and recruited from among the urban, educated middle class, developed as a classic hallmark of the Jamaican labour movement.[180]

At the same time, a contrary pressure had developed within the labour movement – this was the workers' growing recognition of the organically presented power of the strike weapon. The workers' rebellion of 1938 had successfully promoted dramatic reforms in the colony's political structures – structures that had been more or less static since at least the mid-1860s. Furthermore, wartime restrictions promoted greater resistance within the working class, and less tolerance from the colonial government. The island economy was disrupted, the cost of living increased, and workers demanded higher pay.[181]

By the summer of 1940 Bustamante was under pressure from frustrated rank and file workers for greater militancy, and from the government and employers for increased discipline in the work place. Membership in the BITU had declined by some two thousand from the previous year, and the number paying dues had declined even further.[182] Bustamante's followers were beginning to resent his inconsistent attitude to working-class militancy, as demonstrated by his conflicting role as aggressive agitator and conservative negotiator, and his popularity and influence were waning.

As early as August 1938 the BITU had begun to suffer from internal divisions. At that time, a major split occurred between Grant and Bustamante. Grant charged Bustamante's central lieutenants with graft, treachery and corruption, and three days later Bustamante expelled Grant. The schism was not without its reverberations among the union membership. Only three months prior to Grant's expulsion, Bustamante had antagonized many of his supporters by speaking disparagingly of Marcus Garvey. Grant had played a central role in attracting Garvey's supporters into the ranks of the BITU, and Bustamante was justifiably fearful of further repercussions. Bustamante was thus forced to make a concession by allowing Grant to return to the BITU as a general organizer, but continued to bar him from the post of officer.[183]

In 1940, however, colonial repression restored Bustamante's prestige. When Bustamante threatened a waterfront strike in the midst of the wartime economy, Governor Richards immediately sentenced him to jail.[184] During the seventeen-month period of internment, Bustamante's image as the suffering martyr, once again adopting the religious idiomatic form, was reaffirmed. Over these months, Manley and Noel Nethersole, Manley's TUC associate, took over the affairs of the BITU under Bustamante's instruction. The results of their leadership were very impressive. Most notable was the negotiation of Jamaica's first island-wide sugar agreement between the BITU and the Sugar Manufacturers' Association, linking wages to a Labour Department cost-of-living survey.[185] Ironically, despite the atmosphere of restraint, Manley and Nethersole's efforts were favoured by wartime conditions. During this period Britain was offering fixed prices for sugar throughout the Empire, and costs of production, including wages, were included in the price formula.[186] Membership in the BITU soared once again. When recorded six weeks after Bustamante's return to active leadership, membership figures had risen to 20,612 (13,741 dues paying) from 8,133 (5,200 dues paying) only one year before.[187]

Bustamante's prison term marked the last period of cooperation between the "Chief" and Manley. When Bustamante was released in 1942, he immediately began a public campaign denouncing Manley and his associates, and calling for BITU members to have nothing to do with the PNP. Bustamante charged, among other things, that a conspiracy was afoot by the caretaker union officers to extend his detention. Manley denied the allegations, and countered that Bustamante had been responsible for depleting the union's funds and therefore needed to find a scapegoat.[188]

Bustamante's release had not been without conditions. He was forbidden to address gatherings of more than forty-nine people, or to leave Kingston without consulting with the police. Though repeatedly denied by the governor, there was strong suggestion, raised most vocally by Manley and his colleagues, that Bustamante made a private arrangement to sever the BITU's ties with the PNP in return for the right to address mass meetings, even up to a restricted number. Indeed, there were more than one hundred BITU delegates at the first meeting he addressed after his release.[189]

The split between the two men also signalled the split between the BITU and the PNP. After 1942, each organization sought to develop its own affiliate as an alternative. The PNP launched its own offensive on the trade union front, and the BITU became the basis of a new political party, the Jamaica Labour Party (JLP).

Through the connection maintained between the PNP and the TUC, approximately ten new unions were organized between 1942 and 1944. To accomplish this feat, the PNP leadership relied almost entirely upon a small group of Marxist activists operating within the PNP as a caucus, and identifying themselves privately as the "Inner Circle."[190] The style and approach to trade unionism was demonstrably different from Bustamante's, with greater attention to democratic procedure and local union control. Significantly, this type of unionism was able to grow and to challenge the stronghold of Bustamante's labour monopoly in sectors where working conditions were highly collectivized, employment was relatively stable, and links to landholding as a means of bargaining with the employers were most remote. Among such sectors, workers' confidence in their importance as a wage-labour force was relatively high, and the personal appeal of Bustamante was relatively low. These sectors included workers employed in the government railway, the Public Works Department, and the postal and telegraph services, as well as those in private industries such as printing and publishing.[191] Thus the growth of TUC affiliates included sectors of workers new to unionization, such as service employees, as well as those "which had already become, for whatever reason, disillusioned with Bustamante."[192] This portion of the Jamaican working class, however, was small in comparison to the sector that continued to work on the estates with hopes of attaining greater landholdings and the group of urban workers who were employed in small shops and plants. The BITU continued to dominate the field of trade union activity for some years to come.

Bustamante returned to the scene after his internment with a significantly stronger union and a renewed base of support, particularly in the rural districts. By 31 March 1943 the BITU's membership was up a further 8,150 from the previous year. Late in 1943 Bustamante announced the formation of the Jamaica Labour Party to act as the political arm of the BITU. It was at first a party only in name, a label under which Bustamante could appoint and run candidates,[193] a personal right guaranteed to him in the party's constitution.[194]

In the first general election in Jamaica's history, there were three contending parties: the Jamaica Democratic Party (JDP), formed in 1943 as the voice of urban business; the People's National Party, expressing primarily those urban middle class interests that had been previously represented by scattered reform associations; and the Jamaica Labour Party, the party of Alexander Bustamante. There were also a number of independent candidates. The results of the election speak for themselves. The newly formed JLP was swept into power by an overwhelming majority, winning twenty-three of the thirty-two seats in the new House of Representatives. Four of the five elected independents subsequently declared for the JLP. The PNP won only four seats, but gained a fifth when the one remaining independent announced his allegiance to the party.[195] Manley himself lost his constituency to a JLP candidate. The JDP elected no one and every candidate lost his deposit. Moreover, thirty-four of the fifty-one candidates who lost their deposits were independents, and only four out of the twelve members of the old Legislative Council who ran for office were elected.

The lesson of the island's first election was clear: any political alternative to Bustamante and the JLP, whether to the left or right, would have to compete not only at the level of politics and ideology, but also at the level of trade union allegiance. The working class held the majority of votes, and votes remained tied to the BITU's party.

Bustamante's landslide victory was also in part due to the JLP's campaign propaganda. Bustamante attacked the PNP at its weakest areas from the standpoint of the producing classes. He denounced the PNP's social democratic platform as expropriatory, threatening the identification with private landholding which Bustamante knew to be dear to a large portion of Jamaican voters. Moreover, he charged the PNP with being crudely atheistic, and attacked the program for self-government by reminding Jamaicans that it was Britain who emancipated them from slavery.[197] He claimed that independence would mean "brown man rule," with the middle class in power installing a renewed system of slavery.[198] Significantly, it was only after his split with Manley in 1942 that Bustamante used overtly racial arguments to cement his following, and even then it was only as a means to trigger the memory of slavery. Bustamante presented the PNP as a threat to the most central and sensitive elements in the mass ideology of the producing classes: landholding, religion, and the role of the British Crown. In each instance he attempted to paint Manley and the PNP as allies of the most repressive element in Jamaican experience – the old established white plantocracy.

The election results of 1944 defined the pattern organized Jamaican politics was to follow. But these results did not indicate unqualified support for Bustamante and the JLP. Only 52.7 per cent of the electorate cast counted ballots, and only 23.7 per cent of all eligible adults voted for Bustamante and his party.[199] Of the twenty-three electoral seats won in the name of the Jamaica Labour Party, only ten were won with more than 50 per cent of the votes, and only five others were won with between 40 and 50 per cent. Where the victory of the JLP was indeed overwhelming was in those sectors where Bustamante's working-class support was most highly concentrated. The urban parishes, Kingston and St Andrew, and the four sugar parishes of St Thomas, St Catherine, St Elizabeth and Westmoreland showed overwhelming support for the JLP.[200]

The victory of the JLP was nonetheless nothing short of a landslide. There was no other single political alternative that could rally support comparable to the following of Bustamante. The JLP won 41.4 per cent of the popular vote, the PNP followed with a small but respectable 23.5 per cent, the JDP drew 4.1 per cent and independents and other splinter parties[201] combined brought in the remaining 31 per cent.[202]

After the election, the JLP found an additional base of support, one with dubious motives in backing a labour party. With the still-birth of the JDP, the ruling class turned its support to Bustamante and the JLP. The lack of political and ideological hegemony in Jamaican society left the ruling class without any effective official organization through which it could govern directly. In such circumstances, the PNP was perceived as the greater ideological threat. Moreover, still in shock over the rapid expansion of trade unionism, and fearful of any recurrence of events such as those of 1938, employers were "willing to recognize any union leader able to maintain control over the mass of workers."[203] Harrod accurately summarizes this relationship as one based on "the fact that Bustamante did not profess to hold any consistent anti-business ideology and his dealings with businessmen on behalf of his followers tended to be pragmatic."[204]

Thus despite Bustamante's bold and aggressive rhetoric the allegiance of the BITU to the Jamaica Labour Party actually forged an unholy alliance between the trade union and the employing class. It was precisely through Bustamante and the JLP that the interests of local capital finally emerged in a secure hegemonic position. The resistance of the Jamaican working class forced major ideological and superstructural reforms in the modern Jamaican political balance of forces, but the economic fabric of the society was little altered.

Bustamante had learned to use new tools in order to win hegemonic influence among the producing classes. The most important of these were the mass media in the form of popular agitational articles in the press, and, in order to spread his appeal to the illiterate, the mass meeting modelled after a religious revival (in recognition of the importance of the religious idiom). After 1944 political office and the use of governmental authority gave Bustamante an even more centralized and authoritative public platform. In both content and form, therefore, the continuing power of the ruling class was adapted to the experiences of the Jamaican peasant and working classes.

CHAPTER FIVE

Some Implications for the Jamaican Political System

The rebellions of 1831, 1865, and 1938 indicate the existence of a recurrent tradition of resistance among the Jamaican labouring classes. Concepts that became dominant in the era of slavery, particularly the association of African and Christian religious expression with a philosophy of freedom and the association of the British Crown with emancipation, reappeared in subsequent periods. Such ideas were carried through the generations, and were altered or adapted to apply to varying conditions and changing circumstances.

The organization of the Jamaican producing classes changed from collectivized slave labour to private peasant production to collectivized wage labour. These labour forms, however, were neither pure nor static. The relationship between private landholding and mass strike action as an effective means of bargaining with employers also changed according to the particular nature of the labour force.

The argument developed in the previous chapters has illustrated the ideological links from slavery to the work force of the modern era. An attempt has been made to identify broad general trends in mass ideology. In order to highlight this general framework certain important minority perspectives, representing serious options for some members or sections of the producing classes, have not been addressed. In political terms, the emphasis has been placed on a current that may be described as "militant reformism," as distinct from revolutionism. This political tendency is part of a broader tradition of resistance, one which may be referred to as a "rebellious traditional culture."[1] In Jamaica, such a culture combines courageous militancy with a philosophy that tends to seek allies in the church and the state as a means to legitimate protest, even when the dictates of church and state are the very targets of that protest.

Such a tradition contains elements that can surpass the limits of its own purview and encompass a more systematic revolutionary consciousness. In itself, however, such mixed consciousness could not explain, and therefore could not effectively resist, the pressures of repression and co-optation of the colonial capitalist system. Nor could such a view lead to a fundamental and lasting transformation of Jamaican class society. In 1831 and 1865 the objective basis for a fundamental transformation of society did not yet fully exist. In 1938 the strategic power of the working class was far greater, and the impact of the rebellion of that year was far more profound than in the previous rebellions. There was not, however, a sufficiently self-conscious and organized political force, a mass revolutionary party, capable of achieving a revolutionary transformation.

After the 1944 general election, the essential features of the modern Jamaican political system incorporated and institutionalized this tradition of resistance among the producing classes. Superficially, a stable, classic two-party political system emerged, and has continued to characterize Jamaican politics, more or less consistently, to the present day. While a detailed analysis of the emergence of Jamaican institutional politics would take us well beyond the scope of this discussion, some consideration of the implications of the foregoing analysis for understanding the contours of the modern era is in order. By way of conclusion, a brief overview of the process of accommodation and moderation that marked the post-1940s period in the development of the Jamaican labouring classes is presented.

THE GROWING SIMILARITIES OF THE PNP AND THE JLP

After their initial period of division, the two major political parties became increasingly indistinguishable. At last ruling class political hegemony was officially institutionalized through the establishment of a two-party system that incorporated the labouring classes into the electoral process. Each party paid ideological and symbolic tribute to the legacy of the working-class struggle that had catapulted Jamaica into the modern era. In so doing, however, the main ideological features of this tradition – the religious idiom and the identification of the Crown as a benevolent despot – were stripped of their radical content. In the hands of the labouring classes they had been ideological weapons in the struggle against subordination. Now, in the hands of the ruling parties of the society, they became a means of incorporating the labouring classes into the structures of Jamaican capitalism.

Between the late 1940s and the mid-1960s the new institutions of the Jamaican political system crystallized. These years saw the development of mass electoral politics, repeated constitutional reforms, the rise and fall of the Federation of the West Indies, and the island's formal achievement of national independence. It was also during this period that the two main political parties increasingly became mirror images of each other, in class and racial composition, organizational style, and major policy positions. A political system developed "in which both parties, although necessarily structured on a mass basis, [were] fundamentally bourgeois in spirit."[2]

The PNP had learned the lessons of the first general election, in which Bustamante's ideological and organizational links to the working class provided the mass electoral base of the JLP. The PNP proceeded to form a new labour federation of its own, the Trades Union Congress of Jamaica in 1949 (referred to as the TUC, the same acronym as its predecessor of 1939, the Trade Union Advisory Council), in anticipation of the general election that was to take place in the same year. It was the left wing of the PNP, under the direction of such men as Richard Hart and Arthur Henry, that endeavoured to undercut Bustamante's labour and political base. In the 1949 election the PNP secured thirteen seats against the JLP's seventeen, finally establishing itself as a serious opposition party in Jamaican politics.

The credibility gained by the PNP's leftist organizers was hard for even the most enlightened of Jamaica's middle class to tolerate. Under the pressure of local and international anti-communist ideology, the leaders of the TUC were expelled from the PNP in 1952. The ousting of the "Four H's" – Ken Hill, the PNP's Second Vice-President and a Member of the House of Representatives, Frank Hill, Richard Hart, and Arthur Henry, all members of the PNP Executive Committee – was explicitly for activities which were "communistic" and "Marxist."[3] The events surrounding the 1952 conflict brought the party's parliamentary and reformist strategy for social change into sharp relief. Any suggestion inside or outside the PNP that the party's distinction from the JLP was based on a revolutionary or radical perspective was eliminated.

The TUC was abandoned to be replaced by the newly formed National Workers' Union (NWU) as the PNP's labour base. The need for an organized relationship with the trade union movement in order to ensure the PNP's political viability was explicitly recognized.[4] The NWU was organized and led by PNP officials and was closely tied to the party itself. While the PNP struggled to overcome its middle class origins for the sake of electoral success, it became similar to the JLP in its composition and ideology. At the same time, the JLP was compelled by its fundamentally conservative ideology under the leadership of Bustamante, to orient its policies and propaganda increasingly toward the Jamaican middle and ruling classes.

In leadership style, the PNP gradually adopted the messianic imagery characteristic of Bustamante's leadership of the JLP. "The Chief" appealed to the religious idiomatic tradition in order to institutionalize a method of authoritarian political leadership. In an effort to challenge Bustamante, Norman Manley counterposed himself as a "man of destiny" and made a similar effort to use the religious idiomatic tradition to political advantage. Both parties were completely dominated by their leaders and a small group of handpicked advisers. Aspiring members of the coloured middle class who were unable to penetrate the overloaded higher echelons of the PNP were increasingly welcomed into the ranks of the JLP. By 1957 the organized labour movement was almost equally divided between the BITU and the NWU. Thus both parties were led by members of the coloured middle class and supported by a largely passive electoral base among the black working class.

The parties also had similar policies regarding national independence. The historical identification of the Crown as a benevolent despot came to be institutionalized as a conservative adaptation to British colonial rule. In the years between Jamaica's first and second national elections, the PNP, as a minor opposition, took up a defensive posture in the Legislature in order to avoid political destruction. Manley's undying commitment to making the new constitutional experiment appear viable to the British government was also a feature of the PNP's political moderation. Though originally distinguished by its nationalism, the PNP gradually accommodated itself to both the colonial government and the ruling JLP, hence stressing the benevolence rather than the despotism of British imperial domination.

Between 1949 and 1959 (the latter half of these years under a PNP government) three new constitutions were inaugurated, mainly on the initiative of the British government. Despite numerous minor changes, the British retained control over defence, foreign policy, rights of constitutional amendment and, effectively, the island's treasury.[5] In campaigning for re-election in 1959, the PNP nonetheless highlighted its achievements and proudly congratulated itself for winning "self-government" as it had intended.

This process of political accommodation reached the point where the JLP was commended by the PNP for its progressive stance. At the same time, the JLP was undergoing a transition from its earlier conservatism, and this was reflected in Bustamante's more moderate position towards Jamaican independence. Bitter election battles continued, but Bustamante's single-minded pragmatism on major policy questions led him to alter his party's earlier opposition to self-government and state economic intervention. During the JLP's first election campaign "Busta" viciously attacked the PNP's nationalism for being equivalent to "brown-man rule," and charged that self-government would mean a return to slavery. But in 1952 the parliamentary representatives in the JLP unanimously supported a motion in favour of self-government raised in the House by Manley. The motion read: "Be it resolved that the House declares itself in favour of Self-Government for Jamaica and appoints a Committee of seven members of the House forthwith to prepare a Constitution providing for Self-Government to be submitted for approval to the Secretary of State for the Colonies at the earliest possible date."[6] This new stance was a pragmatic response to the increasing acceptance in British ruling circles of constitutional reform throughout the empire. It was not, as the PNP leadership perceived it to be, "an historical occasion in the Legislature and ... a turning point in our fight for Self-Government."[7] Such applause for the JLP's symbolic accommodation was as much an indication of the PNP's weakened conception of self-government, which replaced a commitment to independence with a purely legislative reform within the colonial context, as it was of the JLP's opportunistic approach to politics. Ironically, a few years later Bustamante was able to differentiate the JLP from the PNP on the grounds of Jamaican nationalism, charging the PNP with adapting to British colonialism. The JLP used this argument to defeat Manley's bid for West Indian federation in the 1958 referendum. In 1962 a newly-elected JLP government was able to claim the laurels for winning Jamaican independence.

THE ECONOMIC CONTEXT OF ACCOMMODATION

The composition and policies of the two parties did not, however, result from political forces only. They were also a product of the era of economic growth in which the parties were operating. The institutionalization of the political process arose in the context of a new period of domestic and international economic expansion. The objective basis for recurring social and economic crisis that had characterized Jamaica since the abolition of slavery was now replaced by an era of prolonged capitalist prosperity, albeit a prosperity that benefitted the ruling and middle classes rather than the workers.

The background to the accommodation and stabilization that occurred after the 1940s was the weakening of the organic element of ideological resistance in the development of class action and class consciousness among the producing classes. The willed and organic elements in the ideology of resistance no longer interacted in the same way. Rather than the willed ideological elements of the religious idiom and the identification of the Crown as a benevolent despot serving as elements of a tradition of resistance, they became incorporated more directly as aspects of state ideological authority and domination. Because of the historical importance of the producing classes to the process of Jamaican political transformation, however, both parties were forced to seek the support of the working class through their association with mass trade unions.

The once essentially derived notion of trade unionism had, since the 1938 events, become very much an inherent element in working-class ideology. The trade union leaders, however, were directly linked with the official party leadership of both the JLP and the PNP, and employed this commitment to trade unionism to secure hegemony through a cross-class electoral alliance. The organic notion of strike activity as a means of resistance was retained, but was frequently channelled into the institutionalized process of official trade union activity. The success of legal reform helped to incorporate the producing classes more directly into the operations of governance. Once these important reforms were won, however, the interaction of willed and organic ideology no longer clearly pointed in the direction of radical action against the existing structures of racial and class dominance, but were co-opted to serve the interests of those same structures.

Between 1950 and 1965 gross domestic product increased in Jamaica at an annual rate of 7.2 per cent. Direct foreign investment soared, particularly from US and Canadian investment in the expanding bauxite-alumina industry. By 1957 bauxite-alumina had replaced sugar as the island's major export.[8] Tourism, manufacturing, and construction also became major growth sectors. As leading members of the local ruling class, a group of some twenty-one Jamaican families became more prosperous and influential, and emerged as important contributors to both political parties.[9] The political evolution of the PNP and the JLP as hegemonic parties was thus both cause and effect of the climate of capitalist economic stability and expansion.

The major growth sectors, bauxite-alumina and tourism, provided relatively few jobs, and unemployment continued to be a chronic and serious problem. Unemployment hovered between 15 and 25 per cent, despite a large increase in emigration flows between 1950 and 1961. Net emigration over this period was about 164,000, representing approximately one-third of the total natural growth of the labour force over the same period.[10] Nonetheless, despite a heavily skewed distribution system, per capita income increased as Jamaica experienced its first period of real and sustained economic growth since the eighteenth century. The institution of a series of important democratic rights combined with these factors to mitigate against the recurrence of social upheavals such as the rebellions considered in the previous chapters until the return of crisis in the 1970s. It was the combination of these subjective and objective factors that enabled the development of a political party system based on working-class support to mature without a genuine or consistent working-class political perspective. The relationship of both major parties to the trade unions in Jamaica was part of this process.

THE UNION/PARTY DYNAMIC IN JAMAICAN POLITICS

With the two major parties virtually indistinguishable in composition and orientation, and a situation of chronic unemployment, politics in post-war Jamaica became "simply a struggle for Government money and Government jobs."[11] Party loyalties were strongly influenced by personal ties and access to party favours, attainable through government appointments and the apparatus of the two main trade unions. Each party developed a small base of loyal supporters, but most citizens shifted their allegiance on the basis of immediate benefits. This pattern developed a self-perpetuating dynamic, yielding little political space for third party options within traditional institutional boundaries.

Political patronage developed into an officially accepted practice in both the JLP/BITU and the PNP/NWU. During his first term in office, Bustamante stated in the Legislature that "The Sugar Manufacturers have an obligation to see that unionists are first employed by them in the field and factory, because workers in the field and factory are members of the Bustamante Industrial Trade Union."[12] The PNP was equally blatant. During Manley's first years in office after the election of 1955, political appointments to government positions were so numerous that even the JLP was outraged. In a 1959 official party statement, it was declared that loyal party members should "see that PNP people get work ... of every ten, make it six PNP and four JLP."[13]

Political loyalties and patronage also influenced union allegiances. In conditions where the working class was both poor and new to formal collective bargaining, loyalties to any particular union could shift readily, based on the material benefits offered. When, for example, the newly-formed National Workers' Union challenged the BITU for certification of Reynolds Jamaica Mines, the first poll taken early in January of 1955 resulted in a tie vote. Since the BITU was the original representative of the bargaining unit, the tie meant that the JLP affiliate retained exclusive representation. Within the same month, however, Manley and the PNP dislodged the JLP in a general election, and the PNP took control of the government for the first time. Soon after, a second poll was taken at Reynolds and the NWU won with a comfortable margin.[14] The union tied to the party that had greatest control over funding, legal regulations, and government appointments offered promise of clear advantages to workers concerned about protection of their rights.

The organic idea of strike action also became a political tool of the affiliated party to challenge the trade union base of its opposition. The Report of the International Bank for Reconstruction and Development in 1952 identified this pattern explicitly: "The union connected with the minority party began a campaign to attract members and in several cases demanded recognition from employers hitherto recognizing the other union. Both unions attempted to increase their support by outbidding each other in promises to the workman, and the strike weapon was frequently used to settle the issue."[15] Despite the frequency of strike action as a result of inter-union and inter-party rivalry, the overall tendency in these years was for the trade unions to become more accommodating and less militant. Unions were gradually accepted by the major corporations on the island as "serving a police function ... of value to the company."[16] Foreign investors made it clear that they would not supply capital unless a quiescent labour force and peaceful industrial relations were assured. The report cited above made it clear that Jamaica must "establish a reputation for orderly settlement of Labour disputes," and that, to this end, "the development of good leadership ... is all important."[17]

Such "good leadership" was already in the process of developing in the tradition of Alexander Bustamante. The middle class came to dominate leadership positions in organized labour as they had in organized party politics. This was the result not only of the social, economic and political status obtainable through the labour hierarchy, but also of conscious corporate and state planning.

The bauxite companies brought with them "certain enlightened industrial practices which [were] standard in North America."[18] These practices included extensive in-house training programs, a private industrial relations system for settling grievances, and notably, the acceptance of union contracts with the proviso that no strikes or lock-outs were allowed during the life of the collective agreement. Despite the continued outbreak of illegal strikes even under such provisions, the move towards a more structured and ultimately bureaucratically regulated process of collective bargaining was clear. Such a process was less threatening to the interests of local and foreign entrepreneurs. To encourage the development of a layer of labour leaders trained in such "professional" collective bargaining an educational program was initiated. The Extra-Mural Department of the University College of the West Indies became the centre of labour and industrial relations that was intended to ensure a "reputation for orderly settlement" in contract negotiations, and in 1964 the Trade Union Education Institute (TUEI) of the university was opened. The TUEI was partially financed by a large grant from the US government's Agency for International Development.[19]

The union/party relationship thus developed its own self-perpetuating dynamic. The working class, previously unorganized, was now organizationally divided into two great labour/political competing blocs. Both the JLP/BITU and the PNP/NWU, compelled by the tradition of resistance in Jamaican class development, claimed to represent the interests of the black labouring classes. Yet in reality neither party carried on the tradition of actual class struggle as it had emerged in previous periods of rebellion. The religious idiomatic form and the conception of the Crown as a benevolent despot were removed from the practical working-class struggle and accommodated to secure at last a hegemonic position of authority for the ruling class.

The Jamaican producing classes had a long-established tradition of resistance, characterized by the struggles outlined in the previous chapters. But they had little tradition of collective and sustained organization to ensure the continued preservation and advancement of their interests over long periods of time. The relatively late appearance of mass political parties and organized trade unionism in the aftermath of the 1938 rebellion indicates the contradictory aspects of this process of development. The objective background to the post-war period of accommodation, however, was a prolonged period of international and domestic capitalist prosperity. These conditions were to end in the mid-1970s, with the return of generalized crisis and instability on a global scale.[20] With the return of economic crisis came the return of more intensive ideological polarization between the two main political parties, along with the development of new channels for the expression of discontent. Looking at Jamaica's history, it is impossible to dismiss the possibility of the return of mass rebellion on a scale as great or greater than the highpoint of struggle reached in 1938.

Notes

INTRODUCTION

1 W.H. Knowles, *Trade Union Development and Industrial Relations in the British West Indies* (Berkeley: University of California Press, 1959); G. Eaton, *Alexander Bustamante and Modern Jamaica* (Kingston: Kingston Publishers Ltd., 1975); Z. Henry, *Labour Relations and Industrial Conflict in Commonwealth Caribbean Countries* (Port-of-Spain, Trinidad: Columbus Publishers Ltd, 1972); Major St J. Orde-Browne, *Labour Conditions in the West Indies*, July 1939, Command no. 6070 (London: 1939).
2 Interview with Lloyd Goodleigh, Island Supervisor, National Workers' Union, Kingston (18 May 1981); Lecture by Carlyle Dunkley, Trade Union Education Institute of the University of the West Indies, Kingston (6 May 1981).
3 Richard Hart was central in organizing the trade union movement of Jamaica, especially between 1937 and 1953. R. Hart, *Slaves Who Abolished Slavery*, 2 vols. (Kingston: Institute of Social and Economic Research, 1980, 1985)
4 See in particular S.W. Mintz and D. Hall, "The Origins of the Jamaican Internal Marketing System," *Yale University Publications in Anthropology*, no. 57 (New Haven: Human Relations Area Files Press, 1970), 3–26; and S.W. Mintz, "Slavery and the Rise of Peasantries," *Historical Reflections* 6, no. 1 (Summer 1979): 213–53.
5 For a discussion of post-World War II Jamaica see C. Stone and A. Brown, eds., *Essays on Power and Change in Jamaica* (Jamaica: Jamaica Publishing House, 1977); O. Jefferson, *The Post-War Economic Development of Jamaica* (Jamaica: Institute of Social and Economic Research, 1972); N. Girvan, *Foreign Capital and Economic Underdevelopment in Jamaica* (Jamaica: Institute of Social and Economic Research,

1971); and H. Campbell, *Rasta and Resistance: From Marcus Garvey to Walter Rodney* (Trenton, N.J.: Africa World Press, 1987), ch. 4 ff. For Jamaica during World War II, see K. Post, *Strike the Iron: A Colony at War, 1939–1945*, 2 vols. (The Hague: Humanities Press, 1981).

6 For a classic but notoriously racist discussion of early Jamaican history see E. Long, *The History of Jamaica*, 3 vols. (London: T. Lowndes, 1774).

7 For more on the theory of imperialism see V.I. Lenin, "Imperialism, The Highest Stage of Capitalism: A Popular Outline," *Collected Works* (Moscow: Progress Publishers, 1978), 22: 185–304 and N. Bukharin, *Imperialism and World Economy* (New York: International Publishers, 1929; rpt. Monthly Review Pres, n.d.); for a more contemporary assessment of imperialism see N. Harris, *Of Bread and Guns: The World Economy in Crisis* (Harmondsworth: Penguin Books, 1983), especially chs. 1–3.

8 N. Girvan, *Aspects of the Political Economy of Race in The Caribbean and The Americas: A Preliminary Interpretation*, Institute of Social and Economic Research, University of the West Indies, Working Paper no. 7 (1975), 2.

9 Ibid., 7.

10 "The basic racial system of Jamaica was laid down in the eighteenth century. At the end of the seventeenth century there were an estimated ten thousand whites and forty thousand slaves, principally blacks. Less than a century later the whites numbered about eighteen thousand, but there were a quarter of a million slaves – an increase of over two hundred thousand ... By 1844 there were less than sixteen thousand whites in the Island, and their number has since fluctuated little. The census of 1943 reported 13,400, hardly more than the white population of 1775." L. Broom, "The Social Differentiation of Jamaica," *American Sociological Review* 19 (April 1954): 115

11 T. Munroe, *The Politics of Constitutional Decolonization: Jamaica, 1944–62* (Jamaica: Institute of Social and Economic Research, 1972), 14.

12 Eligibility to vote was based on property and income qualifications far beyond those of the average Jamaican. In 1884, only 9,400 out of a total adult population of approximately 358,000 were eligible to vote (Ibid. and G. Eisner, *Jamaica, 1830–1930: A Study in Economic Growth* [Manchester: Manchester University Press, 1961], 134).

13 F.L. Ambursley, "The Working Class in the Third World: A Study in Class Consciousness and Class Action in Jamaica, 1919–1952" (BA dissertation, University of Birmingham, 1978), 44–5.

14 Ibid.; A. Kuper, *Changing Jamaica* (London: Routledge and Kegan Paul, 1976), 52–70; and M. Burawoy, "Race, Class and Colonialism," *Social and Economic Studies* 23 (Dec. 1974).

15 E.D. Genovese, *The World the Slaveholders Made: Two Essays in Interpretation* (New York: Vintage Books, 1969), 103.
16 P. Alexander, *Racism, Resistance and Revolution* (London: Bookmarks, 1987), 13.
17 G. Lukacs, *History and Class Consciousness: Studies in Marxist Dialectics*, trans. R. Livingstone (Cambridge, Mass.: MIT Press, 1971), 46. On class in Jamaica, see W.B. Vanriel, "The Political Economy of New World Slavery" (M.Sc. dissertation, University of the West Indies, Mona, 1979), 13.
18 "Peasant" classes are notoriously difficult to define with any degree of accuracy, let alone universal applicability. The literature on this issue is extensive. See E. Wolf, *Peasants*, Foundations of Modern Anthropology Series (Englewood Cliffs, N.J.: Prentice Hall, 1966) and "Types of Latin American Peasantry: A Preliminary Discussion," *American Anthropologist* 57, part 1 (June 1955):453–4; S.W. Mintz, "A Note on the Definition of Peasantries," *Journal of Peasant Studies* 1 (Oct. 1973):91–106; T. Shanin, ed., *Peasants and Peasant Studies* (Harmondsworth: Penguin Books, 1971; rpt. 1973, 1976, 1979); R. Frucht, "A Caribbean Social Type: Neither 'Peasant' Nor 'Proletarian'," *Social and Economic Studies* 16 (May 1957):295–300; and C. Stone, "Political Aspects of Postwar Agricultural Policies in Jamaica (1945–1970)," *Social and Economic Studies* 23 (June 1974):145–6.
19 See S.W. Mintz, "The Rural Proletariat and the Problem of the Rural Proletarian Consciousness," in R. Cohen, P.C.W. Gutkind, and P. Brazier, eds., *Peasants and Proletarians: The Struggle of Third World Workers* (London: Hutchinson and Co., 1979), 173–97.
20 E.P. Thompson, "Eighteenth-Century English Society: Class Struggle Without Class?," *Social History* 3 (May 1978): 133–65; see also by Thompson, *The Making of the English Working Class* (New York: Vintage Books, 1963).
21 For an analysis of the general propensity of Jamaican slaves to rebel, see O. Patterson, *The Sociology of Slavery: An Analysis of the Origins, Development and Structure of Negro Slave Society in Jamaica* (London: MacGibbon and Kee; rpt. ed., London: Granada Publishing, 1973), 274–6.
22 On the 1831 slave rebellion see M. Reckord (née Turner), "The Slave Rebellion of 1831," *Jamaica Journal* (June 1969): 25–31; also "The Jamaican Slave Rebellion of 1831," *Past and Present* 40 (July 1968): 108–25; M. Turner, *Slaves and Missionaries: The Disintegration of Jamaican Slave Society 1787–1834* (Urbana: University of Illinois Press, 1982), 148–79; R. Hart, vol. 2 of *Slaves Who Abolished Slavery, Blacks in Rebellion*, 244–337; M. Craton, *Testing the Chains: Resistance to Slavery in the British West Indies* (Ithaca: Cornell University Press, 1982), 291–321;

on the Morant Bay revolt of 1865, see B. Semmel, *Jamaican Blood and Victorian Conscience: The Governor Eyre Controversy* (Britain: Riverside Press, 1963); D. Rowbotham, "'The Notorious Riot': The Socio-Economic and Political Basis of Paul Bogle's Revolt," Working Paper No. 28, Institute of Social and Economic Research, University of the West Indies, Jamaica (1981); E.B. Underhill, *The Tragedy of Morant Bay: A Narrative of the Disturbances in the Island of Jamaica in 1865* (London: Alexander and Shepheard, 1895); and on the 1938 revolt see O.W. Phelps, "Rise and Fall of the Labour Movement in Jamaica," *Social and Economic Studies* 9 (December 1960): 417–68; K. Post, *Arise Ye Starvelings: The Jamaica Labour Rebellion of 1938 and its Aftermath* (The Hague: Martinus Nijhoff, 1978).

23 E.J. Hobsbawm, *Primitive Rebels: Studies in Archaic Forms of Social Movement in the 19th and 20th Centuries* (New York: W.W. Norton, 1959), 146.
24 See C.L.R. James, *The Black Jacobins: Toussaint L'Ouverture and the San Domingo Revolution*, 2nd ed., rev. (New York: Vintage Books, 1963).
25 Cohen, Gutkind, and Brazier, Intro. in *Peasants and Proletarians*, eds. Cohen, Gutkind, and Brazier, 17. For a theoretical discussion of the dialectical relation between reform and revolution, see R. Luxemburg, *Reform or Revolution* (New York: Pathfinder, 1970).
26 G. Rudé, *Ideology and Popular Protest* (London: Lawrence and Wishart, 1980), 15–41.
27 See A. Gramsci, *Selections from the Prison Notebooks*, ed. and trans. Q. Hoare and G.N. Smith (New York: International Publishers, 1971), passim.
28 See Gramsci, *Prison Notebooks*, especially 376–7. For a discussion of this aspect of Gramsci's thought, see Rudé, *Ideology*, 22–5.
29 Gramsci, *Prison Notebooks*, 377. I am aware of the problem of using the term "men" as if to assume women fall under this generic category, and of the sexist bias of modern English. Corrections, however, sometimes can be distorting, while the biased structure of the communication process as a whole remains essentially intact. I have therefore not altered the translation of Gramsci's words, nor have I done so at other points in this text where similar usages are employed.
30 Rudé, *Ideology*, 9–10.
31 Ibid., 28–37.
32 Ibid., 28.
33 Ibid. This framework is vaguely similar to that of Harrod's "evolved" and "imitative" cultures. Whereas Harrod emphasizes the separation of these two spheres, however, Rudé's approach concentrates upon their interaction. See J. Harrod, *Trade Union Foreign Policy: A Study of British and American Trade Union Activities in Jamaica* (New York: Doubleday, 1972), 159–68.

34 Rudé, *Ideology*, 28.
35 Ibid., 35.
36 Ibid.
37 Rudé would undoubtedly attempt to classify such ideas as "inherent." There is an important distinction between ideas that are maintained at the level of folklore, and those that compel action, such as the organization of a mass strike. To place these under the same rubric seems to render the category so general as to lose its essential value. See Rudé, *Ideology*, 30.
38 M.I.P. de Queiroz, "Brazilian Messianic Movements: A Help or a Hindrance to 'Participation'?," *International Institute for Labour Studies Bulletin*, no. 7 (June 1970): 93. See also V. Lanternari, *The Religions of the Oppressed: A Study of Modern Messianic Cults*, trans. L. Sergio (New York: New American Library, 1963) for further discussion of messianic movements in colonial settings.
39 This movement is discussed in greater detail in connection with the labour rebellion of 1938 in chapter 4.
40 N. Cohn, *The Pursuit of the Millenium* (Fairlawn, N.J.: Essential Books, 1957), xiii.
41 For a more detailed analysis and discussion of the Ras Tafarian movement see R. Nettleford, *Mirror, Mirror: Identity, Race and Protest in Jamaica* (Britain: William Collins and Sangster [Jamaica], 1970); L.E. Barrett, *The Rastafarians* (Britain: Sangster's Book Stores, in assn. with Heinemann Educational Books, 1977); and Campbell, *Rasta and Resistance*.
42 In the context of the slave rebellion of 1831, for example, Reckord maintains that the only millenarian element in the struggle was an attempt to turn a leading Baptist missionary, away from the island at the time, into a messianic figure. See Reckord, "Slave Rebellion," 30.
43 In this connection see Herskovits and Herskovits' concept of religion as a "culture focus," in M.J. and F.S. Herskovits, *Trinidad Village* (New York: Alfred Knopf, 1947), 6. It should also be noted that religious concepts have been more the rule than the exception in the history of the expression of discontent. See Hobsbawm, *Primitive Rebels*, 126.
44 Rudé, *Ideology*, 32.
45 Also see Hobsbawm, *Primitive Rebels*, 116 and Thompson, "Eighteenth-Century English Society," 154.

CHAPTER ONE

1 There is some debate as to whether the post-emancipation exodus of the slaves from the estates signified a clear rejection of plantation field labour or took place simply because land was available for occupation. The important point for this study, however, is that where the choice

was presented, private cultivation rather than regular estate employment was overwhelmingly pursued. See D. Hall, "The Flight from the Estates Reconsidered," *Journal of Caribbean Studies* 10/11 (1976): 7–24.
2 The term is taken from Mintz. See S.W. Mintz, "The Question of the Caribbean Peasantries: A Comment," *Caribbean Studies* 1 (October 1961): 32.
3 P. Sheridan, *The Development of the Plantations: An Era of West Indian Prosperity 1750–1775* (Bridgetown: Caribbean Universities Press, 1970), 45–7.
4 See G.E. Cumper, "Population Movements in Jamaica, 1830–1950," *Social and Economic Studies* 5 (May 1956): 267.
5 O. Patterson, *The Sociology of Slavery: An Analysis of the Origins, Development and Structure of Negro Slave Society in Jamaica* (London: MacGibbon and Kee; rpt. ed. London: Granada Publishing, 1973), 218.
6 D. Hall, "The Ex-Colonial Society in Jamaica" in *Patterns of Foreign Influence in the Caribbean*, ed. E. DeKaot (London: Oxford University Press, 1972), 33–4.
7 An account by a visitor to Jamaica in the late seventeenth century, quoted in E.M. Henriques, *Family and Colour in Jamaica* (London: Eyre and Spottiswoode, 1953), 18.
8 This point is taken up in more detail, particularly concerning the theoretical implications of the analogy in my "Plantation Slavery and the Capitalist Mode of Production: An Analysis of the Development of the Jamaican Labour Force" in *Studies in Political Economy* 22 (Spring 1987): 73–101.
9 B. Edwards, *The History, Civil and Commercial, of the British West Indies*, 5 vols. (London: T. Miller, 1819; rpt. ed. New York: AMS Press, 1966), 2:290.
10 Ibid., 292–7.
11 *Jamaica Almanac* (Kingston: 1832), quoted in Cumper, "Population," 263.
12 G. Eisner, *Jamaica, 1830–1930: A Study in Economic Growth* (Manchester: Manchester University Press, 1961), 189.
13 E. Williams, *Capitalism and Slavery* (New York: G.P. Putnam's Sons, 1966), 4.
14 Throughout the latter part of the eighteenth century, male slaves outnumbered female slaves. This was largely because the men were considered stronger and better able to handle the heavy labour on the plantations. Slave women were also frequently pregnant or nursing small children. By the early nineteenth century, as Creole slaves increased in numbers, women constituted closer to half the slave population. See Patterson, *Sociology of Slavery*, 107. However, since male slaves were often selected for "special" tasks, female slaves formed a

large proportion of the field labourers. See M. Craton, *Testing the Chains: Resistance to Slavery in the British West Indies* (Ithaca: Cornell University Press, 1982), 49.
15 D. Hall, *Free Jamaica 1838–1865: An Economic History* (New Haven: Yale University Press, 1959; rpt. ed. Aylesbury: Ginn and Company, 1976), 44–5.
16 Patterson, *Sociology of Slavery*, 59.
17 Ibid., 66–7.
18 J. Stevens, *The State Called Slavery*, vol. 2, ch. 4, cited in Patterson, *Sociology of Slavery*, 67–9.
19 See, for example, the works of such authors as David Brion Davis, Eugene D. Genovese, Richard Hart, C.L.R. James, Orlando Patterson, and Eric Williams among many others.
20 H. Sloane, *A Voyage to the Islands Madera, Nieves, S. Christophers and Jamaica*, 2 vols. (London : 1707), 1:7, quoted in R. Hart, *Slaves Who Abolished Slavery*, vol. 1: *Blacks in Bondage*, 99–100.
21 Cumper, "Population," 267.
22 International Bank for Reconstruction and Development, *The Economic Development of Jamaica* (Baltimore: Johns Hopkins Press, 1952), 11.
23 S.W. Mintz and D. Hall, "The Origins of the Jamaican Internal Marketing System," *Yale University Publications in Anthropology*, no. 57 (New Haven: Human Relations and Area Files Press, 1970), 10–11.
24 Ibid., 5–6.
25 M. Turner, *Slaves and Missionaries: The Disintegration of Jamaican Slave Society 1787–1834* (Urbana: University of Illinois Press, 1982), 43.
26 Colonial Office Files (CO) 139/47, 62, 65. See also Patterson, *Sociology of Slavery*, 84 and 216–59. For an account of West Indian Slave Laws, see E.V. Goveia, *The West Indian Slave Laws of the 18th Century* (Guildford: Caribbean Universities Press, Ginn and Co. Ltd., 1970); R. Hart, *The Abolition of Slavery* (London: Community Education Trust, 1989); and C. Hyett, "Labour, Law and the State: From Slave to Free Labour in Jamaica, 1830–1870," (MA dissertation, Queen's University, 1984).
27 The indications are that Saturday was the standard marketing day until some time in the eighteenth century, when Sunday became the recognized day for the slaves to sell their products. See for example Cundall's remarks in reference to the "usual Saturday market" in 1685, in F. Cundall, *The Governors of Jamaica in the Seventeenth Century*, (London: The West India Committee, 1936), 99.
28 Mintz and Hall, "Origins," 13.
29 E. Long, *The History of Jamaica* (London: T. Lowndes, 1774), 2:486–570.

30 Patterson, *Sociology of Slavery*, 216.
31 Long, *History of Jamaica*, 2:411.
32 See Patterson, *Sociology of Slavery*, 229.
33 Turner, *Slaves and Missionaries*, 46.
34 By 1826, less than a decade before the beginning of emancipation, the slaves were finally granted legal right to this property, though ownership of anything valued over twenty pounds could be challenged in the Supreme Court. See *Acts of Jamaica*, CO 139/65 and Patterson, *Sociology of Slavery*, 80.
35 Turner, *Slaves and Missionaries*, 45.
36 R. Renny, *An History of Jamaica* (London: 1807) quoted in S.W. Mintz and D. Hall, "The Origins of the Jamaican Internal Marketing System," *Yale University Publications in Anthropology*, no. 57 (New Haven: Human Relations Area Files Press, 1970), 20.
37 Edwards, *History of the West Indies*, 2: 160–1 and Mintz and Hall, "Origins," 9–10.
38 Patterson, *Sociology of Slavery*, 221. On the propensity of Jamaican slaves to organize as a class against the planters, see M. Turner, "Chattel Slaves into Wage Slaves," in *Labour in the Caribbean*, ed. M. Cross and G. Heuman (London: Macmillan, 1988).
39 P.D. Curtin, *Two Jamaicas: The Role of Ideas in a Tropical Colony 1830–1865* (n.p.: Harvard University Press, 1955; rpt. ed. New York: Atheneum, 1970), 113. Unoccupied land, however, was considered the communal property of the tribe or king, a belief which was to influence the attitude of the labourers to vacant land after emancipation. See below, this chapter.
40 Turner, *Slaves and Missionaries*, 47. Craton also notes that common family labour predominated on the provision grounds while primarily females laboured in the cane fields. This is described as a factor in the much greater will displayed in the former over the latter. Craton, *Testing the Chains*, 50.
41 Quoted in J. Bigelow, *Jamaica in 1850: or The Effects of Sixteen Years of Freedom on a Slave Colony* (New York: George E. Putnam, 1851), 73n.
42 For a full account of the movement of industrial interests to an anti-slavery position, see Williams, *Capitalism and Slavery*. There is a long-standing debate on Williams' classic work, which, while fascinating, is beyond the scope of this study. See B.L. Solow and S.L. Engerman, eds., *British Capitalism and Caribbean Slavery: The Legacy of Eric Williams* (Cambridge: Cambridge University Press, 1987).
43 Williams, *Capitalism and Slavery*, 150.
44 *A Statement of Facts, Illustrating the Administration of the Abolition Law, and the Sufferings of the Negro Apprentices, in the Island of Jamaica* (London: n.p., 1837) 4.

45 See for example, *Statement of Facts*, 4–5.
46 See Patterson, *Sociology of Slavery*, 78–9.
47 *Statement of Facts*, 6.
48 Bigelow, *Jamaica in 1850*, 73n.
49 Ibid., 94n.
50 This was despite the fact that Jamaica received the highest percentage of total compensation awarded among all the British colonial possessions, and held slaves who carried the highest relative value. See Bigelow, *Jamaica in 1850*, 93n.
51 Eisner, *Jamaica, 1830–1930*, 196 and 203.
52 S.W. Mintz, Foreword to *Sugar and Society in the Caribbean: An Economic History of Cuban Agriculture*, by R. Guerra y Sanchez (New Haven: Yale University Press, 1964), xx.
53 Hall, *Free Jamaica*, 20.
54 D. Rowbotham, "Agrarian Relations in Jamaica," in *Essays on Power and Change in Jamaica* (Jamaica: Jamaica Publishing House, 1977), 50.
55 Hall, *Free Jamaica*, 20.
56 E.B. Underhill, *The Tragedy of Morant Bay: A Narrative of the Disturbances in the Island of Jamaica in 1865* (London: Alexander and Shepheard, 1895), 55. Such were the conditions in St Thomas-in-the-East in 1865, where the major peasant rebellion in Jamaican history took place. See chapter 3.
57 See for example, J. Phillippo, *Jamaica: Its Past and Present State*, intro. P. Wright (London: 1843; rpt. ed. London: Dawsons of Pall Mall, 1969), passim.
58 See Hart, *Abolition of Slavery*, 40–2.
59 Eisner, *Jamaica, 1830–1930*, 221–5. The Morant Bay events are discussed in chapter 3.
60 Ibid., 220.
61 Hall, *Free Jamaica*, 183.
62 W.K. Marshall, "Notes on Peasant Development in the West Indies Since 1838," *Social and Economic Studies* 17 (May 1968): 254.
63 Eisner, *Jamaica, 1830–1930*, 234. Over this period cultivated acreage as a percentage of total acreage remained fairly constant at about 22 per cent (Eisner, *Jamaica, 1830–1930*, 349).
64 Ibid.
65 CO 137/390, The Reverend Magnan and W.M. Anderson to the Bishop of Jamaica, 1865.
66 P. Wright, Introduction, *Jamaica: Past and Present*, 4.
67 Eisner, *Jamaica, 1830–1930*, 346.
68 W.G. Sewell, *The Ordeal of Free Labor in the British West Indies* (London: Sampson Low, Son, and Co., 1862; rpt. ed. New York: A.M. Kelley, 1968), 269–70. The conclusion that free labour was less costly to the

planter than slave labour is also supported by Bigelow, (*Jamaica in 1850*, 125) and Eisner, (*Jamaica, 1830–1930*, 346).
69 Eisner, *Jamaica, 1830–1930*, 193.
70 Hall, *Free Jamaica*, 50–1.
71 I. Carlyle, *An Occasional Discourse on the Nigger Question*, (London: 1869) quoted in Eisner, *Jamaica, 1830–1930*, 213.
72 For a complete description of the rise and fall of this effort, see D. Hall, "Bountied European Immigration into Jamaica," *Jamaica Journal* 8 (1974): 48–54, 9 (1975): 2–9.
73 D.W.D. Comins, *Note on Emigration from the East Indies to Jamaica* (Calcutta: Bengal Secretarial Press, 1893), 10. See also *Correspondence Relative to the Financial Arrangements for Coolie Immigration Into Jamaica*, Command 14 August 1879 (London: 1879) and *Report of the Committee on Emigration from India to the Crown Colonies and Protectorates*, Command June 1910 (London: 1910).
74 Hall, *Free Jamaica*, 47.
75 Ibid., 70, and Eisner, *Jamaica, 1830–1930*, 303.
76 Hall, *Free Jamaica*, 27–8.
77 CO 137/293, Sir Charles Grey, no. 99, 22 October 1847.
78 Eisner, *Jamaica, 1830–1930*, 204.
79 After 1865, Jamaica's political structure was changed by the adoption of Crown Colony status. However, this fact has little bearing on points discussed here.
80 After 1838, suffrage was open to sane adult males owning and paying taxes on land valued at six pounds, or paying an annual rent of thirty pounds, or paying direct taxes of three pounds per year. All voters were required to register on the official voters' list. See Phillippo, *Jamaica: Past and Present*, ch. 7.
81 CO 137/332, Barkly to Newcastle, no. 37, 22 March 1854.
82 For statistics on racial composition from 1834 to 1921, see Eisner, *Jamaica, 1830–1930*, 153.
83 Bigelow, *Jamaica in 1850*, 115.
84 Hall, *Free Jamaica*, 19. Craton identifies landholding as a defining feature of "freedom" among West Indian slaves. Craton, *Testing the Chains*, 252.
85 J.E. Henderson and W. Bancroft Espeut, *The Labour Question in, and the Condition of Jamaica* (n.p.: Office of the "Colonial Standard and Jamaica Despatch," 1876), 5.
86 See Eisner, *Jamaica, 1830–1930*, 164, 168, 348.; Marshall, "Peasant Development," 254, 257–66; Cumper, "Population," 271, 274; and K. Post, *Arise Ye Starvelings: The Jamaica Labour Rebellion of 1938 and its Aftermath* (The Hague: Martinus Nijhoff, 1978), 40.

87 See Eisner, *Jamaica, 1830–1930*, 348; and *West India Royal Commission Report*, Lord W.E. Moyne, Chairman, Command June 1945, no. 6607, (London: 1945), 9 (Hereafter referred to as the *Moyne Report*).
88 Eisner, *Jamaica, 1830–1930*, 348.
89 C. Stone, "Political Aspects of Postwar Agricultural Policies in Jamaica (1945–1970)," *Social and Economic Studies* 23 (June 1974): 151.
90 N. Girvan, *Foreign Capital and Economic Underdevelopment in Jamaica* (Jamaica: Institute of Social and Economic Research, 1971), 10.
91 See D. Edwards, *An Economic Study of Small Farming in Jamaica* (Kingston: Institute of Social and Economic Research, 1961), 95, for a detailed explanation of land division and inheritance practices. Besson discusses the contradiction between diminishing individual access to land, and the perception of limitless "family land" in the district of Martha Brae in Trelawney Parish, Jamaica. See J. Besson, "A Paradox in Caribbean Attitudes in Land," in *Land and Development in the Caribbean*, ed. J. Besson and J. Momsen (London: Macmillan, 1987), 13–45.
92 Girvan, *Foreign Capital*, 10.
93 F.L. Ambursley, "The Working Class in the Third World: A Study in Class Consciousness and Class Action in Jamaica, 1919–1952," (BA dissertation, University of Birmingham, 1978), 13. This statistic must also be considered against the background of declining sugar and rum exports.
94 R. Hart, *The Origin and Development of the People of Jamaica* (Kingston: By the Author, 1952), 19.
95 *Moyne Report*, 19.
96 Cumper, "Population," 271.
97 An address by Mr. Graham Hawkins to the Jamaica Imperial Association, in *Annual Report*, Jamaica Imperial Association (1936): 37–40. Also quoted in Stone, "Political Aspects," 153.
98 *Annual Report on the Work of the Labour Department for the Year 1943*, (n.p.: 1943), 1. Each year's banana crop during World War II was, however, paid for by the British government, though never shipped, to protect the Jamaican economy from wartime disaster.
99 Post, *Arise Ye Starvelings*, 38.
100 Eisner, *Jamaica, 1830–1930*, 245; and Girvan, *Foreign Capital*, 10.
101 Eisner, *Jamaica, 1830–1930*, 245–6.
102 Stone, "Political Aspects," 151. With the exception of an aborted attempt to enter the sugar industry in 1928, United Fruit Company investments were concentrated in banana production.
103 Post, *Arise Ye Starvelings*, 88. This purchase included the sugar estates that had been owned previously by the United Fruit Company.

104 K. Stahl, *The Metropolitan Organization of British Colonial Trade*, 41 quoted in S.St A. Clarke, *The Competitive Position of Jamaica's Agricultural Exports* (Kingston: Institute of Social and Economic Research, n.d.), 62n.
105 O. Jefferson, "Some Aspects of the Post-War Economic Development of Jamaica" in *Readings in the Political Economy of the Caribbean*, ed. N. Girvan and O. Jefferson (Kingston: New World Group, 1971; rpt. ed. 1974), 112.
106 Stone, "Political Aspects," 150–1.
107 Eisner, *Jamaica, 1830–1930*, 206; R. Hart, Correspondence to A. Bakan, (7 July 1985); Clarke, *Competitive Position*, 62 and 62n; and Stone, "Political Aspects," 150.
108 *Report on an Economic Survey Among Field Workers in the Sugar Industry, Jamaica, B.W.I.* (Kingston: Labour Department, 1946), 5 and 69.
109 K. Post, *Strike the Iron: A Colony at War 1939–45* (The Hague: Humanities Press, 1981) 1:18. After about 1950, there was a decline in the production of both traditional peasant export crops, such as bananas, and locally consumed items such as yams, corn, peas, and breadfruit. The land crisis and the increased pressure to seek wage work at home or abroad meant a net decline in the amounts of land and labour used in agricultural properties with areas under five hundred acres. At the same time, domestic food demand was increasing significantly as a result of post-war growth. The result was that the market in food imports grew rapidly, and patterns of domestic consumption, particularly among the higher income groups, shifted accordingly. See Girvan, *Foreign Capital*, 138–45, and N. Adams, "An Analysis of Food Consumption and Food Import Trends in Jamaica, 1950–1963," *Social and Economic Studies* 17 (March 1969): 1–22.
110 Post, *Strike the Iron*, 1:16.
111 *Moyne Report*, 35. It should be noted that this report was not published until 1945, because of the outbreak of World War II.
112 Ibid., 7.
113 Census figures cited in Hart, *Origin*, 21, 29.
114 *Moyne Report*, 15.
115 Stone, "Political Aspects," 151.
116 See D. Rowbotham, *Our Struggles* (Kingston: Workers' Liberation League, 1975), 70 ff. "Tenants-at-will" were bound to work on the estates as rent payment, on pain of eviction.
117 International Bank, *Economic Development*, 14.
118 Hart, *Origin*, 21–2.
119 See R.B. Davison, "The Labour Force in the Jamaican Sugar Industry" in *Work and Family Life: West Indian Perspectives*, ed. and intro.

L. Comitas and D. Lowenthal (Garden City: Anchor Books, 1973), 130.
120 Rowbotham, *Our Struggles*, 70 ff.
121 Hart, *Origin*, 21.
122 E. Williams, *The Negro in the Caribbean* (Washington: Panaf Publications, 1942), 21.
123 Post, *Arise Ye Starvelings*, 132.
124 Eisner, *Jamaica, 1830–1930*, 147.
125 This rebellion is considered in further detail in chapter 4.
126 See Cumper, "Population," 271–2.
127 The elaboration of Kingston's expansion is drawn largely from Hart, *Origin*, 22–4.
128 Cumper, "Population," 272–5. Cumper maintains that all of these trends are consistent, even in the light of variable statistical guidelines and possible errors in estimation methods.
129 Hart, *Origin*, 22.
130 The state became increasingly involved in the economy as centralization increased. This began with the outbreak of World War I, but was considerably accelerated during and after World War II. See Girvan, *Foreign Capital*, passim, and Clarke, *Competitive Position*, 157.
131 Jamaica Central Bureau of Statistics, *Economic Conditions in Jamaica 1939–48*, Bulletin no. 20 (Kingston: 1949), 6.
132 *Annual Report of the Labour Department for the Year Ended 1939* (Kingston: 1939), 8.
133 Eisner, *Jamaica, 1830–1930*, 164.
134 Major St J. Orde-Browne, *Labour Conditions in the West Indies*, July 1939, Command no. 6070 (London: 1939), 30.
135 Ibid., 39.
136 Ibid., 28.
137 Ibid., 28 and 75. See also *Annual Report, 1939*, 2.
138 Post, *Arise Ye Starvelings*, 135.
139 One indication of the early growth of the tourist industry is that the number of hotels and boarding houses grew from 54 in 1910 to 114 in 1930. (See Eisner, *Jamaica, 1830–1930*, 287–8).
140 T. Munroe, *The Politics of Constitutional Decolonization: Jamaica 1944–62* (Jamaica: Institute of Social and Economic Research, 1972), 4.
141 Post appropriately applies Marx's term of the "lazarus layer" of the population to this stratum *(Arise Ye Starvelings*, 135).
142 Stone, "Political Aspects," 156.
143 T. Munroe, *The Marxist 'Left' in Jamaica 1940–1950*, University of the West Indies Working Paper Series, no. 15 (Kingston: Institute of Social and Economic Research, 1977), 57.
144 *Annual Report 1950*, 3.

145 Munroe, *Politics*, 5.
146 Computed by L. Broom, "The Social Differentiation of Jamaica," *American Sociological Review*, 19 (April 1954): 120. The remaining groups are Chinese and East Indian.
147 Munroe, *Politics*, 5. It appears that these figures are for 1943, though no specific date is provided.
148 Orde-Browne, *Labour Conditions*, 38. See also M.G. Smith, "Patterns of Rural Labour," in L. Comitas and D. Lowenthal, eds. and intro., *Work and Family Life: West Indian Perspectives* (Garden City: Anchor Books, 1973), 79, for an analysis of the social impact of this generational disparity.
149 See Orde-Browne, *Labour Conditions*, 73–4.
150 Ibid., 77.
151 Ambursley, "Working Class," 17.
152 K. Post, Unpublished Mimeograph quoted in Ambursley, "Working Class," 17; also cited in Post, *Strike the Iron*, 1:19.
153 See M.F. Katzin, "The Jamaican Country Higgler," *Social and Economic Studies* (Dec. 1959): 421–40 and "The Business of Higglering in Jamaica," *Social and Economic Studies* 9 (Sept. 1960): 297–331. These studies were conducted after the period under review, but are not time-bound in their findings.
154 Post, *Strike the Iron*, 1:21.
155 S. Reid, "Economic Elites in Jamaica: A Study of Monistic Relationships," presented to the Conference of the Canadian Sociology and Anthropology Association (July 1979), 5.
156 See Post, *Strike the Iron*, 1:15–18.
157 See chapter 4.
158 Post, *Arise Ye Starvelings*, 124.
159 *Moyne Report*, 35.
160 *Annual Report on the Work of the Labour Department for the Year 1945* (n.p.: 1945), 2.
161 D.T. Edwards, "The Development of Small Scale Farming: Two Cases from the Commonwealth Caribbean," *Caribbean Quarterly* 18 (March, 1972): 63. See also D. Edwards, *An Economic Study of Small Farming in Jamaica* (Kingston: Institute of Social and Economic Research, 1961) and Stone, "Political Aspects," 168.
162 See Smith, "Patterns of Rural Labour," 79, 128.
163 See R. Lewis, *Marcus Garvey: Anti-Colonial Champion* (Trenton, N.J.: Africa World Press, Inc., 1988).

CHAPTER TWO

1 Lanternari points this out in reference to religious sects in modern Africa. See V. Lanternari, *The Religions of the Oppressed: A Study of*

Modern Messianic Cults, trans. L. Sergio (New York: New American Library, 1963), 20.
2 P.D. Curtin, *Two Jamaicas: The Role of Ideas in a Tropical Colony 1830–1865* (n.p.: Harvard University Press, 1955; rpt. ed. New York: Atheneum, 1970), 237, n. 2.
3 Ibid., 25.
4 O. Patterson, *The Sociology of Slavery: An Analysis of the Origins, Development and Structure of Negro Slave Society in Jamaica* (London: Mac-Gibbon and Kee; rpt. ed. London: Granada Publishing, 1973), 188. For a more detailed account of the beliefs and practices associated with African tradition in Jamaican life see M.W. Beckwith, *Black Roadways* (Chapel Hill: University of North Carolina Press, 1929).
5 Curtin, *Two Jamaicas*, 26.
6 See P. Taylor, "Hegel, Afro-Caribbean Religion, and the Struggle for Freedom," *North/South: Canadian Journal of Latin America and Caribbean Studies* 13:26 (1988); M. Schuler, "Myalism and the African Religious Tradition in Jamaica," in *Africa and the Caribbean: The Legacies of a Link*, ed. M. Crahan and F. Knight (Baltimore: Johns Hopkins University Press, 1979); E. Brathwaite, *The Development of Creole Society in Jamaica: 1770–1820* (Oxford: Oxford University Press, 1971); and N. Erskine, *Decolonizing Theology: A Caribbean Perspective* (New York: Orbis, 1981).
7 R. Hart, *Slaves Who Abolished Slavery*, vol. 1, *Blacks in Bondage* (Kingston: Institute of Social and Economic Research, 1980), 117 and R. Bickell, *The West Indies as They Are; or a Real Picture of Slavery: but More Particularly as It Exists in the Island of Jamaica* (London: J. Hatchard and Son, 1825), 89–91.
8 Curtin, *Two Jamaicas*, 32.
9 The Church of England was in certain respects more inhumane regarding the issue of slavery than the Catholic Church. For an insightful discussion of the historical reasons for this divergence and its implications, see Hart, *Blacks in Bondage*, 114–51.
10 Curtin, *Two Jamaicas*, 168.
11 Craton, "What and Who to Whom and What: The Significance of Slave Resistance," in B.L. Solow and S.L. Engerman, (eds.) *British Capitalism and Caribbean Slavery: The Legacy of Eric Williams* (Cambridge: Cambridge University Press, 1987), 272. It should be recalled that Christianity was also widely employed as a justification for slavery. See N. Girvan, *Aspects of the Political Economy of Race in The Caribbean and The Americas: A Preliminary Interpretation*, Institute of Social and Economic Research, University of the West Indies, Working Paper no. 7 (1975), 5.
12 Erskine, *Decolonizing Theology*, 48; see also Craton, "Slave Resistance," 273 and M. Turner, *Slaves and Missionaries: The Disintegration of Jamai-*

can Slave Society 1787–1834 (Urbana: University of Illinois Press, 1982), 10–11.

13   There is some difference of opinion among historians concerning Lisle's origins. Turner maintains that Lisle was from Savannah, Georgia, in contradiction to Hart who places his origin as Virginia (Turner, *Slaves and Missionaries*, 113; Hart, *Blacks in Bondage*, 118). Hart maintains that Lisle's mistress, resident in Kingston, allowed him to peddle wares in return for a monthly fee, which gave him far more mobility and autonomy than that usually granted (*Blacks in Bondage*, 118). Curtin, however, assigns these same conditions to the life of George Lewis (*Two Jamaicas*, 32).

14   See Curtin, *Two Jamaicas*, 32. I have relied heavily on Curtin's research for information on the Afro-Christian tradition.

15   Turner, *Slaves and Missionaries*, 11.

16   Ibid. Also see Bickell, *The West Indies*, 89–91 and J. Clark, W. Dendy and J.M. Phillippo, *The Voice of Jubilee* (London: John Snow, 1865), 30–1.

17   Turner, *Slaves and Missionaries*, 52–7.

18   The first mission was established near Falmouth using Baker's converts as the core group. The second mission was established in 1816 at Old Harbour, again in response to a request from Native Baptists in the region. See Curtin, *Two Jamaicas*, 36–7.

19   Ibid., 37.

20   Besides the Established and Baptist Churches, there were other churches in Jamaica, but they appealed mainly to the middle classes.

21   The Wesleyans were also committed to emancipation by this date. Turner, *Slaves and Missionaries*, 171.

22   Hart, *Blacks in Bondage*, 119.

23   H.M. Waddell, *Twenty-Nine Years in the West Indies and Central Africa, 1826–1858* (London: Nelson, 1863), 79.

24   M. Reckord, "The Slave Rebellion of 1831," *Jamaica Journal* (June 1969): 26.

25   See for example H. Temperley, *British Anti-Slavery 1833–1870* (London: Longman, 1972); and D.B. Davis, "James Cropper and the British Anti-Slavery Movement, 1821–1823," *Journal of Negro History* 45 (1960): 241–8 and "James Cropper and the British Anti-Slavery Movement, 1823–1833," *Journal of Negro History* 46 (1961): 153–73. The best single overview of the abolition movement is R. Blackburn, *The Overthrow of Colonial Slavery, 1776–1848* (London: Verso, 1988).

26   See Reckord, "Slave Rebellion," 27.

27   As quoted in [B.M. Senior], *Jamaica as it was, as it is, and as it may be ... An Authentic Narrative of the Negro Insurrection in 1831* ... (London:

T. Hurst, 1835), 183. (Authorship is sometimes attributed to B. Martin, Sr.)
28 Curtin, *Two Jamaicas*, 85.
29 H. Bleby, *Death Struggles of Slavery: Being a Narrative of Facts and Incidents, Which Occurred in a British Colony, During the Two Years Immediately Preceding Emancipation* (London: Hamilton, Adams and Co., 1853), 115.
30 Bleby, *Death Struggles*, 110–12.
31 R. Hart, *Slaves Who Abolished Slavery*, vol. 2, *Blacks in Rebellion* (Kingston: Institute of Social and Economic Research, 1985), 253 and Bleby, *Death Struggles*, 110–12.
32 The most notable of such arguments was the claim that emancipation had already been declared in Britain. This point is considered later in this chapter. Hart also identifies some examples of coercion to recruit participants, not directly by Sharpe but by his less persuasive agents. Hart, *Blacks in Rebellion*, 257.
33 Reckord, "Slave Rebellion," 20, and Hart, *Blacks in Rebellion*, 257.
34 G. Blyth, *Reminiscences of Missionary Life* (Edinburgh: Partridge, 1853), 58, Curtin, *Two Jamaicas*, 86 and [Senior], *Jamaica*, 164.
35 Reckord, "Slave Rebellion," 28.
36 Bleby, *Death Struggles*, 119; [Senior], *Jamaica*, 215.
37 As quoted in Turner, *Slaves and Missionaries*, 155. Also see Waddell, *Twenty-Nine Years*, 51, and Bleby, *Death Struggles*, 119.
38 *Scottish Missionary Society and Philanthropic Register* (March, 1832), 198, as quoted in Reckord, "Slave Rebellion," 28.
39 See E. Williams, *Capitalism and Slavery* (New York: G.P. Putnam's Sons, 1966), for an insightful discussion and analysis of the roots of this conflict.
40 Bleby, *Death Struggles*, 111.
41 See E. Halevy, *The Triumph of Reform 1830–1841*, trans. E.I. Watkin, 2nd ed. (London: Benn, 1950), 3–15, and Blackburn, *Overthrow of Colonial Slavery*, 419–72.
42 [Senior], *Jamaica*, 160.
43 Curtin, *Two Jamaicas*, 83.
44 [Senior], *Jamaica*, 170–3, and Bleby, *Death Struggles*, passim.
45 Hart, *Blacks in Rebellion*, 245.
46 *Parliamentary Accounts and Papers*, 47, 276–7; *Votes of the Jamaican Assembly 1831*, 111–112 as quoted in ibid., 246.
47 Bleby, *Death Struggles*, 116.
48 Ibid., 116.
49 Turner, *Slaves and Missionaries*, 149–50.
50 Hart, *Blacks in Rebellion*, 258. On the association of "freedom" with peasant production, see M. Craton, *Testing the Chains: Resistance to*

Slavery in the British West Indies (Ithaca: Cornell University Press, 1982), 332 and passim.
51 W.G. Sewell, *The Ordeal of Free Labor in the British West Indies* (London: Sampson Low, Son and Co., 1862; rpt. ed. New York: A.M. Kelley, 1968), 216. Curtin sees the planters' encouragement of these activities as representative of their interest in an "item of local color." (*Two Jamaicas*, 26).
52 Long was the first to use the spelling "Connu". See E. Long, *The History of Jamaica* (London: T. Lowndes, 1774), 2: 424–5. For a history of the John Canoe dance see Patterson, *Sociology of Slavery*, 243–8.
53 J. Phillippo, *Jamaica: Its Past and Present State*, intro. P. Wright (London: 1843; rpt. ed. London: Dawsons of Pall Mall, 1969), 242–3.
54 An analogy can be drawn here to the Sunday market. Sunday was given to the slaves as their official "day of rest," but many of them used this day for provision grounds cultivation and marketing. The Baptist missionaries in particular vehemently disapproved of the slaves' failure to observe the Sabbath. See Phillippo, *Jamaica: Past and Present*, 274–5.
55 Bleby, *Death Struggles*, 110–12.
56 Curtin, *Two Jamaicas*, 86.
57 This description of events relies largely on Reckord, "Slave Rebellion," [Senior], *Jamaica*, Curtin, *Two Jamaicas*, 83–9, Hart, *Blacks in Rebellion*, 244–337, and Bleby, *Death Struggles*.
58 "Trash" is the term applied to the unuseable part of the sugar cane plant. The trash houses were where this waste was kept.
59 Kensington Estate is identified by Reckord ("Slave Rebellion," 28) as the first site of the rebellion, as stated in the Parliamentary Papers 1831–32, vol. 47, no. 561, p. 200, on the evidence of J.H. Morris. This is confirmed by Hart, *Blacks in Rebellion*, 276–7 and Waddell, *Twenty-Nine Years*, 53–4. Senior, however, (*Jamaica*, 178) identifies Bellefield Estate as the first point of the outbreak.
60 [Senior], *Jamaica*, 179.
61 Bleby describes Sharpe's despair over the destruction of property instigated by the slave rebels. *Death Struggles*, 116–17.
62 [Senior], *Jamaica*, 180. This pro-slavery author suspects that this was because the slaves thought they could use the shops to forge weapons as the revolt continued.
63 See Waddell, *Twenty-Nine Years*, 56–7.
64 CO 137/185, "General Return of Slaves and Whites Killed and Wounded"; Bleby, *Death Struggles*, 37; W.L. Burn, *Emancipation and Apprenticeship in the British West Indies* (London: Jonathan Cape, 1937), 94; Curtin, *Two Jamaicas*, 85.
65 Reckord, "Slave Rebellion," 28–9.

66 The concept is Rudé's developed in connection with pre-industrial popular rebellions. See *The Crowd in History: A Study of Popular Disturbances in France and England 1730–1848* (New York: John Wiley and Sons, 1964), 253 and passim.
67 Reckord, "Slave Rebellion," 30. On the Maroons' involvement in the repression, see Bleby, *Death Struggles*, 20.
68 [Senior], *Jamaica*, 250.
69 CO 137/185; Hart estimates the high figure. *Blacks in Rebellion*, 327.
70 Bleby, *Death Struggles*, 116.
71 Hart, however, maintains that it was not until April 1832 that the revolt was completely crushed (*Blacks in Bondage*, 232).
72 CO 137/185. Bleby estimates as many as fifty thousand were "more or less concerned in the insurrection." (*Death Struggles*, 42).
73 Patterson, *Sociology of Slavery*, 273.
74 CO 137/827/68868/2, Letter from Dunn to Nathan, 13 June 1938. This myth was maintained over the generations, and was widely believed a hundred years later.
75 Craton, *Testing the Chains*, 316.
76 The coloured population largely supported the repression of the slave revolt, and had served in the militia. In fact some coloured regiments were reported to be more active in the massacre of slaves than were the white residents. Once the repression was complete, however, the coloured population refused to continue to support the planters' anti-emancipation movement. Among the most prominent representatives of the coloured middle class was Edward Jordon, who was indicted for "constructive treason" for printing an anti-slavery article in the newspaper he published, though he was acquitted. See Bleby, *Death Struggles*, 9, 133–5 and Turner, *Slaves and Missionaries*, 164–5, 184.
77 Prior to Mulgrave, the Earl of Belmore was the governor of Jamaica. He had remained inactive in the face of the growing conflict provoked by the Colonial Church Union.
78 See Turner, *Slaves and Missionaries*, 197.
79 Eisner, *Jamaica, 1830–1930*, 211.
80 Knibb as quoted in Curtin, *Two Jamaicas*, 116.
81 Phillippo, *Jamaica: Past and Present*, 228.
82 Eisner, *Jamaica, 1830–1930*, 211.

CHAPTER THREE

1 P.D. Curtin, *Two Jamaicas: The Role of Ideas in a Tropical Colony 1830–1865* (n.p.: Harvard University Press, 1955; rpt. ed. New York: Atheneum, 1970), 101.

2 See Lenin, "The State and Revolution: The Marxist Theory of the State and the Tasks of the Proletariat in the Revolution," *Collected Works*, 25: 381–492, and R. Miliband, *The State in Capitalist Society: An Analysis of the Western System of Power* (London: Quartet Books, 1969).
3 See A. Gramsci, *Selections from the Prison Notebooks*, ed. and trans. Q. Hoare and G.N. Smith (New York: International Publishers, 1971), passim.
4 Curtin, *Two Jamaicas*, 103.
5 See H. Campbell, *Rasta and Resistance: From Marcus Garvey to Walter Rodney* (Trenton, N.J.: Africa World Press, 1987), 39.
6 The number of seats in the Council and the Assembly varied over time, and was an issue of some debate. When Crown Colony government was first instituted in 1865, the Assembly was dissolved and only the nominated Council remained. In 1884, however, the Council was divided into elected and nominated portions. In 1895, the number of elected members was raised to fourteen, one member for each parish, but the right to increase the number of nominated seats to an equivalent number (from its traditional nine) was retained by the governor. See section on "Aftermath." For more on the structure and organization of colonial government in Jamaica and the West Indies see H. Wrong, *Government of the West Indies* (London: Oxford University Press, 1923) and D.J. Murray, *The West Indies and the Development of Colonial Government 1801–1834* (London: Oxford University Press, 1965).
7 Figures are according to Governor Eyre, as quoted in E.B. Underhill, *The Tragedy of Morant Bay: A Narrative of the Disturbances in the Island of Jamaica in 1865* (London: Alexander and Shepheard, 1895), 3.
8 J. Bigelow, *Jamaica in 1850: or the Effects of Sixteen Years of Freedom on a Slave Colony* (New York: George E. Putnam, 1851), 38–9. The conversion to pound equivalents is not provided.
9 "Parliamentary Debates of Jamaica," 1865, 47 as quoted in Underhill, *Tragedy of Morant Bay*, 5.
10 The two exceptions were laws concerning vaccination and the formation of industrial schools. Underhill, *Tragedy of Morant Bay*, 4, 43. The list of restrictive legislation included laws against vagrancy and trespass that gave licence to vicious repression. Campbell, *Rasta and Resistance*, 34.
11 Quoted in Underhill, *Tragedy of Morant Bay*, 9.
12 The organ of local government based on the plantations as the prime social and economic unit.
13 Murray, *West Indies and Colonial Government*, 29–33 and Curtin, *Two Jamaicas*, 193.

14 *Facts and Documents Relating to the Alleged Rebellion in Jamaica and the Measures of Repression; Including Notes of the Trial of Mr. Gordon*, Jamaica Papers, no. 1 (London: Jamaica Committee, 1866), 7 and Curtin, *Two Jamaicas*, 163.
15 One of the effects of the lack of medical services was the death of 20–30,000 Jamaicans from cholera between 1850 and 1851. Campbell, *Rasta and Resistance*, 34. Curtin points out that health care and education were also low priorities in Britain (*Two Jamaicas*, 161).
16 Gramsci, *Prison Notebooks*, 210.
17 Curtin, *Two Jamaicas*, 162.
18 The following data provide a breakdown of church involvement in education in Jamaica. (Drawn from *Jamaica Blue Book*, 1863 as cited in *Facts and Documents*, 3).

No. of Schools	No. of Scholars
127 Established Church	8,552
47 Moravians	3,578
66 Jamaica Baptist Union	3,456
42 Wesleyan Methodist	2,530
43 United Presbyterians	3,126
19 London Missionary Society	1,108
26 Endowed Schools	2,592
8 United Methodist Free Church	502
9 American Mission	388
5 Roman Catholic	215
1 Church of Scotland	120
	26,167

(It should be noted that this is a gross indicator only, because it does not reflect attendance by class, nor is it clear whether there were universal criteria for the definition of "scholars").

19 G. Price, *Jamaica and the Colonial Office: Who Caused the Crisis?* (London: Sampson Low, Son, and Marston, 1866), 20. Eisner maintains that in 1896, one-third of the population could read and write (*Jamaica, 1830–1930: A Study in Economic Growth* [Manchester: Manchester University Press, 1961], 231).
20 Curtin, *Two Jamaicas*, 162. The slave population in 1831 was approximately 315,000 (B.W. Higman, *Slave Population and Economy in Jamaica 1807–1834* [Cambridge: Cambridge University Press, 1976], 62); in 1844 the total population, white and black, was something over 377,000 (Eisner, *Jamaica, 1830–1930*, 134). Other churches also showed numerical increases, but none approached the rate of growth displayed by the Baptists.

21 Turner, *Slaves and Missionaries*, 202.
22 Curtin, *Two Jamaicas*, 168 and D. Rowbotham, "The 'Notorious Riot': The Socio-Economic and Political Basis of Paul Bogle's Revolt," Working Paper no. 28, Institute of Social and Economic Research, University of the West Indies, Jamaica (1981): 15–19, 79–92.
23 It should, however, be noted that various missions responded differently to this pressure. Again, the Baptists were the most prepared to intervene directly. See Curtin, *Two Jamaicas*, 114–15, 163.
24 Ibid.
25 Eisner, *Jamaica, 1830–1930*, 213.
26 Rowbotham, *Notorious Riot*, 82.
27 In 1857, merely consulting with an obeah man was punishable by three months of hard labour. See Curtin, *Two Jamaicas*, 168–70, 260 and Campbell, *Rasta and Resistance*, 39.
28 See J. Phillippo, *Jamaica: Its Past and Present State*, intro P. Wright (London: 1843; rpt. ed. London: Dawsons of Pall Mall, 1969), 243–4, 267–79 for an example of the contempt for traditional African customs displayed by the missionaries in Jamaica.
29 E.B. Underhill, *Life of J.M. Phillippo, Missionary in Jamaica* (London: Yates and Alexander, 1881), 302–13. Rowbotham sees the Revival as "part of the tradition of the popular struggle for freedom and equality" in Jamaica (*Notorious Riot*, 18).
30 Underhill, *Tragedy of Morant Bay*, 24.
31 Social and economic conditions are further discussed in this chapter.
32 Underhill, *Tragedy of Morant Bay*, xiv.
33 Ibid., xvi.
34 The Rev. D. East's "Reminiscences," cited in Underhill, *Tragedy of Morant Bay*, 13–14.
35 The Baptist missionaries' report filled thirty-three pages in the *Jamaica Blue Book*, and was completed on the basis of a survey of seventy-three congregations. See Underhill, *Tragedy of Morant Bay*, 35.
36 B. Semmel, *Jamaican Blood and Victorian Conscience: The Governor Eyre Controversy* (Britain: Riverside Press, 1963), 42; D. Hall, *Free Jamaica 1838–1865: An Economic History* (New Haven: Yale University Press, 1959; rpt. ed. Aylesbury: Ginn and Company, 1976), 243.
37 Underhill, *Tragedy of Morant Bay*, 22.
38 Ibid., 180–1 and Rowbotham, *Notorious Riot*, 80.
39 It is not clear how large Bogle's landholdings actually were. They were at least large enough to allow Bogle to vote in the island's elections. See Lord Olivier, *Jamaica: The Blessed Island* (New York: Russell and Russell, 1946), 177.
40 K. Post, *Arise Ye Starvelings: The Jamaica Labour Rebellion of 1938 and its Aftermath* (The Hague: Martinus Nijhoff, 1978), 34.
41 Semmel, *Jamaican Blood*, 38.

42 D. Fletcher, *Personal Recollections of the Honorable George W. Gordon* (London: Elliot Stock, 1987) as cited in Rowbotham, *Notorious Riot*, 83–5. Rowbotham also notes that the Revival in Kingston was launched in Gordon's tabernacle (*Notorious Riot*, 83).
43 Semmel, *Jamaican Blood*, 40.
44 Underhill, *Tragedy of Morant Bay*, 60. It should be remembered that the missionaries were ineffective in reversing the course of the slave rebellion in 1831, in conditions where Baptist mission influence appeared to be greater.
45 Blue Books Despatch, 19 August 1865, 247 as quoted in Underhill, *Tragedy of Morant Bay*, 39.
46 Underhill, *Tragedy of Morant Bay*, 30–2.
47 As quoted in Semmel, *Jamaican Blood*, 45.
48 Underhill, *Tragedy of Morant Bay*, 55.
49 Rowbotham, *Notorious Riot*, 85 and Semmel, *Jamaican Blood*, 45–6.
50 *Facts and Documents*, 12; Underhill, *Tragedy of Morant Bay*, 59.
51 *Colonial Standard*, 21 October 1865, in *Facts and Documents*, 12.
52 *Facts and Documents*, 12; Underhill, *Tragedy of Morant Bay*, 59.
53 As quoted in Hall, *Free Jamaica*, 246 and Campbell, *Rasta and Resistance*, 36.
54 The Royal Commission that investigated the Morant Bay events concluded that if stones were in fact thrown, the action was most likely taken by some women standing by, not by the main participants in the incident (*Royal Commission Report*, 12, as cited in Underhill, *Tragedy of Morant Bay*, 62).
55 *Facts and Documents*, 14; Hall, *Free Jamaica*, 247. Estates at Amity Hall and Golden Groves were captured by rebels. Campbell, *Rasta and Resistance*, 36.
56 As quoted in Hall, *Free Jamaica*, 246.
57 Hall, *Free Jamaica*, 250–1. Curtin also maintains that the Morant Bay revolt focused on class rather than racial divisions (*Two Jamaicas*, 175). See also B. Semmel, "The Issue of 'Race' in the British Reaction to the Morant Bay Uprising of 1865," *Caribbean Studies* 2 (October 1962). The history of struggle of the Jamaican Maroons represents a study in the transition from armed resistance against, to armed defense of, the colonial authorities. For a detailed history see R.C. Dallas, *The History of the Maroons* (London: A. Strahan, 1803).
58 See Olivier, *Jamaica: The Blessed Island*, 176.
59 Underhill, *Tragedy of Morant Bay*, 63. It is unclear what church the Reverend Herschell was connected with, but he was under severe criticism from Underhill, who represented the Baptists.
60 *Facts and Documents*, 15. Baron von Ketelhodt's name is here spelled "Ketelholdt" in the original in both places where it is quoted. I have corrected it.

61 Campbell, *Rasta and Resistance*, 36, and *Facts and Documents*, 14.
62 Hall, *Free Jamaica*, 248.
63 Underhill, *Tragedy of Morant Bay*, 48.
64 *The Freeman*, 3 January 1866, as quoted in Underhill, *Tragedy of Morant Bay*, 51.
65 As quoted in Underhill, *Tragedy of Morant Bay*, 50; and J. Gorrie, *Illustrations of Martial Law in Jamaica. Compiled from the Report of the Royal Commissioners, and Other Blue Books Laid Before Parliament*, Jamaica Papers, no. 6 (London: Jamaica Committee, 1867), 44–5.
66 *Commissioners' Report*, 37, as quoted in Gorrie, *Illustrations*, 44–5.
67 See Gorrie, *Illustrations*, 29–102.
68 Semmel, *Jamaican Blood*, 36–7.
69 Underhill, *Tragedy of Morant Bay*, 181.
70 See ibid., 158–84.
71 Quoted in *Missionary Herald*, 1866, 8.
72 Underhill, *Tragedy of Morant Bay*, 170–1.
73 It is also significant that obeah men were summarily executed during the repression. See M. Craton, *Testing the Chains: Resistance to Slavery in the British West Indies* (Ithaca: Cornell University Press, 1982), on the similarities between the revolts of 1831 and 1865 regarding the links between "religious revival" and social resistance (327).
74 Olivier, *Jamaica: The Blessed Isle*, 178, 182; T. Munroe, *The Politics of Constitutional Decolonization: Jamaica, 1944–62* (Jamaica: Institute of Social and Economic Research, 1972), 17; Underhill, *Tragedy of Morant Bay*, 24–5.
75 Eisner, *Jamaica, 1830–1930*, 211.
76 Eyre and the Custos of St Ann's parish maintained that the petition actually appeared only as the result of the climate of discontent sparked by Underhill's letter (CO 137/390, Royes to Austin, 18 April 1865). This interpretation is also held by Semmel (*Jamaican Blood*, 43). Underhill points out, however, that his letter was not distributed until several days after the drafting of the St Ann's petition (*Tragedy of Morant Bay*, 164).
77 CO 137/390.
78 CO 137/392.
79 Semmel, *Jamaican Blood*, 44.
80 Ibid. See also Rowbotham's discussion of the peasantry in the 1860s (*The Notorious Riot*, 36ff.) and Campbell, (*Rasta and Rebellion*, 33). Though Rowbotham stresses the "lumpen" character of the masses and Campbell overstates the element of proletarianization, these authors identify the role of land as a means of bargaining with the planters. See "Organic Ideology" in this chapter.
81 Semmel, *Jamaican Blood*, 41, 45.

82 Hall points out that emotional outbursts cannot be the sole subject of political analysis, however, (*Free Jamaica*, 250).
83 Olivier, *Jamaica: The Blessed Island*, 173; Underhill, *Tragedy of Morant Bay*, 60.
84 Semmel, *Jamaican Blood*, 45. Rowbotham chastises the Jamaican people for holding to a "naïve monarchism," but he fails to see the character of this adherence to the Crown as a tool of struggle against the Colonial system as well as a source of its survival. *Notorious Riot*, 22–3.
85 Cited in Underhill, *Tragedy of Morant Bay*, 159.
86 Curtin, *Two Jamaicas*, 110.
87 Ibid., 194. In a detailed examination of local crime data in the years prior to the 1865 events, Rowbotham convincingly indicates the extent of crimes committed not only across class, but among sections of the exploited themselves. The general rise of plunder, prostitution, and vagabondage leads Rowbotham to conclude that "it was not widespread anti-colonial militancy nor the flourishing of popular organizations, but deep despair, social chaos and a deterioration in their very moral fibre which spread as the main tendency amongst the people" (*Notorious Riot*, 78). Virtually every situation of failed ruling class hegemony is accompanied by a general decay of social norms and a rise of despair, but this is also the precondition to an alternative form of social organization that inspires resistance. Rowbotham's point therefore seems overstated. He sees such an alternative rallied under the leadership of Bogle, and identifies the religious element as an important feature. The anti-colonial sentiment harboured under the ostensible love for the Crown, however, is not identified, though it is recognized on page 15 of this same work. This appears to be a contradiction in the analysis, misguided in the first instance, accurate in the second.
88 Parliamentary Papers, 1866, 21 [C.3683–I], 1099–1100, cited in Curtin, *Two Jamaicas*, 194.
89 Eisner, *Jamaica, 1830–1930*, 217–18; Underhill, *Tragedy of Morant Bay*, 5, 8, 26; CO 137/390, "The Humble Petition of the Poor people of Jamaica and parish of Saint Anns."
90 *Facts and Documents*, 32.
91 Eisner, *Jamaica, 1830–1930*, 366–7.
92 CO 137/390 "The Humble Petition"; *Facts and Documents*, 9.
93 Price, *Jamaica and the Colonial Office*, iv; W.G. Sewell, *The Ordeal of Free Labor in the British West Indies* (London: Sampson Low, Son, and Co., 1862; rpt. ed. New York: A.M. Kelley, 1968), 286; Rowbotham, *Notorious Riot*, 51.
94 CO 137/390, Royes to Austin.
95 Eisner, *Jamaica, 1830–1930*, 231.

96 As quoted in Olivier, *Jamaica: The Blessed Island*, 177.
97 Semmel, *Jamaican Blood*, 46.
98 Underhill, *Tragedy of Morant Bay*, 59.
99 *Daily News*, n.d., cited in *Facts and Documents*, 14.
100 As quoted in *Facts and Documents*, 17. There is considerable debate regarding the amount of planning and organization involved in the revolt itself, however, because Eyre's supporters were compelled to exaggerate the insurrectionary threat as a justification for the extent of the repression. See Rowbotham, *Notorious Riot*, 88–91.
101 Underhill, *Tragedy of Morant Bay*, 62–3.
102 Hall, *Free Jamaica*, 253; Rowbotham, *Notorious Riot*, 88; and Campbell, *Rasta and Resistance*, 35.
103 Hall, *Free Jamaica*, 252. "Demagogues" was the term applied to the vocal middle class political opponents within the government.
104 Ibid., 251; Curtin, *Two Jamaicas*, 196–7.
105 Eyre's address to the Legislature, 7 November 1865, as quoted in Curtin, *Two Jamaicas*, 198.
106 Hall, *Free Jamaica*, 251–2.
107 Underhill, *Tragedy of Morant Bay*, 80.
108 Ibid., 80–1.
109 Ibid., 182–3.
110 It should also be noted that the Church of England was disestablished in 1870.
111 R. Hart, *The Origin and Development of the People of Jamaica* (Kingston: By the Author, 1952), 15–16.
112 Underhill, *Tragedy of Morant Bay*, 79.
113 Curtin, *Two Jamaicas*, 202.
114 Underhill, *Tragedy of Morant Bay*, 78.
115 Grant was appointed following the temporary governorship of Sir Henry Storks, sworn in earlier in the same year.
116 Eisner, *Jamaica, 1830–1930*, 358–9, 340, 344 and 372.
117 Ibid., 218.
118 Munroe, *Politics*, 11.
119 Rowbotham, *Notorious Riot*, 15; see also Hall, *Free Jamaica*, 263.
120 As quoted in Semmel, *Jamaican Blood*, 67.
121 Cited in W.F. Finlason, *A History of the Jamaica Case, Founded upon Official or Authentic Documents ... Arising Out of the Case* (London: Chapman and Hall, [1868]), Preface, n.p.
122 Eyre was finally acquitted. For full details of the British response to the Morant Bay rebellion, see Semmel, *Jamaican Blood*, 56–180.
123 Ibid., 169.
124 Eisner, *Jamaica, 1830–1930*, 368–9.

CHAPTER FOUR

1 M. St Pierre, "The 1938 Jamaica Disturbances, A Portrait of Mass Reaction Against Colonialism," *Social and Economic Studies* 27 (June 1978): 173. St Pierre also points out that of those eligible, only 36 per cent voted in 1930 and 41 per cent in 1935, reducing the percentages of the population that actually voted to 3 per cent and 2.5 per cent respectively (St Pierre, "Jamaica Disturbances," 173).
2 G. Eisner, *Jamaica, 1830–1930: A Study in Economic Growth* (Manchester: Manchester University Press, 1961), 362.
3 J. Carnegie, *Some Aspects of Jamaica's Politics: 1918–1938*, Cultural Heritage Series, vol. 4 (n.p.: Institute of Jamaica, 1973), 28.
4 Ibid., 29.
5 Ibid., 30.
6 F.L. Ambursley, "The Working Class in the Third World: A Study in Class Consciousness and Class Action in Jamaica, 1919–1952" (BA dissertation, University of Birmingham, 1978), 32.
7 The word is coined by Simpson. See G.E. Simpson, "Jamaica Revivalist Cults," *Social and Economic Studies* 5 (June 1956): 337.
8 See A.A. Brooks, *History of Bedwardism or the Jamaica Native Baptist Free Church* (Kingston: The Gleaner Co., 1917); K. Post, *Arise Ye Starvelings: The Jamaica Labour Rebellion of 1938 and its Aftermath* (The Hague: Martinus Nijhoff, 1978), 6–8; G. Eaton, *Alexander Bustamante and Modern Jamaica* (Kingston: Kingston Publishers Ltd., 1975), 21–2; and M.W. Beckwith, *Black Roadways* (Chapel Hill: University of North Carolina Press, 1929), 157–75.
9 Ambursley, "Working Class," 20.
10 As quoted in ibid., 20.
11 Simpson, "Jamaica Revivalist Cults," 337 n.
12 Ibid.
13 See Beckwith, *Black Roadways* on the revivalist tradition. The charge of insanity was useful to the authorities in repressing Bedward's political message. See B. Chevannes, "Jamaican Lower Class Religious Struggles Against Oppression," (MA Thesis, University of the West Indies, 1971), cited in H. Campbell, *Rasta and Resistance: From Marcus Garvey to Walter Rodney* (Trenton, N.J.: Africa World Press, 1987), 49.
14 Post, *Arise Ye Starvelings*, 8.
15 A.J. Garvey, *Garvey and Garveyism*, intro. J.H. Clarke (New York: Collier Books, 1963), 14. See also for further biographical information on Marcus Garvey, T. Mackie, *The Great Marcus Garvey* (London: Hansib Publishing, 1987); R. Lewis, *Marcus Garvey: Anti-Colonial Champion* (New Jersey: Africa World Press, 1988); E.D. Cronon, *Black Masses: The Story of Marcus Garvey* (Wisconsin: University of Wisconsin Press, 1969).

16 Garvey, *Garvey*, 48.
17 *Daily Gleaner*, 12 December 1928 as quoted in R. Lewis, "Political Aspects of Garvey's Work in Jamaica 1929–35," *Jamaica Journal* 7 (March-June 1973): 32.
18 Eaton, *Alexander Bustamante*, 23.
19 Ibid.
20 For a more detailed account of Garvey's politics see Lewis, "Political Aspects"; "A Political Study of Garveyism in Jamaica and London: 1914–1940" (MA dissertation, University of the West Indies, 1971); and in particular, *Marcus Garvey*.
21 For example, see Carnegie, *Some Aspects*, 111.
22 K. Post, "The Politics of Protest in Jamaica, 1938: Some Problems of Analysis and Conceptualization," *Social and Economic Studies* 18 (December 1969): 387.
23 Garvey's political activities, particularly the relative emphasis of his politics regarding class, racial, and anti-colonial issues, has become a subject of considerable debate among contemporary scholars. Lewis and Campbell have argued against Cronon that the implications of Garvey's back-to-Africa movement have been exaggerated, a reflection of a failure to understand the importance of the message of black pride in conditions of the 1920s in both the colonial and imperial worlds. The danger in simply dismissing those who criticize Garvey for his undeniable, if inconsistent, illusions in both black and white capitalist governments, however, is a similar dismissal of the contradictory directions pursued by later black nationalist movements. For a very clear and balanced account of the relationship between black nationalism and class politics from a Marxist perspective, see P. Alexander, *Racism, Resistance and Revolution* (London: Bookmarks, 1987), 58–159.
24 Carnegie, *Some Aspects*, 96. This number excludes trade unions.
25 Ibid., 65–69.
26 CO 137/820/68868, Denham to Gore, 20 September 1937.
27 R. Hart, *The Origin and Development of the People of Jamaica* (Kingston: By the Author, 1952), 26. Hart further notes that in 1929 the Jamaica Trade and Labour Union was formed as a result of this effort, though the union failed to operate after a few months.
28 Lord W.E. Moyne, Chairman, *West India Royal Commission Report*, Command June 1945, no. 6607 (London: 1945). (Hereafter referred to as the *Moyne Report*), 422.
29 See ibid., 197–8.
30 Carnegie, *Some Aspects*, 28.
31 R. Hart, correspondence to A. Bakan, 7 July 1985.
32 Eaton, *Alexander Bustamante*, 19.

33 Attempts to form trade unions occurred as early as 1898, when the Artisans' Union was formed by craft workers. The Printers' Union (in which Marcus Garvey was active for a short period before leaving Jamaica for the first time), was formed in 1907, and organization among workers in the tobacco trade developed in 1908. There were several other attempts to form lasting trade unions in the early 1900s but by and large they did not survive. The unions often lacked internal cohesion and were unable to pose a lasting threat to the employing class. Furthermore, the most promising working-class leaders were among the first to emigrate when opportunities for more secure employment arose. See G. Eaton, "The Development of Trade Unionism in Jamaica–W.I." (Ph.D. dissertation, McGill University, 1961), 198–242.

34 It should be noted that the Jamaica Union of Teachers, founded in 1894, was not a labour union as such, but "the vehicle of a prestige profession which almost alone among professions of colonial Jamaica provided an avenue of social-occupational mobility." G.K. Lewis, *The Growth of the Modern West India* (New York: Modern Reader, 1968), 173. For a detailed analysis of the development and evolution of teachers in Jamaica as political actors, see H. Goulbourne, *Teachers, Education and Politics in Jamaica 1892–1972* (London: Macmillan, 1988).

35 Coombs had served in the Jamaica Constabulary from 1919 to 1922, and in the West India Regiment until 1926. In 1936 he worked as a contractor for the Public Works Department, where he formed the JWTU among his fellow labourers. Coombs was among the "few truly working-class agitators and trade union leaders" to rise from the ranks of Jamaican labour (Eaton, "Development of Trade Unionism" 237–8). Buchanan, a fellow contractor with Coombs, had lived and worked in Cuba, where he was influenced by both the Communist Party and the Cuban section of the UNIA in the 1930s. He earned the mantle of "Jamaica's first real Marxist," and became an active trade union leader (Post, *Arise Ye Starvelings*, 5).

36 Eaton, "Development of Trade Unionism," 237.

37 Ibid., 238.

38 See Eaton, *Alexander Bustamante*, 32; and "A Personal Memoir by Norman W. Manley," in *Bustamante and his Letters*, F. Hill, intro. and ed., (Kingston: Kingston Publishers, 1976), 47–9. Significant portions of Hill's contribution to this collection appear nearly verbatim in the pages of Eaton's *Alexander Bustamante*, which was published one year prior to Hill's work. Cf. Hill, *Bustamante and his Letters*, 21–5, and Eaton, *Alexander Bustamante*, 31–5. Hill's collection has only been drawn upon for works by Bustamante and Manley.

39 "Personal Memoir," 47.

40 Eaton, *Alexander Bustamante*, 15.
41 Ibid.
42 Carnegie, *Some Aspects*, 102.
43 Eaton, *Alexander Bustamante*, 34.
44 Ibid., 35.
45 *Richard Hart Papers*, Hart to O'Meally, 1 June 1938. (The *Hart Papers* will hereafter be abbreviated *H.P.*)
46 See Eaton, "Development of Trade Unionism," 242–3.
47 St Pierre, "Jamaica Disturbances," 172–3.
48 Post, *Arise Ye Starvelings*, 277.
49 Eaton, *Alexander Bustamante*, 40.
50 *H.P.*, Diary of Sunday and Monday.
51 As quoted in Eaton, *Alexander Bustamante*, 43.
52 O.W. Phelps, "Rise and Fall of the Labour Movement in Jamaica," *Social and Economic Studies* 9 (December 1960): 431.
53 During the brief period that Bustamante was in jail, Kenneth Hill recommended in an emergency session of the National Reform Association – an organization which ceased to function soon after the founding of the People's National Party, which attracted its core membership – that the dock workers should form a new union with Bustamante as leader. The Association voted in favour of the proposal and began the work of signing up members, but the new union was under the sole authority and direction of Bustamante from its inception.
54 Phelps, "Rise of the Labour Movement," 444.
55 W.H. Knowles, *Trade Union Development and Industrial Relations in the British West Indies* (Berkeley: University of California Press, 1959), 144.
56 Phelps, "Rise of the Labour Movement," 440.
57 This "movementist" tendency among trade unions had been identified as characteristic of the Commonwealth Caribbean. See B.C. Roberts, *Labour in the Tropical Territories of the Commonwealth* (London: Bell, 1964), 27.
58 G.T. Daniel, "Labour and Nationalism in the British Caribbean," in *Annals of the American Academy of Political and Social Sciences* 310 (March 1957): 165.
59 E.J. Hobsbawn, *Primitive Rebels: Studies in Archaic Forms of Social Movement in the 19th and 20th Centuries* (New York: W.W. Norton, 1959), 126–50.
60 Ibid., 127.
61 Ibid., 130.
62 Ibid., 132.

63 For a historical assessment of the dual role played by trade unions under capitalism as organs of both working-class struggle from below, and control over the working class from above, see R. Hyman, *Marxism and the Sociology of Trade Unionism* (London: Pluto Press, 1971), and T. Cliff and D. Gluckstein, *Marxism and Trade Union Struggle: The General Strike of 1926* (London: Bookmarks, 1986), 7–79.
64 Hobsbawm, *Primitive Rebels*, 132–3.
65 The religious vocabulary of Bustamante's agitation has been widely identified, if rarely analysed. See for example, Ambursley, "Working Class," 32 and Eaton, *Alexander Bustamante*, 53.
66 B.St J. Hamilton, intro. and ed., *Bustamante: Anthology of a Hero* (Kingston: Publications and Productions, n.d.), 68.
67 F. Henriques and C. Rickards in *Latin America and the Caribbean: A Handbook*, ed. C. Veliz (Blond, 1968), 329, as quoted in Ambursley, "Working Class," 37.
68 Such a perspective was of course compatible with Bustamante's own class interests as a small businessman.
69 The JBPA was formed in the late 1920s. Though it included some peasants in its numbers, it was essentially an organization of large banana producers and was designed to protect their position on the international market.
70 Letter to *Daily Gleaner*, 3 July 1935, in Hill, *Bustamante and his Letters*, 62.
71 Letter to *Daily Gleaner*, 27 June 1935, in ibid., 58.
72 Eaton, *Alexander Bustamante*, 223; Knowles, *Trade Union Development*, 59; Phelps, "Rise of the Labour Movement," 432.
73 Letter to *Daily Gleaner*, 18 October 1935, in Hill, *Bustamante and his Letters*, 73. In this edition, the word "soul" is misspelled "sould". I have corrected it.
74 Eaton, *Alexander Bustamante*, 55.
75 See Ambursley, "Working Class," 32.
76 *Daily Gleaner*, 4 June 1938.
77 Ibid., 27 August 1938.
78 See Knowles, *Trade Union Development*, 59.
79 As quoted in Eaton, *Alexander Bustamante*, 62–3.
80 Letter to *Daily Gleaner*, 23 August 1938, in Hill, *Bustamante and his Letters*, 120.
81 Eaton, *Alexander Bustamante*, 73–5.
82 Hamilton, *Bustamante: Anthology*, 64.
83 Letter to *Daily Gleaner*, 23 August 1938, in Hill, *Bustamante and his Letters*, 120.
84 Letter to *Daily Gleaner*, 4 November 1937 in ibid., 114.

85 See Hamilton, *Bustamante: Anthology*, 68.
86 Eaton, *Alexander Bustamante*, 73.
87 Carnegie, *Some Aspects*, 93.
88 Ibid., 111.
89 CO 137/827/68868/2, Garvey to McDonald, 26 May 1938.
90 Letter to *Daily Gleaner*, 20 September 1935, in Hill, *Bustamante and his Letters*, 68.
91 *Daily Gleaner*, 27 August 1938.
92 See J.T. Murphy, *Preparing for Power: A Critical Study of the History of the British Working Class Movement* (1934; rpt. London: Pluto Press, 1972); R. Miliband, *Parliamentary Socialism* (London: Allen and Unwin, 1972); and T. Cliff and D. Gluckstein, *The Labour Party – A Marxist History* (London: Bookmarks, 1988).
93 The second Labour Government was in office from 1929 to 1931; the first was elected in 1924. During World War II, the Labour Party was part of a Coalition Government and was re-elected with a clear majority in 1945. The party stayed in office until 1951.
94 J. Harrod, *Trade Union Foreign Policy: A Study of British and American Trade Union Activities in Jamaica* (New York: Doubleday, 1972), 207.
95 Ibid., 208. The ILO is the International Labour Office.
96 See M. Cole, *The Story of Fabian Socialism* (Stanford: Stanford University Press, 1961; rpt. 1978) and A.M. McBriar, *Fabian Socialism and English Politics 1884–1918* (Britain: Willmer Brothers and Haram, 1962; rpt. Cambridge: Cambridge University Press, 1966) for more on the Fabian tradition and its influence in British politics.
97 *Labour in the United Kingdom Dependencies* (London: British Government Publication, 1957), 8, as quoted in Harrod, *Trade Union Foreign Policy*, 208.
98 Eaton, *Alexander Bustamante*, 20.
99 *Labour Supervision in the Colonial Empire, 1937–1943* (London: HMSO, 1943), 1. Harrod also draws attention to this report (*Trade Union Foreign Policy*, 209).
100 See R. Nettleford, ed. with notes and intro., *Manley and the New Jamaica: Selected Speeches and Writings 1938–68* (London: Longman Caribbean, 1971), editor's intro., 8.
101 Nettleford, *Manley and the New Jamaica*, 11.
102 This was indicated by the poor showing of the PNP in the first general election held in 1944, which followed Bustamante's breach with Manley and the PNP and the formation of the Jamaica Labour Party as a political competitor. See section on "Aftermath."
103 The local commission appointed to investigate the disturbances of 1938 heaped praise upon Manley, but made little mention of Bustamante except to note his inflammatory speeches. See *Report (with Ap-*

pendices) of the Commission appointed to enquire into Disturbances which Occurred in Jamaica Between the 23rd May and the 8th June, 1938 (Kingston: Jamaica Government Printing Office, 1938); see also Eaton, "Development of Trade Unionism," 279–80.

104 The turnabout came in 1961, when Bustamante was leading the JLP as the Opposition in the Jamaican House. At this point the JLP opposed Jamaica's participation in a West Indian Federation, advocated by the PNP, in a national referendum. The JLP position won out, and in the election that took place in April 1962, the party was swept back into power. In August 1962, Jamaican independence was declared, with Bustamante at the helm championing the cause that had previously been backed exclusively by the PNP and Norman Manley.

105 Letter to *Daily Gleaner*, 15 April 1935 in Hamilton, *Bustamante: Anthology*, 50.

106 Letter to *Daily Gleaner*, 16 May 1935, in Hill, *Bustamante and his Letters*, 57.

107 Letter to *Daily Gleaner*, 24 January 1936, in ibid., 86.

108 *Daily Gleaner*, 14 May 1938.

109 As quoted in Hamilton, *Bustamante: Anthology*, 46.

110 *Daily Gleaner*, 13 April 1938.

111 H.P., Hart to O'Meally, 1 June 1938.

112 Ibid.

113 CO 137/827/68868/7, "Disturbances, Restoration of Order Indemnity Law," 5 August 1938.

114 Ambursley, "Working Class," 27.

115 Post, "Politics," 389 and *Arise Ye Starvelings*, 279.

116 St Pierre, "Jamaica Disturbances," 186–7.

117 Ibid., 188, and *Report ... into Disturbances*, 7.

118 *Annual General Report of Jamaica* (Kingston: 1939), 39.

119 *Report of Board of Conciliation appointed by Governor Sir Edward Denham* (Jamaica: Jamaica Government Printing Office, 26 May 1938), 1.

120 Eaton, *Alexander Bustamante*, 56.

121 St Pierre, "Jamaica Disturbances," 189.

122 H.P., Diary of Sunday and Monday.

123 K. Marx, *The Poverty of Philosophy*, intro. F. Engels (New York: International Publishers, 1847 ed.; rpt. 1963) 172–3.

124 Hart, *Origin*, 14.

125 See Post, *Arise Ye Starvelings*, 282.

126 St Pierre, "Jamaica Disturbances," 185.

127 Ibid., 187.

128 Phelps, "Rise of the Labour Movement," 425; Post, *Arise Ye Starvelings*, 295.

129 Post, *Arise Ye Starvelings*, 276–7.

130 See ibid., 295–6.
131 Jamaican Government Commission to investigate conditions in August 1935, (no ref.), as quoted in Major St J. Orde-Browne, *Labour Conditions in the West Indies*, July 1939, Command no. 6070 (London: 1939), 79.
132 *Jamaica Standard*, 8 June 1938 as quoted in Post, *Arise Ye Starvelings*, 295.
133 Post, *Arise Ye Starvelings*, 296.
134 CO 137/827/68868/2, Dunn to Nathan, 13 June 1938.
135 Ibid.
136 *Plain Talk*, 30 April 1938.
137 Post, *Arise Ye Starvelings*, 249.
138 This is the exchange equivalent provided by St Pierre ("Jamaica Disturbances," 177). It is commonly translated into an even four shillings.
139 Ibid., 177–8.
140 As quoted in Phelps, "Rise of the Labour Movement," 425.
141 *Jamaica Standard*, 4 June 1938, quoted in Post, *Arise Ye Starvelings*, 263.
142 Post, *Arise Ye Starvelings*, 70.
143 Eaton, *Alexander Bustamante*, 56.
144 Ibid.
145 As quoted in Post, *Arise Ye Starvelings*, 283.
146 CO 137/820/68868, Denham to Gore.
147 See Post, *Arise Ye Starvelings*, 295.
148 V.I. Lenin, "What is to be Done? Burning Questions of Our Movement," *Collected Works*, 5:347–529.
149 Hart, *Origin*, 14.
150 See Eaton, "Development of Trade Unionism," 203–13.
151 Other factors besides the objective conditions of the labour process affected the development of a trade union tradition on the Kingston waterfront – exposure to international influences and local leadership, for example – though to expand upon these points would take us beyond the scope of this discussion.
152 Eaton, *Alexander Bustamante*, 44–6.
153 Phelps, "Rise of the Labour Movement," 440.
154 Post, *Arise Ye Starvelings*, 296.
155 Eaton, "Development of Trade Unionism," 237.
156 Phelps, "Rise of the Labour Movement," 444.
157 Eaton, "Development of Trade Unionism," 348.
158 Ibid., 349.
159 *Daily Gleaner*, 24 July 1938.
160 St Pierre, "Jamaica Disturbances," 179–81.

161 Phelps, "Rise of the Labour Movement," 436.
162 The proposed constitution was prepared in consultation with a delegation to London that included Manley, but excluded Bustamante, much to the latter's outrage. See *Daily Gleaner*, 27 January 1943.
163 Stone, "Political Aspects," 156.
164 Post, *Arise Ye Starvelings*, 311.
165 Knowles, *Trade Union Development*, 44.
166 Carlyle Dunkley, *Lecture*, Trade Union Education Institute, University of the West Indies, Mona (6 May 1981).
167 See Lewis, *Growth of the Modern West Indies*, 91.
168 "Mass Strike, Party and Trade Unions," in R. Luxemburg, *Selected Political Writings*, ed. and intro., D. Howard (New York: Monthly Review Press, 1971), 236–7.
169 Orde-Browne, *Labour Conditions*, 43–4.
170 Ibid., 50, and *Moyne Report*, 44.
171 Orde-Browne, *Labour Conditions*, 46. Harrod points out that the Moyne Report had a somewhat different view of the role of the Labour Department, seeing its function as the protection of workers' interests (*Trade Union Foreign Policy*, 220–31). Both reports, however, perceived the Labour Department to be a state regulatory body, including significant representation from employers.
172 Ambursley, "Working Class," 31.
173 Harrod, *Trade Union Foreign Policy*, 209.
174 See R. Dahrendorf, *Class and Class Conflict in Industrial Society* (Stanford: Stanford University Press, 1959), 65–6.
175 R. Hyman, *Strikes*, 2nd. rev. ed. (n.p.: Fontana/Collins, 1972), 79.
176 H.P., *Jamaica Standard*, 6 August 1938. Kirkwood was the Managing Director of the West Indies Sugar Company in Jamaica.
177 *Moyne Report*, 204.
178 *Daily Gleaner*, 15 February 1939.
179 4 November 1937, in Hill, *Bustamante and his Letters*, 114.
180 There are numerous theories that attempt to explain this phenomenon. Some emphasize the workers' disdain for leadership representatives from among their own ranks (Knowles, *Trade Union Development*, 61; Eaton, *Alexander Bustamante*, 54). Other more convincing analyses identify the source in the structural and ideological traditions within the Jamaican working class, allowing middle class opportunistic leadership to come forth without challenge (Post, "Politics," 383; Ambursley, "Working Class," 32). The latter approach recognizes the complex interaction of class forces in the relationship between trade union leadership and membership, though it fails to identify the specific historical elements and traditions in Jamaican working-class consciousness that engendered this interaction.

181 Phelps, "Rise of the Labour Movement," 448.
182 Ibid.
183 Eaton, *Alexander Bustamante*, 62.
184 The waterfront strike took place despite the union leader's internment, closing all of Kingston's wharves except for the United Fruit Company's between 8 and 19 September.
185 *Labour Position – Annual Report from the Year Ended 1940* (Jamaican Government Department of Labour, 1940); see also Phelps, "Rise of the Labour Movement," 449.
186 Knowles, *Trade Union Development*, 12.
187 Phelps, "Rise of the Labour Movement," 449.
188 This charge became a recurring argument in the PNP's opposition to Bustamante and the BITU/JLP. See for example, *Public Opinion*, 1 November 1944.
189 See Eaton, *Alexander Bustamante*, 82–3 and Phelps, "Rise of the Labour Movement," 450.
190 See Munroe, *Marxist 'Left'*.
191 Ibid., 37.
192 Ibid., 36–7.
193 Richard Hart, Letter to A. Bakan, 7 April 1979.
194 Eaton, *Alexander Bustamante*, 88.
195 K. Post, *Strike the Iron: A Colony at War, 1939–1945*, 2 vols. (The Hague: Humanities Press, 1981), 491.
196 Munroe, *Politics*, 43.
197 Eaton, *Alexander Bustamante*, 89.
198 In raising this charge Bustamante was attempting to reconfirm the historical association of the coloured middle class with the white planters in the minds of Jamaica's poor. See L. Lindsay, "The Myth of Independence: Middle Class Politics and Non-Mobilization in Jamaica," Institute for Social and Economic Research, University of the West Indies, Working Paper no. 6 (1975).
199 These and subsequent election figures drawn from Post, *Strike the Iron*, 2: 490–5.
200 Ibid., 494.
201 These included the Jamaica Liberal Party, the United Rentpayers Party, the Jag Smith Political Party, and the Federation of Citizens Associations. See Post, *Strike the Iron*, 2: 502 n.32, and *Strike the Iron*, 1: 66.
202 Post, *Strike the Iron*, 1: 490.
203 Knowles, *Trade Union Development*, 68.
204 Harrod, *Trade Union Foreign Policy*, 202–3.

CHAPTER FIVE

1 The term is borrowed from E.P. Thompson, "Eighteenth-Century English Society: Class Struggle Without Class?," *Social History* 3 (May 1978): 154.
2 G.K. Lewis, *The Growth of the Modern West Indies* (New York: Modern Reader, 1966), 78.
3 Hart Papers, PNP *Newsletter*, 1, no. 16 (February-March 1952); PNP *Newsletter* 1, no. 21 (August 1952); *Daily Gleaner*, (3 March 1952); *Public Opinion* (3 March 1952).
4 H.P., PNP *Newsletter* 1, no. 21 (August 1952).
5 See T. Munroe, *The Politics of Constitutional Decolonization: Jamaica, 1944–62* (Jamaica: Institute of Social and Economic Research, 1972), Munroe develops the argument regarding the increasing similarity of the two main parties in Jamaica in considerable detail, relying on original party and legislative documents. I have relied on his analysis, which is only asserted here in order to illustrate the conditions under which the ideological traditions of the producing classes became incorporated into the institutionalized political system.
6 H.P., PNP *Newsletter* 1–21 (August 1952).
7 Ibid.
8 O. Jefferson, "Some Aspects of the Post-War Economic Development of Jamaica," *Readings in the Political Economy of the Caribbean*, ed. N. Girvan and O. Jefferson (Kingston: New World Group Ltd., 1974), 109.
9 See C. Holzberg, "Social Stratification, Cultural Nationalism and Political Economy in Jamaica: The Myths of Development and the Anti-White Bias," *Canadian Review of Sociology and Anthropology* 14, no. 4 (November 1977): 384.
10 Ibid., 111.
11 N. Girvan et al, "Unemployment in Jamaica," *Readings in the Political Economy of the Caribbean*, 267.
12 As quoted in G. Eaton, *Alexander Bustamante and Modern Jamaica* (Kingston: Kingston Publishers, Ltd., 1975), 115.
13 *People's National Party Group Leaders Training Course*, as quoted in Munroe, *Politics*, 93.
14 M. Manley, *A Voice at the Workplace – Reflections on Colonialism and the Jamaican Worker* (London: Andre Deutsch Ltd., 1975), 133–4. Michael Manley, son of PNP leader Norman Washington Manley, was head of the NWU at the time of these events.
15 International Bank for Reconstruction and Development, *The Economic Development of Jamaica* (Baltimore: Johns Hopkins Press, 1952), 79.

16 G. Eaton, "The Development of Trade Unionism in Jamaica – W.I." (Ph.D. dissertation, McGill University, 1961), 624.
17 *Economic Development*, 82.
18 H.P., "Jamaica's Bauxite and Labour," *West Indian Economist* 1, no. 4 (October 1958): 32–3.
19 Harrod, *Trade Union Foreign Policy*, 320.
20 It is beyond the scope of this argument to project a detailed analysis of the highly complex socio-political situation that has marked Jamaica's recent history. For more on this subject, see M. Kaufman, *Jamaica Under Manley: Dilemmas of Socialism and Democracy* (London: Zed Books Ltd., 1985); H. Campbell, *Rasta and Resistance: From Marcus Garvey to Walter Rodney* (Trenton, N.J.: Africa World Press, 1987); and E.H. Stephens and J.D. Stephens, *Democratic Socialism in Jamaica: The Political Movement and Social Transformation in Dependent Capitalism* (Princeton N.J.: Princeton University Press, 1986).

Index

African Orthodox Church, 97
African religion, 15, 50–1, 52, 53, 62–3, 73–4; adaptation of Christian theology to, 53, 54
Afro-Christian religion, 62–3, 73–4, 96
Alves, A. Bain, 100
apprenticeship system, 27, 66

Baker, Moses, 52, 54
bananas, 29–30, 35, 37
Baptist, 15, 29, 51–7, 66, 72–5, 89; "leader system," 52–3; missionaries in Morant Bay Rebellion, 82
"Baptist War," 55
bauxite, 5, 139, 141
Bedward, Alexander, 16, 95–6, 98
Black Star Line, 97
Bogle, Paul, 77, 78–80, 82, 85, 87, 89
British Crown, 15, 16–17, 58, 83–5, 90, 114, 125; as benevolent despot in Rebellion of 1831, 57–60; "Queen's Advice," 84–5; in Rebellion of 1865, 83–5; in Rebellion of 1938, 111–15
Buchanan, H.C. 101, 102, 111

Burchell, Thomas, 54, 56, 73
Bustamante, Alexander, 5, 101–11, 113–17, 122, 123–4, 127, 128, 129–33, 137–8, 140–1; and his influence on labour reform, 112–13; in Rebellion of 1938, 102–3, 108, 120
Bustamante Industrial Trade Union (BITU), 104–6, 109, 110–11, 113, 122, 123, 124, 127, 128–30, 140, 141, 142

class: analysis, 4, 8, 10, 30; conflict, 63, 103; middle, growth of, 45
clerical workers, 44
Coombs, A.G.S., 101, 102, 111, 171n35

Denham, Sir Edward, 108, 121
Dick, Lewis, 80
dock workers, 44, 100–1, 103, 122, 123
domestic servants, 44, 47

emancipation: movement, 57, 58, 59, 60; problems following, 68–72
Emancipation Act, 26–7
emigration 42, 139; and returns, 42, 100

Eyre, Edward, 75–80, 82, 83, 84–5, 88–9, 90–2

franchise, 33–4, 70, 124, 144n12
free villages, 67, 73

Garvey, Marcus, 49, 95, 96–8, 111, 129, 170n23
Gibb, George, 52
Gordon, George William, 77, 78, 79, 80, 85, 87, 89
Gramsci, Antonio, 13–14
Grant, St William, 103–4, 108, 111, 117, 128–9
Great Revival, 73, 74, 77

Henriques Brothers, 47
Herschell, the Rev. Mr 81
higglers, 9, 46
Hobsbawm, E.J., 12, 106

ideology: derived, 13–15, 52, 54, 56, 57, 60, 63, 73, 99, 128, 138–9; inherent, 13–15, 50, 54, 57, 60, 63, 73, 74, 83, 95, 139
immigration program, 31

Jamaica
– Assembly of, 67–71, 83, 162n6; after emancipation, 68–9

– churches of, 94–5, 163n18
– economy of, 74, 138–40
– education in, 94
– effect of Emancipation Act on, 18, 68–72
– election of 1944, 131–3
– government of, 69–70, 71, 72, 90–1; British control of, 137; crisis of hegemony in, 68–9, 72, 90–1; as Crown Colony, 91, 92, 93; self-government in, 124, 138
– international system in, 5, 47
– labour: organization of, 5, 99–113; reform, 99–100, 112, 124
– parishes of: Clarendon, 43, 119; Hanover, 56; Kingston-St Andrew, 97–8, 132; Manchester, 56; Portland, 37, 43, 119, 120; St Andrew, 18, 35, 97–8; St Ann's, 79, 83–4, 86, 119, 120; St Catherine, 43, 132; St Elizabeth, 56, 132; St James, 43, 56, 57, 64; St Mary, 37, 43, 119, 120; St Thomas, 43, 132; St Thomas-in-the-East, 76, 77, 78, 79, 85, 90; Trelawney, 56, 63; Westmoreland, 39, 43, 56, 103, 132
– politics in, 5, 111, 140–1
– population of: current, 3; in 1930, 94; patterns of, 43
– social programs in, 71–2, 91, 94
– taxation policies of, 86
– working class in, 9, 10, 71
– World War II and, 5, 128, 154n109
Jamaica Banana Producers' Association (JBPA), 107, 173n69

Jamaica Democratic Party, 131–2
Jamaica Imperial Association, 99
Jamaica Labour Party (JLP), 130–3, 135–8, 140–1, 142, 175n104
Jamaica Representative Government Association, 99
Jamaica Workers and Tradesmen Union (JWTU), 101, 102
John Canoe (Connu) dance, 62–3

Ketelhodt, Baron von, 78, 79, 81
Kingston, 18, 35, 97, 122; growth of, 42–3; as seat of government, 43
Knibb, William, 54, 57, 67, 73; and free villages, 67

labour force: complaints of, 86–7; and planters, 34–5; social and economic forces on, 33. See also wage workers
labour organization, 3, 49. See also trade unions
landholding, 3, 8, 35, 36, 48, 121; decline of, 4, 18, 119; desire for, 85–7; after Emancipation, 28–9; production on, 28, 37; in Rebellion of 1938, 119, 120; size of, 36–7
land settlement, 124
Lewis, George, 52
Lisle, George, 52, 53, 158n13
Longshoremen's Unions, 100

Manley, Norman Washington, 5, 104, 111, 113, 117, 120, 127, 129, 131, 137–8, 140–1

Marxism, 8, 130, 136
missionaries, 7–8, 51, 67, 74; and emancipation, 54–5, 72–3; and free villages, 29; and Rebellion of 1831, 57, 66–7; role of, in education, 72
Montego Bay, 54, 55
Morant Bay, 77, 82; Rebellion, 74, 78–83, 88–9, 167n87; Royal Commission on, 85
Moyne Commission, 40, 125, 126, 127
Mulgrave, Lord, 66
myalism, 50–1, 53, 56, 73

National Workers' Union (NWU), 136–7, 140–1, 142
Nethersole, Noel, 129
Norman, F.A., 126

obeah, 50–1, 53, 73, 166n73
Orde-Browne Commission, 46, 125, 126

Panama disease, 37
peasant class, 3, 8, 9, 86, 91; decline in prosperity of, 35, 39, 86; development into wage-labour force of, 39–40, 47; and landholdings, 36; as "reconstituted peasantry," 28, 31
People's National Party (PNP), 5, 113, 120, 129–32, 135–8, 140–1, 142
People's Political Party, 98
plantocracy, 6, 30; and apprenticeship, 66; concessions to, 93; and the decline of plantations, 27, 28; and emancipation, 27, 57, 58, 59; and missionaries, 55, 66; and Morant Bay Rebellion, 82; and multinationals, 38–9;

and Rebellion of 1831, 65
political parties, 49, 69, 135–8, 140–1, 179n5; Country Party, 69, 77; Town Party, 69, 77. *See also* Jamaica Labour Party and People's National Party
Poor Man's Improvement Land Settlement and Labour Association, 119–20
provision grounds, 22, 23, 25, 26, 28, 61

racism, 6–8, 30, 31, 45
Ras Tafari movement, 16
Rebellion of 1831, 4, 11, 12, 55, 56, 60, 62–7, 161n76; as "Baptist War," 55; religious aspects of, 16, 54, 62
Rebellion of 1865, 4, 11, 12; religious aspects of, 16. *See also* Morant Bay Rebellion
Rebellion of 1938, 4, 11, 12, 102–4, 116–20; casualties in, 116; effects of, 115; preconditions of, 96; religious aspects of, 16
religion: in Rebellion of 1831, 50–7; in Rebellion of 1866, 72–83; in Rebellion of 1938, 95–111; religious idiom, 15, 16, 17, 50, 82; traditions of, 73. *See also* African religion and Baptist
Report of the International Bank for Reconstruction and Development, 141
Reynolds Jamaica Mines, 140–1
Rudé, George, 13–14
Rumble, Robert E., 119, 120

scuffling, 44–5, 47
Sharpe, Samuel, 55–6, 60, 63, 64, 65
Simpson, H.A.L., 99
slave gangs, 21, 61
slave markets, 23–4
slaves, 8, 14, 19–26, 148n14; Christmas celebration of, 62; collectivism of, 20; and Emancipation Act, 18; families of, 25; forms of, 19–20; laws governing, 23, 25; exodus from plantations of, 67, 147n1; and provision grounds, 22–3, 25, 26, 61; punishment of, 22; and Rebellion of 1831, 60–1, 63–5; work of, 20–1, 61
Sligo, Lord, 66
Smith, J.A.G., 99, 111
Stony Gut, 77, 80, 88
strikes, 49, 100, 117–18, 122, 127–8; in Rebellion of 1831, 60–2, 63; in Rebellion of 1938, 103–4, 108–9, 117
sugar, 19, 38–9, 45, 129
sugar plantations, 19–20; decline of, 27, 28; labour on, 18, 28, 30, 31; production of, 18, 31–3; slavery on, 19–26
sugar workers, 122–3, 129

Tate and Lyle, 18, 38, 39, 103, 127
tourism, 44, 139, 155n139
trade unions, 5, 99, 100, 122, 126–7, 171n33; effect of British policy on, 111–12
Trade Union Congress, 136
Trade Union Council (TUC), 127, 130
Trade Union Educational Institute (TUEI), 142

Underhill, E.B., 75–7, 83
Underhill meetings, 76, 79
unemployment, 40, 41, 42, 44, 47, 139
United Empire Loyalists, 51
United Fruit Company, 18, 30, 38, 99, 107, 127
Universal Negro Improvement Association (UNIA), 96–8

wage workers, 18, 28, 30–1, 46–7; in agriculture, 41–2; collectivization of, 40–1, 48; in Rebellion of 1938, 102–3, 120
West India Royal Commission. *See* Moyne Commission
West Indian Sugar Company (WISCO), 38, 103
Woolley, C.C., 121, 124